Liberalism, Nationalism, Citizenship

Ronald Beiner

Liberalism, Nationalism, Citizenship:
Essays on the Problem
of Political Community

UBCPress · Vancouver · Toronto

09 08 07 06 05 04 03   5 4 3 2 1

Printed in Canada on acid-free paper. ∞

National Library Cataloguing in Publication Data

Beiner, Ronald, 1953-
Liberalism, nationalism, citizenship : essays on the problem of political community

  Includes bibliographical references and index.
  ISBN 0-7748-0987-6

  1. Citizenship. 2. Liberalism. 3. Nationalism. 4. Civil society. I. Title.
JF801.B44 2002   323.6'01   C2002-910735-0

Canadä

UBC Press gratefully acknowledges the financial support for our publishing program of the Government of Canada through the Book Publishing Industry Development Program (BPIDP), and of the Canada Council for the Arts, and the British Columbia Arts Council.

UBC Press
The University of British Columbia
2029 West Mall
Vancouver, BC V6T 1Z2
604-822-5959 / Fax: 604-822-6083
www.ubcpress.ca

To the memory of Liam O'Sullivan

Contents

Liberalism, Nationalism, Citizenship

Introduction

The purpose of this book is to articulate, in different theoretical contexts and in response to a variety of theorists of political community, a notion of citizenship that can provide a normative standard for critical judgment concerning liberalism and critical judgment concerning nationalism. In the chapter devoted to Richard Flathman's work (chapter 2), I write that political philosophy "is a form of reflection that is uncompromisingly focused on an intellectual epicentre." I think that one could apply the same dictum to my own endeavours as a political theorist, except that in my case the gravitational centre is not the idea of individuality but the idea of citizenship.

The essays in this collection are intended to pursue a consistent line of reflection on themes related to the idea of citizenship. Chapter 12 is a new essay, not previously published. I have deliberately held back from updating two of the previously published chapters – chapter 7 and chapter 10 – in order to preserve the time-bound character of the context in which they were written. All the other chapters have been published previously in various versions but were revised for this book.

Chapter 1 airs the full range of themes concerning citizenship and nationalism that are treated in more detail and often with greater (but never perfect) clarity of understanding in the other chapters of the book.[1] It was written out of a sense of the crisis of citizenship in the early 1990s, the years immediately following the close of the Cold War: the collapse of several notable multi-nation states in succession; heightened concerns about large-scale migrations from poor oppressed societies to rich free ones; the redefinition of citizenship in the EU. Rather than taking advantage of the end of Cold War tensions to build up bonds of civic solidarity crossing ethnic and ideological divisions, many societies quickly succumbed to *intensified* conflict along ethnic and religious cleavages. It was and remains a shock to see those expectations of a civically healthier world broken so cruelly by harsh new ideologies. Writing at the present moment, when "McWorld" is literally going to war against

"Jihad" (to use Benjamin Barber's categories), one can hardly allow oneself to imagine that this crisis of citizenship is over.[2]

Chapter 2 considers the work of Richard Flathman, who offers a version of liberal theory that is at the opposite extremity from the kind of "civic liberalism" discussed in chapter 3. What drives Flathman is both a positive conception of individuality and a negative conception of the modern state; because he sees the idea of citizenship as aligned with the latter, he views citizenship not as expressive of individuality but as a threat to it. I think Flathman is right that we cannot embrace an affirmative concept of citizenship without also embracing a fairly affirmative concept of the state and of the citizen's duties and responsibilities toward the state. But I disagree with his view that an endorsement of the contemporary state is too bitter a pill to swallow, and that, in consequence, the notion of robust citizenship is poisoned by its association with the state. At least with respect to this militant version of liberal theory, appeal to the idea of citizenship helps to expose problems and deficiencies in certain important grounding concepts of liberalism.

In 1992 I published a book in which I claimed that there was something in the very nature of contemporary liberalism that seemed resistant to doing justice to the theme of citizenship and civic membership *(What's the Matter with Liberalism?* chapter 5). My point seemed to be proved by the chapter on citizenship in Bruce Ackerman's book *Social Justice in the Liberal State,* devoted as it was to trying to vindicate the civic credentials of talking apes. (Ackerman's point was to emphasize the minimalist requirements of liberal citizenship: if a talking ape could debate fair entitlements, one could consider it to have suitably surpassed the threshold of liberal civic membership.) In the decade since I published my book on liberalism, liberals have been writing books trying to prove me wrong, starting with John Rawls's *Political Liberalism* (published one year later: in 1993), which is a kind of treatise on liberal citizenship. Chapter 3 is devoted to Stephen Macedo's book *Diversity and Distrust,* which, it seems to me, goes a lot further than Rawls in proving me wrong.[3] Though it may seem a paradox to some, the civic critique of liberalism invites a more robust (that is, less parsimonious) version of liberalism (as the chapter on Macedo should help to make clear).

One important insight (or set of insights) to be drawn from Macedo's book is that we require a better understanding of possible tensions between multiculturalism and citizenship. Cultural diversity is the norm today in almost all societies, and it is a condition to be celebrated. But multiculturalist political philosophies don't simply celebrate cultural diversity, they also privilege it politically in ways that sometimes threaten to undermine the idea of shared citizenship. To be sure, cultural diversity should be embraced as a positive aspect of contemporary citizenship, but not at the cost of losing sight of the requirements of a common civic community. That is, we need a *reciprocal* understanding of how the notion of citizenship is enriched by taking better account of differences of cultural identity *and* of how group identity and group allegiance should moderate their claims so that they do not derogate from an experience of what all citizens in a political community share in common.[4] As Brian Barry writes in his trenchant critique of the politics of multiculturalism, "political life presupposes citizens who think of themselves as contributing to a common discourse about their shared institutions."[5] What we desire is not a politics that divides citizens on an ascriptive basis, but rather a "politics of solidarity" where "citizens [are understood to] belong to a single society, and [to] share a common fate."[6] Insofar as multiculturalist politics undermines "this conception of politics as a society-wide conversation about questions of common concern," it must be challenged.[7]

The title of chapter 4 ("From Community to Citizenship") is relevant here. The chapter is devoted to the work of Michael Sandel, the most forceful critic of the procedural liberalism of Rawls and the most eloquent advocate for a thicker "communitarian" understanding of civic and moral membership. But framing a critique of liberalism in terms of an appeal to community involves significant perils. It can lead in a variety of political directions, depending on the types of community that one relies upon to inject thicker substance into personal and political identity. If the locus of communal identity is the local community and its associated institutions (school, church, clinic, guild), then we have a "politics of local community" *à la* Alasdair MacIntyre (see chapter 5). If the locus of identity politics is the nation in an ethnocultural sense or the subnational ethnic or cultural group, then we move toward either the politics of nationalism or the politics of multiculturalism; therefore it isn't surprising that Charles Taylor's communitarianism has evolved into a philosophical defence of multiculturalism and liberal nationalism (the same is true of Michael Walzer). If what strengthening community means is beefing up the experience of citizenship in the modern state, then we have a politics pointing more in a civic or civic-republican direction (as is the case for Sandel and me). But each of these notions of community is grounded in a quite different normative vision of politics; in this respect, communitarianism as such presents itself as an incoherent political philosophy.

It is much clearer in *Democracy's Discontent* than in Sandel's earlier work that citizenship in the standard sense is the privileged site of constitutive community (although Sandel's talk at the end of *Democracy's Discontent* about "multiply-situated selves" and "diffusion of sovereignty" suggests renewed ambiguity about the location of politically relevant community).[8] However, as sympathetic as I am to Sandel's theoretical project, I think he understates the gap between civic republicanism as a critical standard and civic republicanism as a practical possibility. Sandel tends to suggest that the United States *could have* continued to remain faithful to a regime of robust citizenship had it not been lured astray by the kind of procedural-liberal public philosophy eventually articulated fully in the political philosophy of Rawls. That is, Sandel characterizes the triumph of a procedural-liberal public philosophy in abstraction from the economic and sociological realities that are so powerfully at play in the evolution of a political way of life. Nor does he rule out – given the adoption of the right public philosophy – a possible return to a regime of "high citizenship."[9] We need to reflect more toughmindedly than Sandel does (and more toughmindedly than I have done in some of my writings on citizenship) on the utopian character of a civic-republican regime.

It is easy to see why the civic-republican vision of politics is normatively attractive, and why, having enjoyed a long and illustrious tradition of articulations within the history of political philosophy, it continues to find defenders today, or at least those reluctant to close the door on its ideals: citizens motivated by the apprehension of a common good rather than by merely private interests; civic unity rather than an aggregate of subcommunities at cross-purposes to each other; engaged citizens rather than passive and indifferent ones; citizens who treat each other *as* co-citizens rather than as strangers, competitors, or parties to a contractual arrangement – in short, an ideal of civic friendship played out within a shared public forum about which all the participants care deeply and genuinely. It's easy to see why all of this would be desirable as a theoretical ideal. The question is whether it's a meaningful option, given the conditions of modern life and the constraints of modern politics. Is it just a pipe dream?

It is not hard to grasp that ours would be a wonderful world if we were all committed and enthusiastic citizens concerned with a general good shared by all our fellow citizens, but it is no less readily discernible that basic features of social and political life in the modern world militate strongly against the realization of such an ideal. We live in large and complex societies. All of us are deeply immersed in the demands of our private lives, which rarely provide the huge measures of leisure and disinterestedness that a fully committed civic-mindedness would require. We belong to subgroups tied to particularistic and very real interests that draw us away from shared polity-wide interests. The intense pluralism of contemporary social reality means that members of a political community see the world very differently, and lack the time or motivation to enter deeply into the very different experiences and life horizons of citizens differently situated. Moreover, few people living in the kind of societies we now have possess anywhere near the kinds of expertise one would need in order to weigh alternative policies for the regulation of a modern economy, or the regulation of international affairs, or most other issues with which contemporary states must wrestle (biotechnology, global warming, nuclear defence systems, bio-terrorism ...). Most of us are simply not equipped for informed deliberation about these issues, and lack the time and motivation to equip ourselves more adequately. People living in modern circumstances are unlikely to view politics and public deliberation as the core meaning of their lives, since endless conversation about the public good would generate not "public happiness" (Hannah Arendt's phrase) but frustration with "too many meetings" (Oscar Wilde's phrase). Instead, we settle for arbitration of sectional interests delegated to politicians who we assume work for the interests of the constituents who elect them and the lobbyists who court them rather than genuinely debate a common good.[10]

The utopianism of the civic-republican ideal is not something for which we should apologize, for political theory would fall short of its mission if it failed to supply utopian ideals. But it would also fall short of its mission if it failed to own up to them *as* utopian. The idea of citizenship appealed to in the following chapters therefore tries to preserve an echo of the civic-republican legacy (with a suitable awareness of the genuine radicalness of that theoretical legacy); at the same time, it tries to acknowledge that in practice we have no choice but to settle for scaled-down and less ambitious forms of civic life. Our purpose is to salvage a bit of civicness in the context of a political world where the odds tend to be stacked against citizenship. We can draw upon republicanism and civicism to criticize the "diluted citizenship" that is currently on offer, but we should temper our theorizing with realism about the objective constraints on a wholesale transformation of our civic practices.[11] The appeal to citizenship is both a residue of utopia and a grudging concession to social and political reality.

Alasdair MacIntyre certainly doesn't see himself as a liberal, and readers of his work are unlikely to view him as anything other than a trenchant critic of liberalism. Still, a focus on the question of citizenship exposes strange and paradoxical affinities between his theoretical position and familiar versions of liberalism. As an Aristotelian, MacIntyre believes that moral philosophy must orient itself according to conceptions of the good, not conceptions of the right. These conceptions of the good get realized in necessarily communal settings; yet the modern state is not, and cannot be, the kind of political entity worthy of being entrusted with the pursuit of collective goods. In fact, MacIntyre's hostility to the state as a dispensation of the modern world is no less fierce than that of Richard Flathman (though on the basis of social assumptions that are radically opposed to Flathman's). Therefore, although MacIntyre believes that liberalism's conception of the neutrality of the liberal state is a sham, he also thinks (unlike communitarians with whom he is usually grouped) that it would be better if the state *could be* neutral – since it habitually botches up whatever collective goods are placed in its clumsy hands. Hence he describes himself as an Aristotelian but not a communitarian. It is a human requirement that human beings deliberate together on the proper ends of life, and modern political community as we know it is not an eligible location for this moral deliberation. (This strikes us as a pretty harsh view of contemporary citizenship, but see the preceding two paragraphs for considerations that arguably lend weight to MacIntyre's view.)

MacIntyre looks at other so-called communitarians (Taylor, Sandel, Walzer) and sees decisive theoretical differences between them and himself. However, rather than concluding that they are communitarians and he isn't, we might more reasonably consider that MacIntyre is, relative to this group, the *only* fully rigorous communitarian thinker. This is so, not because MacIntyre believes that community is an end in itself – a view that he (rightly) rejects – but because he thinks that moral practices that unfold within forms of local community are the uniquely privileged site for the virtues that he conceives to be humanly desirable.

In part 2 I switch my critical attention to the seductions of nationalism. The core argument in chapter 6 is that contemporary liberal defenders of nationalism shouldn't rush to assume that the concept of liberal nationalism fully captures what moves committed nationalists. Consider, for instance, what Will Kymlicka says in a recent treatment of nationalism: "Over the past few years ... an increasing number of theorists have been ... arguing that national cultures and polities provide the best context for promoting Enlightenment values of freedom, equality, and democracy. What we increasingly see, therefore, is not a debate between liberal cosmopolitanism and illiberal particularism, but rather a debate between liberal cosmopolitanism and liberal nationalism."[12]

As Kymlicka frames the contemporary debate about nationalism, then, the relevant normative debate is between liberal cosmopolitanism and liberal nationalism. But it may be that the more interesting normative horizons are opened up by forms of nationalism that aren't trying to satisfy liberal standards of moral legitimacy.[13] As Margaret Canovan sharply puts it, "When the sleeping dogs of nationalism first woke up at the beginning of the [1990s], quite a few political theorists were inclined to make pets of them"; to which we can add that undomesticated and undomesticable forms of nationalism can sometimes open up more interesting normative horizons (because they offer a more radical challenge to liberal moral-cultural horizons) than "the domesticated nationalism that liberal theorists wanted to support."[14] Nationalism, like contemporary theocracy, is in important measure a reaction against the banalities of liberal culture, and liberals will fail to see what is driving these nationalists and other anti-liberals if they simply liberalize on their behalf what is in fact a quite different view of the world.

We've adverted above to the fact that there are civic versions of liberalism; it's worth noting that there are also civic versions of the politics of nationality. The first and still-influential civic argument for nationalism (of an at least qualified liberal variety) is to be found in John Stuart Mill's *Considerations on Representative Government,* chapter 16.[15] A recent version has been offered by a contemporary Millian: Brian Barry. Consider the following interesting analysis of how a multination state such as Belgium is difficult to sustain as a civic community:

> Belgium functions like a microcosm of the European Union, which is commonly accused of suffering from a "democratic deficit." The charge is certainly sustainable if the model of a democratic polity is taken to be one in which there is a single comprehensive realm of discourse giving rise to a unified "public opinion" – unified not in the sense that everybody thinks the same but in the sense that everybody is aware of what the others think and takes it into account. This model seems to me largely inapplicable to the European Union, now and for the foreseeable future. For even if the trend within the countries of the European Union toward ever more widespread knowledge of English continues until it is universal, most people will still read newspapers and watch television in their native language. There will therefore continue to be parallel national discourses, and governments will continue to be expected to pursue within the European Union policies arrived at through national politics.
>
> ... Political communities are bound to be linguistic communities, because politics is (in some sense) linguistically constructed. We can negotiate across language barriers but we cannot deliberate together about the way in which our common life is to be conducted unless we share a language.[16]

This is a powerful argument – in my view the *most* powerful argument – in favour of uni-national (or at least uni-linguistic) polities, an argument much more compelling than appeals to rights of national self-determination (see chapter 9). Yet Barry is no less committed than Jürgen Habermas to what the latter calls "the normative achievements of a national self-understanding that is no longer based on ethnicity but founded on citizenship."[17]

Anyone who wants to experience the full agony of nationalist conflict can scarcely pick a better society than Israel for fathoming what's at stake. In chapter 6 I quote Conor Cruise O'Brien, an unswerving opponent of Irish nationalism, to make the point that even resolute anti-nationalists can feel the tug of their own national identities. I experienced something of this in Israel, and chapter 7 offers a few personal reflections. I include this little piece in the collection more as a record of what prompted me to think about nationalism in the following decade than as an adequate analysis. As a non-Zionist Jew (not exactly an anti-Zionist Jew, but certainly a non-Zionist one), I cannot help being preoccupied with how the philosophy of nationalism applies to the civic life of Israel. An Israeli state defined in terms of Jewish national self-expression and clothed in the public symbols of Jewish national history inevitably impugns the citizenship of Arabs and other non-Jews who also happen to be citizens of the state of Israel, and who are therefore also entitled to be included in its civic vision. (The people I have in mind here are not Arabs living on territory that will revert to what is already an incipient Palestinian state; rather, they are Palestinians and other non-Jews who are citizens of Israel and will continue to be citizens of Israel after the founding of a Palestinian state.) It's out of appreciation for this normative insight that some in Israel have begun to speak of a "post-Zionist" definition of the Israeli state.

The overall thrust of this book is Arendtian insofar as it is critical both of liberalism and of nationalism as comprehensive political visions, on the grounds that neither of these conceptions of political life fully honours citizenship as a normative standard. However, Hannah Arendt herself presented an account of nationalism that is in various ways confusing and less than fully fleshed out philosophically: on the one hand, for instance, she holds the strong conviction that nationally defined polities had outlived their usefulness in guarding the human rights of particular peoples, and, on the other hand, she makes the decisive admission that the Jews had obtained much greater security for their human rights by winning precisely a nation-state for themselves. But the most striking weakness of Arendt's theorizing about nationalism is that, for a thinker who was sanguine about very few things in political life, she was overly sanguine about what she conceived to be the inevitable eclipse of nationalist ideologies. As Judith Shklar revealingly writes: the strict distinction that Arendt erects between citizenship and nationality was "one of her blind spots. By the time she wrote *The Origins of Totalitarianism* she had made up her mind that nationalism was a thing of the past – it was dead and not to be confused or compared with the living ideologies of the age. This notion, which her Marxist inclinations reinforced, was immune to evidence; nothing could persuade her that nationalism was still a very great force in the present. On this point, I speak from personal experience."[18] Arendt offers powerful criticisms of the basic nationalist idea. But she never sufficiently clarified what she meant in claiming that the nation-state system had broken down in the twentieth century, and she never gave persuasive reasons for thinking that nationalism had spent its force as a modern ideology.

Chapter 9 offers a sequel, relevant to the politics of nationalism, to the argument offered in chapter 4 of my book *What's the Matter with Liberalism?* There are many political contexts in which the language of rights is an indispensable protest against violence and illegitimate power. But there are also limits to this moral language that political philosophers haven't always appreciated. It is an adversarial language – the "sign of breakdown in a relationship," as Mary Ann Glendon puts it[19] – rather than a language of community. The liberal idea of rights is that individuals, even in a liberal society, need to be protected from each other (women need to be protected from abusive husbands, children need to be protected from neglectful parents, and so on). The communitarian critique of rights flows from the idea that one will not be able to enter into satisfying moral relationships based on the premise that fellow members of one's moral community are to be thought of in the first instance as potential intruders upon one's basic personal integrity. Transposing this into the arena of philosophical debates about nationalism, we can say that although it's true that in some cases one nation inexcusably tramples on another nation's prerogative to decide its own destiny, it is not helpful to frame *all* situations of national conflict in this language of universal and inviolable rights. National self-determination framed in the language of rights is a dangerous idea because it absolutizes political claims that might otherwise be resolved in a spirit of compromise and accommodation.

VIP

In chapter 10 I make explicit the Canadian preoccupations that in fact run through the book as a whole. Pierre Trudeau's political career was a kind of living instantiation of Elie Kedourie's root-and-branch theoretical critique of nationalism, and the Trudeau-Lévesque agon from the 1960s to 1980s gave political embodiment to the debates about nationalism that continue to exercise political philosophers. No politically aware Canadian can be indifferent to the opposing conceptions of nationality wielded by a René Lévesque or Jean Chrétien, by a Brian Mulroney or Lucien Bouchard. Canadian citizenship is a perennial instruction in the political philosophy of nationalism. This is not to say that Canada as a political community is unique in this respect: many other political societies also contend never-endingly with their own "national question." But for me, as a Canadian, theoretical reflection on nationalism is inseparable from my civic membership in what Quebec sovereigntists refer to as an "abnormal" political community.

Politically speaking, I'm far from being a diehard opponent of Quebec nationalism: like Charles Taylor, I believe that francophone Quebeckers are quite legitimately anxious about their cultural survival within an anglophone North America, and are entitled to employ political instruments to promote their prospects of cultural survival; I'm not moved especially by the slogan of "anglophone rights"; and I would welcome a greater willingness on the part of English-speaking Canada to constitutionalize a recognition of francophone Quebec as a bona fide "people" or "nation." However, philosophically, I believe that the vocation of political philosophy requires the clarification of ultimate normative principles, and at this level of "first principles," Quebec nationalism, like any nationalism, raises troubling normative questions about the ethnic definition of citizenship in multiethnic societies. Quebec nationalists are clearly anxious to portray their nationalism as expressing the aspirations of a nation that is *not* defined ethnically. On the other hand, those opposed to Quebec nationalism (especially anti-nationalists living within Quebec, including Aboriginal Quebeckers) see it as a bid for ethnic hegemony. What's at stake in this debate is a normatively crucial principle:

namely, whether certain members of a society should have a privileged citizenship (and correlatively, others should have a diminished citizenship) by virtue of the culture to which they belong.[20]

Those sympathetic to the idea of liberal nationalism will likely object to my identification of nationalism *per se* with an ethnic definition of citizenship. They might pose the challenge: What about civic nationalism? Doesn't it redeem the nationalist idea? I'm not without sympathy for the notion of civic nationality, as chapter 6 makes clear, but I worry that the term itself will simply add confusion to the debate, as I also explain in that chapter:

> A big part of the problem in pursuing [the] project [of upholding civic na-
> tionalism as an alternative to ethnic nationalism] is that different people use
> the term *civic nationalism* for radically different purposes (nationalists use
> it to fend off accusations that their nationalism is exclusionary and ethno-
> centric, whereas critics of nationalism use it to cast a moral cloud over "real"
> nationalism, i.e., ethnic nationalism). Wayne Norman rightly points out
> that when someone like Michael Ignatieff describes himself as committed
> to civic nationalism, it suggests, misleadingly, that this is a particular species
> of nationalism, whereas Ignatieff himself, of course, intends it as a reproach
> to all forms of nationalism strictly speaking ... Therefore it might clarify the
> debate somewhat simply to drop the term *civic nationalism* and replace it
> with references to citizenship (or Habermas's constitutional patriotism).

In chapter 12 I coin the term *civicism* partly in order to avoid reference to civic nationalism, because both nationalists and anti-nationalists struggle to use the term for their own (conflicting) purposes. (My purpose is also partly to designate a strong concept of citizenship that doesn't presume to fulfill the full-blown ambitions of the civic-republican tradition.) It's true, for instance, that many people speak of "Canadian nationalism" as if a "civic nation" such as Canada can equally be an appropriate object of nationalist fervour. But here I think we have good reason to resist common usage of the term *nationalism*. I find it hard to see much that's interestingly in common between the fleeting and generally feeble episodes of "Canadian nationalism" (i.e., anti-Americanism), on the one hand, and, on the other hand, the kind of hunger for ethnocultural self-determination that drives Irish republicans, Quebec sovereigntists, Zionists in Israel, or members of the Scottish National Party.[21] As I have already suggested, one of the most important theoretical motivations for reflecting philosophically on nationalism is to expand our view beyond the liberal horizon, and civic nationalism cannot contribute to this theoretical purpose for the simple reason that so-called civic nationalism is located squarely within the liberal horizon, not beyond it.

Interesting normative challenges to liberalism are offered only by forms of nationalism that make a much more robust appeal to culture and ethnos. In

Canada as a political community there is far too much cultural diversity to be able to do this in a meaningful way (and the same is true of the United States), which helps explain why Quebec nationalists find Canadian citizenship so unsatisfying and unimpressive. It's true, of course, that Canadian cultural identity does have some substance, and also true that this cultural identity expresses itself politically from time to time in relation to threats of American hegemony. Yet the aspiration toward the kind of uni-national basis of political community sought by Quebec nationalists and Scottish nationalists is meaningless for a type of political community as culturally diverse as Canada's. Therefore, in Canada any strong appeals to "the nation" as the focus of political agency sound rather inflated, whereas such appeals sound much less contrived in the Quebec context. It seems to me that it only makes sense to speak of "real" nationalism in cases where politics is driven by really deep cultural attachments of a kind that are untypical in contemporary liberal societies.[22] In any case, nationalism by definition (so I am convinced) does not apply to a binational state, and that is what Canada is.

The watershed year for political-philosophical reflection on nationalism was 1989. Starting in that year, hopes for post-Cold War global peace and political convergence rapidly gave way to new anxieties concerning ethnic conflict. World politics, instead of being defined by the confrontation between opposing economic systems, was now defined by the clash of opposing nationalities: no longer Karl Marx versus Adam Smith, but Azeris versus Armenians, Slovaks versus Czechs, Macedonians versus Albanians. In chapter 11 I juxtapose one radical defender of nationalism (Tom Nairn) and one radical adversary of nationalism (Eric Hobsbawm), drawing them into a somewhat more explicit dialogue with each other (although elements of this dialogue already feature in their own work). In this way, I deploy the time-honoured resource of political philosophers, namely the dialogical encounter (dialectic), in order to shed light on the philosophical challenge of nationalism. Ernest Gellner, a powerful theorizer of nationalism, also hovers over this debate between Nairn and Hobsbawm.

A Gellnerian sociology of nationalism certainly yields indispensable insights into modernity's privileging of nationally organized political units; but this same sociology involves a tacit deprecation of the *politics* of nationalism (i.e., nationalism conceived as a mode of civic agency expressing a set of political choices that could be other than they are). Consider the following apt summary by Nairn of Gellner's perspective on nationalism:

> Nationalism ... is not really about the past. It is about the difficult transition to modernity, a process in which people often have to recreate a more suitable past for themselves. To become modern (or postmodern) beings, they need a new identity, and to get that they must re-imagine their community as being (and always having been) worthy of the change. Thus new

nations and pasts are "invented" – but not by whim or arbitrarily. However cruel and uneven, modern development is inescapable and all societies are called to opt into it in their own way – predominantly the way of separate or independent growth. Where such development is abruptly reimposed – as in eastern Europe after 1989 – nationalism becomes as inevitable as it was at earlier stages of modernisation.[23]

If it were literally true that modern societies *must* re-imagine their community according to nationalist categories, nationalism would not present itself as a distinct political alternative, because all modern politics would be nationalist politics. But in fact nationalist outcomes ensue only when partisans of nationalist politics prevail over their non-nationalist or anti-nationalist adversaries. Slovakia's divorce from its Czech partner was not sociologically preordained (though Nairn may be of the opinion that it was), and if Quebeckers decide to secede from Canada, this will represent a triumph of one kind of politics over a rival politics, not the unavoidable dispensation of a sociologically determined fate. One can make similar points about globalization, for which there are, equally, various accounts presenting it as an inexorable and universal social process. But surely there are political choices here, a possibility of civic agency, that we cannot allow to be trumped by the claims of sociological determinism. To think of these phenomena strictly on the level of sociological explanation would be an insult to our nature as political beings.

Chapter 12 attempts to offer a re-statement of the themes and problems addressed in the rest of the book, while remaining vividly conscious that these theoretical dilemmas are anything but satisfactorily resolved. In response to chapter 11, Margaret Canovan sent me a postcard in which she posed the following challenge: "I wonder ... whether you are right to conclude that the issue is 'normative-philosophical'? What strikes me is (1) that views on nationalism seem to be a matter of personal experience and identity, and (2) that the pros and cons of particular cases are a matter for political judgment ... rather than philosophical generalisation." Chapter 12 begins with a response to this challenge; and this book as a whole only makes sense if Canovan's challenge can be answered. In fact, one can state parallel challenges with respect to *all* political phenomena and the political philosophies that respond to them. *All* aspects of political life draw on "personal experience and identity," and call for the exercise of contingent political judgment. But there is nonetheless an indispensable role for the philosophical generalizations offered by (or at least considered by) political philosophy.

Despite the endless complexities we encounter in working through a philosophical position – distinguishing it from rival views, identifying tensions and inconsistencies in our own theoretical perspective, and trying to fashion a consistent view – an essentially simple core idea lies at the base of every political philosophy. The liberal idea is that individuals should not face unfair impediments in pursuing the lives they choose for themselves, and the purpose of politics is to guarantee that such impediments are removed. The nationalist idea is that membership in an ethnos is an essential aspect of a properly human life, and the purpose of politics is to open up a space of collective sovereignty where such membership can be given political effect. The communitarian idea is that the attainment of character in one's moral life and full engagement in one's civic life require thick identities, and that the liberal conception of the free agency of individuals pulls up short with respect to this normative standard. The multiculturalist idea is that it is with respect to differences of power between cultural groups, not individuals, that the idea of social justice is most importantly tested, and that politics should be subservient to this standard of justice in the relationship between majority and minority cultures. The civic idea is that citizenship is an essential human calling, and that insofar as liberal, nationalist, communitarian, and multiculturalist understandings of politics cramp the idea of shared citizenship, they must be called before the bar of judgment provided by the ideal of citizenship as a critical standard. And so on. Each of these ideas has a significant normative attraction, yet political philosophy would be a vain pursuit if it supplied no intellectual resources for weighing the relative attraction of each vis-à-vis the others. What defines political philosophy as a non-trivial intellectual activity is the hope of discerning decisive reasons for preferring one of these normative conceptions (or some other one not included here), and subsequently apprehending the truth of political life in the light of that philosophically triumphant idea.

Notes

1 One question that is not sufficiently clarified in chapter 1 is why I subsume nationalism under the rubric of a "communitarian" vision of political community. The reason for this is spelled out better in chapter 8: "If ... a properly communitarian argument emphasizes the collective constitution of selfhood, and the political salience of the shared identity so constituted, one would expect communitarians to exhibit significant sympathy for the politics of nationalism – a form of politics that places shared identity and thick communal attachments at the very core of its understanding of political life."

2 For an excellent supplement to the themes concerning citizenship surveyed in chapter 1, see Alan C. Cairns's introduction to *Citizenship, Diversity, and Pluralism: Canadian and Comparative Perspectives*, ed. Alan C. Cairns et al. (Montreal and Kingston: McGill-Queen's University Press, 1999), 3-22. For reasons that should be obvious to readers of the following chapters, I'm heartened by Cairns's claim that "societies in the midst of a major paradigm shift concerning the fate and rehabilitation of a troubled institution such as citizenship can gain more assistance from scholars who do not profess to have found the answers than from the simplifiers who pretend to have done so" (17).

3 Other excellent liberal theories of citizenship are offered in Jeff Spinner, *The Boundaries of Citizenship: Race, Ethnicity, and Nationality in the Liberal State* (Baltimore, MD: Johns Hopkins University Press, 1994); and Richard Dagger, *Civic Virtues: Rights, Citizenship, and Republican Liberalism* (New York: Oxford University Press, 1997).

4   Cf. Bhikhu Parekh, *Rethinking Multiculturalism: Cultural Diversity and Political Theory* (London: Macmillan, 2000): "[Multicultural societies] need to find ways of reconciling the legitimate demands of unity and diversity, achieving political unity without cultural uniformity, being inclusive without being assimilationist, cultivating among their citizens a common sense of belonging while respecting their legitimate cultural differences, and cherishing plural cultural identities without weakening the shared and precious identity of shared citizenship" (343).

5   Brian Barry, *Culture and Equality: An Egalitarian Critique of Multiculturalism* (Cambridge: Polity Press, 2001), 301.

6   Ibid., 300.

7   Ibid., 302. What Barry says about the British political community applies to the attenuated experience of citizenship in liberal societies more generally: "The problem is ... that the criteria for membership in the British nation may be so undemanding as to render membership incapable of providing the foundation of common identity that is needed for the stability and justice of liberal democratic polities" (ibid., 83). Barry clearly doesn't intend this as a warrant for a more nationalistic conception of citizenship.

8   Michael J. Sandel, *Democracy's Discontent: America in Search of a Public Philosophy* (Cambridge, MA: Belknap Press, 1996), 350, 345-7.

9   See Richard E. Flathman, "Citizenship and Authority: A Chastened View of Citizenship," in *Theorizing Citizenship,* ed. Ronald Beiner (Albany: State University of New York Press, 1995), 105-51.

10 For an incisive discussion of problems such as those summarized above, see Daniel A. Bell, "Is Republicanism Appropriate for the Modern World?" (forthcoming in a volume of essays devoted to the work of David Miller).

11 "Diluted citizenship" is a phrase borrowed from the essay by Daniel Bell cited in the previous note.

12 Will Kymlicka, "From Enlightenment Cosmopolitanism to Liberal Nationalism," in Kymlicka, *Politics in the Vernacular: Nationalism, Multiculturalism, and Citizenship* (Oxford: Oxford University Press, 2001), 204.

13 Kymlicka writes: "Liberals cannot endorse a notion of culture that sees the process of interacting with and learning from other cultures as a threat to 'purity' or 'integrity,' rather than as an opportunity for enrichment" (ibid., 211). But Kymlicka doesn't acknowledge that there are elements of this tendency toward closure in *all* nationalisms, including the kinds of liberal nationalism that he is defending.

14 Margaret Canovan, "Sleeping Dogs, Prowling Cats and Soaring Doves: Three Paradoxes in the Political Theory of Nationhood," *Political Studies* 49, 2 (2001): 206, 207. For one example of the contrast between domesticated (theoretical) and undomesticated (real) versions of nationalism, consider what Margaret Moore writes about Charles Stewart Parnell in her book, *The Ethics of Nationalism* (Oxford: Oxford University Press, 2001), 40.

15 See the discussion of Mill's argument in chapter 12.

16 Barry, *Culture and Equality,* 227. Citizenship is problematical in multilinguistic political communities because in such states (Barry refers not only to Belgium but also to Switzerland and Canada), "the linguistic communities tend to carry on parallel conversations confined largely to their own members" (ibid., 226). Cf. Kymlicka, "From Enlightenment Cosmopolitanism to Liberal Nationalism," 212-16, 217-18. Kymlicka notes the discouraging outcome of efforts to promote personal bilingualism in multination states: "The goal was that Belgian citizens, for example, would read a Flemish newspaper in the morning, and watch the French news on television at night, and be equally conversant with, and feel comfortable contributing to, the political debates in both languages. However, these efforts have been uniformly unsuccessful" (ibid., 217; cf. 214 n. 9).

17 Jürgen Habermas, "Struggles for Recognition in the Democratic Constitutional State," in *Multiculturalism: Examining the Politics of Recognition,* ed. Amy Gutmann (Princeton, NJ: Princeton University Press, 1994), 148. Cf. Parekh, *Rethinking Multiculturalism:* "A multicultural society cannot be stable and last long without developing a common sense of belonging among its citizens. The sense of belonging cannot be ethnic or based on shared cultural, ethnic and other characteristics, for a multicultural society is too diverse for that,

but political in nature and based on a shared commitment to the political community" (341).

18 Judith N. Shklar, "Hannah Arendt As Pariah," in Shklar, *Political Thought and Political Thinkers*, ed. Stanley Hoffmann (Chicago: University of Chicago Press, 1998), 367.

19 Mary Ann Glendon, *Rights Talk: The Impoverishment of Political Discourse* (New York: Free Press, 1991), 175.

20 The principle at stake here is well stated by Will Kymlicka: "The boundaries of state and nation rarely if ever coincide perfectly, so viewing the state as the possession of a particular national group can only alienate minority groups. The state must be seen as equally belonging to all people who are governed by it, regardless of their nationality." "Misunderstanding Nationalism," in *Theorizing Nationalism*, ed. Ronald Beiner (Albany: State University of New York Press, 1999), 139. Cf. Cairns, "Introduction": "The number of ethnic groups and nations will for any foreseeable future be vastly greater than the number of states. Coexistence of more than one ethnic group, people, or nation within the same state is, therefore, the inescapable norm. To think of citizenship as if its holders did, should, could belong to a single people who can view the states as 'theirs' and turn it into an instrument to express their culture alone is to live in an imaginary world, or to be willing to sacrifice democracy for the sake of those who have gained control of the polity" (18).

21 Perhaps of some relevance here is the fact that the National Party in Canada, referred to in chapter 1, no longer exists.

22 It is not without reason that Michael Walzer refers to contemporary neo-nationalism as "the new tribalism" (*Theorizing Nationalism*, ed. Beiner, chapter 11) – and note that this label isn't intended by Walzer as pejorative. The basic idea of nationalism is that each "tribe" demands and gets its own state. Therefore, Walzer is of the view (rightly, I think) that the category of nationalism doesn't apply to a fundamentally immigrant society such as the United States.

23 Tom Nairn, "Nationalism Is Not the Enemy," *Observer Review,* 12 November 1995, 4.

Part 1:
Citizenship versus Liberalism

1
Liberalism, Nationalism, Citizenship: Three Models of Political Community

For Canadians, this seems like a timely moment for a systematic reconsideration of the idea of citizenship, for the 1992 referendum demonstrated, if proof was indeed required, that Canadians have especially good reasons to be anxious about whether modern citizenship is in a sound condition.[1] The crisis of contemporary citizenship, however, is of course not a local phenomenon but a global one, and warrants an ambitious effort of theorizing proportionate to the many-layered crises that day by day are rendering citizenship ever more problematical. With our experience today of nationalism, ethnic strife, the fragmentation of previously united multinational political communities such as Yugoslavia, the Soviet Union, Czechoslovakia, and perhaps even at some point our own political community, the problem of citizenship – of what draws a body of citizens together into a coherent and stably organized political community, and keeps that allegiance durable – is placed at the centre of theoretical concerns. But once we put it on the agenda, and begin to examine the problem with some attention, we soon see manifold difficulties starting to unfold. In terms of our own society, we are committed socially and economically to capitalism, whether in a milder or harsher version, and we are committed intellectually to some variety of liberalism. But capitalism is certainly no respecter of civic boundaries; on the contrary, to the extent that our lives today are shaped by the modern corporation, we are driven to attend to market imperatives that transgress and subvert civic boundaries.[2] (This is so pervasive that in Canada a new fringe party such as the "National Party" needs to arise in order to lodge a protest.) As for liberalism, it is a philosophy concerned with upholding the dignity and inherent rights of individuals, understood as instantiations of a *universal* humanity, and so it is unclear why this philosophy would accord any special moral status to the claims of citizenship. Why concern ourselves with the quality of civic life within *our own* national boundaries rather than with, say, human rights violations within some society halfway around the globe?[3] So we see that the two defining commitments of our modern, more-or-less-capitalist, liberal society tend to render the meaning of citizenship deeply problematical, rather than help to dispel what puzzles us here.

In the first half of this essay I want to draw attention to a few of the salient challenges to the idea of citizenship in the modern world, and then in the second half come back again to the question of a principled theoretical response (or perhaps the lack thereof).

Let me begin with Jürgen Habermas's very helpful summary of three contemporary developments that have rendered deeply problematical the relation between national identity and citizenship:

> First, the issue of the future of the nation state has unexpectedly become topical in the wake of German unification, the liberation of the East Central European states and the nationality conflicts that are breaking out throughout Eastern Europe. Second, the fact that the states of the European Community are gradually growing together, especially with the impending *caesura* which will be created by the introduction of a common market in 1993, sheds some light on the relation between nation state and democracy, for the democratic processes that have gone hand in hand with the nation state lag hopelessly behind the supranational form taken by economic integration. Third, the tremendous influx of immigration from the poor regions of the East and South with which Europe will be increasingly confronted in the coming years lend the problem of asylum seekers a new significance and urgency. This process exacerbates the conflict between the universalistic principles of constitutional democracies on the one hand and the particularistic claims of communities to preserve the integrity of their *habitual* ways of life on the other.[4]

These political crises identified by Habermas are indeed central to an understanding of why the problem of citizenship is especially salient in our day. Ethnic and sectarian conflict in northeastern and southeastern Europe; a redefining of national states at the heart of Europe, in a post-Cold War epoch that might have been expected to diminish political turbulence but seems instead to have generated *more* of it; dislocating shifts of identity provoked by mass migration and economic integration, accompanied by defensive reactions to bolster these jeopardized identities: all these political dilemmas have raised anew deep questions about what binds citizens together into a shared political community. To these formidable challenges may be added what is probably the greatest challenge of all to contemporary citizenship, namely persistent mass unemployment, which offers the surest prospect of excluding tens of millions of people even within the richest nations on earth from a sense of full membership in civic community.[5]

With respect to the issue of national identity, the basic problem as I see it is that national citizenship is being simultaneously undermined by globalizing pressures and localizing pressures. These two opposing challenges are by no means unrelated. In fact, particularistic identities assert themselves most forcefully just when globalist tendencies present real threats to such identities. It is no accident, for instance, that nationalism rises up again in Europe simultaneously with a movement toward European integration.[6] Nationalism is typically a reaction to feelings of threatened identity, and nothing is more threatening in this respect than global integration. So the two go together, and although they push in opposite directions, both undercut the integrity of the state, and the civic relationship it defines. This is what I elsewhere refer to as the dialectic of globalism and localism.[7] By calling this a "dialectical" relationship, what I mean is that the two are inseparable tendencies; they are opposites that nonetheless mirror each other, two sides of the same coin.[8] Hence there is an unsuspected correlation between liberalism and nationalism. This thesis, I believe, admits of a more generalized formulation, namely, that the attraction of ideologies generally is a function of deracination; as deracination spreads in modern societies, individuals are increasingly exposed to the grip of ideologies of all kinds (whether universalistic or anti-universalistic).[9]

As I said earlier, I want to come back toward the end to this question of "nation" in the civic sense, as opposed to "nation" in the ethnic sense, and of how the latter subverts the former. So let me turn now to some other issues that pose contemporary challenges to the idea of citizenship. Since my space is limited, let me concentrate on three (related) challenges to the idea of citizenship:

1 what Michael Walzer has called "the civil society argument"
2 what I call "groupism," or "groupist" ideologies, but which might also be called radical pluralism (not the old liberal pluralism, but a new, trendy left-wing pluralism)
3 as a generalization of (1) and (2) above: the postmodernist challenge.

(1 *Civil society*) In the 1970s and 1980s, "civil society" was raised as one of the most prominent banners in the struggle against the Stalinist regimes of Eastern Europe. The basic idea here was that active involvement in an autonomous civil society, one that is composed of a multitude of voluntary associations separate from (or opposed to) the sphere of the state, represents a superior form of citizenship as compared with the decayed citizenship of subservience to an all-pervasive paternalistic state. More recently, this slogan of Eastern European intellectuals has been picked up and embraced by theorists in the West.[10] These theorists argue that given the character of the modern state, with its anonymity, its bureaucratic remoteness, its imperviousness to democratic agency, the modern state is not the vehicle of citizenship but a bar to genuinely democratic citizenship. Citizenship, then, must be *localized*. This is of course a new formulation of an old argument, for all forms of liberalism invoke some version of the civil society argument.

This kind of argument certainly has a lot of force to it. In a very illuminating essay on the topic, Michael Walzer explains the force of this idea, but also traces its limits. As Walzer rightly argues:

> Here is the paradox of the civil society argument. Citizenship is one of many roles that members play, but the state itself is unlike all the other associations. It both frames civil society and occupies space within it. It fixes the boundary conditions and the basic rules of all associational activity (including political activity). It compels association members to think about a common good, beyond their own conceptions of the good life. Even the failed totalitarianism of, say, the Polish communist state had this much impact upon the Solidarity union: it determined that Solidarity was a Polish union, focused on economic arrangements and labour policy within the borders of Poland.[11]

Although Walzer is plainly sympathetic to the civil society vision, he understands that, as he puts it, "citizenship [i.e., political, state-centred citizenship] has a certain practical pre-eminence among all our actual and possible memberships."[12] It is surely highly significant in this connection (as is noted by Walzer as well) that the Solidarity movement in Poland, the most sensational model of the civil society vision, and the one that helped most to inspire this line of theorizing, did *not* confine itself to civil society once the totalitarian state had collapsed, but went on to turn itself into a political party, quickly assuming the reins of government, and the leader of the original Solidarity movement eventually became the president of Poland. This was not a sell-out by Solidarity, but a natural response to the "built-in" insufficiency of the kind of "localized" citizenship made available to us at the civil society level alone.[13]

(*2 Pluralism*) A more radical version of the same argument is made by theorists like Iris Marion Young in the name of group identity, invoking popular slogans such as "the politics of difference."[14] Here the cultural fragmentation of citizenship is seen not as a danger, but as a positive advantage. Debates about multiculturalism in Canada and the United States obviously draw upon this sort of radical pluralist argument. Will Kymlicka has pointed out the central perplexity to which we are led when we follow through this way of thinking to its ultimate limit: "On the one hand, many of these groups are insisting that society officially affirm their difference, and provide various kinds of institutional support and recognition for their difference,

e.g., public funding for group-based organizations ... On the other hand, if
society accepts and encourages more and more diversity, in order to promote
cultural inclusion, it seems that citizens will have less and less in common.
If affirming difference is required to integrate marginalized groups into the
common culture, there may cease to be a common culture."[15]

The pluralist vision poses a threat to the idea of citizenship because
groupism taken to its logical conclusion amounts to a kind of ghettoization.
That is to say, each group in the society withdraws behind the boundaries
of its own group, its own groupist identity, with no need to acknowledge
a larger common culture. Citizenship is then reduced to an aggregate of
subnational ghettoes.[16]

In order to clarify the range of theoretical options, I want to distinguish
three possibilities. The first of these options I will call "nationalism." In a
provocative essay entitled "In Defense of the Nation," Roger Scruton defines
national identity in terms of ethnic-cultural identity.[17] According to Scruton's
argument, groups must assimilate to the "national idea," or if they cannot,
ought not to belong to the political community, but instead should belong to
one that offers them a sense of home and rootedness. The thrust of Scruton's
argument is that what ultimately sustains the liberal state is not a sense of
political membership in the state but the *social* loyalties and allegiances that
define nationhood, and therefore that citizenship as a political concept is
ultimately parasitic upon nationhood as a social concept. In other words, a
relation to the nation as a pre-political community is more basic than any
relation to the state precisely because the former is situated on the social
side of the social/political dichotomy. For instance, Scruton's argument is
that the United States "works" as a liberal state not on account of a sense
of shared political commitment to the Constitution, but rather, because it
has successfully instilled the sense of itself as a genuine "nation," albeit one
defined non-ethnically.[18] It is at the social level, the level at which national
identification reposes, that one secures the sense of pre-political community
without which the liberal state, no less than any other kind of state, dissolves. While Scruton defends the liberal state, he attacks liberals because
liberalism, as he conceives it, is defined by blindness to or willful ignorance
of this essential truth.[19]

Scruton repudiates any association between nation and race. As he defines it, "nation" refers to the development of a people's destiny, preferably
within definite territorial boundaries, embracing shared language, shared
associations, shared history, and a common culture (including, often but not
always, the culture of a shared religion). The idea of a multinational state,
according to this conception, is inherently unsustainable, for such states
either move in the direction of forging a unitary sense of nationhood or
cease to exist. Admittedly, the sustainability of multinational states appears
at present to warrant a great deal of pessimism. (Scruton refers to Lebanon,

Cyprus, and India, but he seems to have been premature in his judgment that Czechoslovakia had solved its problem of common nationhood).[20]

The second option is multiculturalist. In various writings, Bhikhu Parekh offers a strong defence of multiculturalism.[21] According to his argument in its most robust version, the state is obliged to serve the particularistic identities of subgroups, not vice versa. In one passage, he goes so far as to argue that immigrant communities in Britain are bound by no obligation to conform to a larger host culture, on the grounds that British society not only admitted but positively recruited them to help rebuild its postwar economy "in full knowledge of who they were and what they stood for."[22] How far is a society really obliged to go in order to accommodate minority cultures? Is a liberal society required to condone the wearing of veils by Islamic schoolgirls forced by their families to do so? Ought France to exempt North Africans from French military service and allow them to substitute service for countries that in given circumstances may be militarily opposed to France? Should Rastafarians in Britain be exempt from marijuana laws that apply to the rest of the population? Should the Hispanic population in the United States not be required to adapt to English as the primary language of daily life? If there were no limit whatever to cultural pluralism, clearly we would approach the point where the very notion of common citizenship as an existential reality dissolves into nothingness.[23]

Having summarized Scruton's nationalist option and Parekh's multicultural option, I want to propose a third possibility, which I would develop under the heading of citizenship. According to this third conception, there is a requirement that all citizens conform to a larger culture, but this culture is national-civic, not national-ethnic.[24] It refers to political, not social, allegiance, or, to employ the classical liberal dichotomy, it identifies membership in the state, not membership in civil society. I think this conception is captured very well in Jürgen Habermas's notion of "constitutional patriotism."[25] Admittedly, it can be quite tricky to separate out these two senses of nationhood, for the social and the political, culture and state, unavoidably overlap in all kinds of ways. Still, I think this approach offers a helpful way of mediating the debate between nationalists such as Scruton and multiculturalists such as Parekh. As I try to spell out at further length below, what I'm searching for under the title of citizenship is an elusive middle term between opposing alternatives that I find unacceptable.[26]

3 *Postmodernism* In recent years, certain French intellectual fashions have caught on in North America, and the most familiar umbrella term for these new theoretical tendencies is "postmodernism."[27] The basic theoretical challenge here is that the philosophical universalisms that we know from the canonical tradition of the West all involve what we might call a hegemonic function, which is to suppress various particularistic identities. Appeals to universal reason typically serve to silence, stigmatize, and marginalize groups

and identities that lie beyond the boundaries of a white, male, Eurocentric hegemon. Universalism is merely the cover for an imperialistic particularism. If all of this is correct, then the debunking of Western rationalism, and the universalism it presupposes, serves to liberate oppressed groups that are then free to express and articulate their authentic, but suppressed, identities. Postmodernism, thus defined, is actually an encompassing theoretical statement of the claims of localism and pluralism reviewed above. But if we were right to criticize the idea of a localizing and pluralizing citizenship, we ought to be disturbed by the claim by postmodern social theory that *all* social reality is untranscendably local, plural, fragmentary, episodic, and infinitely re-arrangeable.

Postmodern philosophy has sought to do for social theory what the postmodern movement has done in art and architecture: to turn pastiche into a distinctive style; to splice and tape cultural identities so that any comforting sense of fixity or essence is subverted – perhaps to turn the necessities of our modern condition into virtues.[28] In Salman Rushdie's phrase, this involves seeing cultural "mongrelization" as a positive and enriching thing.[29] I certainly agree that there is something attractive and refreshing about this notion that we are all hybrids. Still, there is something worrying here as concerns the possibility of sustaining a coherent idea of citizenship. This worry is captured very well in the following response by John Pocock:

> A community or a sovereign that demands the whole of one's allegiance may be foreclosing one's freedom of choice to be this or that kind of person; that was the early modern and modern danger. A plurality of communities or sovereignties that take turns in demanding one's allegiance, while conceding that each and every allocation of allegiance is partial, contingent, and provisional, is denying one the freedom to make a final commitment which determines one's identity, and that is plainly the post-modern danger ... We may have to resist this, and say that we have decided and declared who we are, that our words have gone forth and cannot be recalled, unspoken, or deconstructed. To say this is an act of citizenship, or rather an act of affirming citizenship.[30]

A postmodern world is one where various "unmakers, deconstructors, and decenterers" tell us "that there is no choice of an identity, no commitment of an allegiance, no determination of one's citizenship or personality that they regard as other than provisional (or may not require one at any moment to unmake)." In response, Pocock insists: "our citizenship may have to be our means of telling them where they get off."[31] So we might hope; but more and more we find today that it is the deconstructors who tend to be successful in telling citizenship where it gets off.

It is doubtless true that the primary motivation behind the politics of difference is to secure inclusion for traditionally excluded groups and marginalized voices. But does it make sense to speak of inclusion if all is particularity, and there is no possibility of rising above the contest of rival particularisms? Inclusion in what? If citizenship doesn't involve a kind of universality, how can there be a community of citizens to which the hitherto excluded and marginalized gain entry? Here, postmodernism leaves us at a loss, and to recover a coherent idea of citizenship we must go back to older categories of political thought (available from Aristotle, Rousseau, or Hegel, for instance, rather than from Nietzsche or Foucault).[32]

We might hope that pillars of the republican tradition such as Aristotle and Rousseau were mistaken in thinking that ethnic and cultural homogeneity is a necessary condition of civic identity. On the other hand, it should be clear that the more that citizens become fixated on cultural differences within the political community, the more difficult it becomes to sustain an experience of common citizenship. In other words, what we share as citizens must have a power to shape identity that at some point overrides, or is more salient than, our local identities. Consider as an example the recent controversy concerning gays in the US military. The argument here, surely (namely, the Clinton argument), is that the willingness and capacity of gay soldiers to contribute to the defence of the American nation pertains to a shared civic identity that is larger, more comprehensive, and possessing a more egalitarian foundation than the more local allegiances of homosexual identity or heterosexual identity. From this point of view, gay activists or gay theorists who want to lay such emphasis on their partial identity as gays that it excludes the possibility of a more general ("sex-blind") citizenship cannot help but undermine the egalitarian argument that Clinton is trying to make on their behalf. Shared citizenship entails egalitarianism, and this egalitarianism is undercut by too much emphasis upon particularistic identity insofar as the egalitarian conception presupposes an appeal to what is shared across divergent cultural or ethnic groups. An obvious parallel is the case of Arab Israelis' exclusion from the Israeli army. I think that there is a compelling egalitarian argument for the full participation of Arab-Israeli citizens in the Israeli Defence Forces. But such an argument presupposes that what Jews and Arabs share as citizens transcends their ethnic identity. One would not be at all surprised if many or most Arabs were unwilling to embrace this egalitarian argument, precisely for the sake of giving priority to their Arab identity (which mirrors perfectly the Jewish motivation that denies them equal citizenship in the first place). This would simply be another way of saying that for them Israeli citizenship is impossible. Yet one would like to think that a citizenship that transcends ethnicity *is* a possibility.[33]

The affirmation of particularity is by no means limited to the sphere of ethnic conflicts and national identity. Certain brands of feminism present the appearance of a kind of "gender nationalism," that is, a self-conception involving the same kinds of narrow particularism we encounter in the realm of ethnic divisions. Another example would be identification with one's own social class, to the exclusion of other classes within society.[34] Yet I think the events of our day entitle us to give special attention to national particularism. After all, no feminists as far as I know are proposing a gender equivalent of ethnic cleansing, and even in the days when class warfare was being waged on behalf of class-based ideologies in Russia and China, this was done in the name of a higher universalism that was supposed to be the ultimate outcome of the struggle of one class against another. But today nationalists are indeed killing one another, and doing so without any appeal to a higher transnational universalism; on the contrary, they do so in brutal rejection of any kind of universalism. Let us, then, probe further the relation between citizenship and nationalism.

Our problem today is that we seem to be locked into a choice between two mutually exclusive alternatives, neither of which strike me as satisfactory. On the one hand, there are the various kinds of universalism that exalt the inviolable moral worth of individuals, seen as human beings *as such*, above and beyond any collective or civic identity that would "particularize" human beings, so to speak. This universalistic vision, as we discussed early on in this essay, tends to render morally dubious any privileging of citizenship, which implies, after all, an exclusive and particularistic identity. On the other hand, we have those forces of exclusivity and particularism that celebrate and affirm just those forms of group identity that distinguish sets of individuals from one another, and which tend, again as we referred to at the outset, to generate those ethnic and nationalistic outbursts whose outcome, as we have seen more and more in the last few years, is the self-dissolution of citizenship. So we are left with two competing visions – liberal universalism and anti-liberal particularism – *both* of which tend to subvert, from opposing directions, the idea of a civic community. Mutually exclusive, but not – one hopes – exhaustive. However, anyone who wants to show that these alternatives do not exhaust the possibilities would have to make available a full-fledged theory of citizenship. And here, I'm sorry to confess, I simply don't have in my possession such a theory of citizenship. (I wish I did.)

Lying at the heart of this dilemma is what I would call the universalism/ particularism conundrum. To opt wholeheartedly for universalism implies deracination – rootlessness. To opt wholeheartedly for particularism implies parochialism, exclusivity, and narrow-minded closure of horizons. Yet it is by no means clear that a viable synthesis of particularistic rootedness and universalistic openness is philosophically or practically available. In practice, and perhaps even in theory, we always seem to get drawn to one unsatisfactory extreme or the other. This elusive synthesis of liberal cosmopolitanism and illiberal particularism, to the extent that it is attainable, is what I want to call "citizenship."

The conundrum sketched here is the same conundrum that we find Rousseau struggling with at the end of the *Social Contract,* where we are left with two unhappy alternatives: political particularism, which is false and inhuman, and moral universalism, which is morally and religiously true but is politically useless and ultimately uncivic.[35] Rousseau criticizes that phoney cosmopolitanism that allows individuals to "boast of loving everyone in order to have the right to love no one."[36] Yet by the same token, Rousseau is as critical as any universalist liberal of the spirit of national exclusivity and parochialism. In the *Second Discourse,* the very thinkers who in the *Geneva Manuscript* are condemned for their cosmopolitanism are praised as "great cosmopolitan souls, who surmount the imaginary barriers that separate peoples"![37] Rousseau is anti-cosmopolitan *and* anti-particularist.[38] The *via media* between universalism and particularism remains inaccessible. The key here, of course, is to distinguish genuine cosmopolitanism from phoney cosmopolitanism (or: to distinguish "the liberal spirit," in the sense of openness to the real diversity of social experience, from "liberal tolerance" in the sense of a shallow acceptance of whatever the existing social order happens to have cast up), but to draw these distinctions is by no means easy, at least theoretically.

In order to help clarify the alternatives here, I want to distinguish three theoretical perspectives:

(1) The liberal perspective emphasizes the individual, and the individual's capacity to transcend group or collective identity, to break the shackles of fixed identity (social station, hierarchy, traditional roles, and so forth), to define and redefine one's own purposes, and so on.

(2) The communitarian perspective emphasizes the cultural or ethnic group, solidarity among those sharing a history or tradition, the capacity of the group to confer identity upon those otherwise left "atomized" by the deracinating tendencies of a liberal society.

(3) Finally, the republican perspective emphasizes "civic" bonds. From my point of view, both of the above two competing perspectives (liberalism and communitarianism) jeopardize the idea of a political community that is reducible neither to an aggregation of individuals nor to a conjunction of identity-constituting groups. That is, both liberal and communitarian theories pose threats to the idea of citizenship as I understand it. The decisive question, of course, is whether there really exists some third possibility that is theoretically coherent and practically viable. I think that Jürgen Habermas is groping in the direction of such a theoretical perspective with his idea of "constitutional patriotism," an idea of citizenship that is intended to be neither individualist nor communitarian, neither liberal nor anti-liberal. But it remains highly uncertain whether one can give sense to such an idea

relative to the realities of life at the end of the twentieth century (or indeed whether such an idea of citizenship has *ever* made sense).

My threefold schema yields two instrumental approaches and one non-instrumental approach to citizenship. According to the liberal perspective, ①
political community is instrumental to the strivings of individuals to give to their lives an authentic meaning or sense that they are happy with as individuals. For example, the idea here would be that membership in "Canada" is justified by the Charter of Rights and Freedoms. According to the com- ②
munitarian perspective, political community is instrumental to the strivings of communities to elaborate a collective identity that can be constitutive of the selfhood of its members (to use Sandel's terms). Here the idea would be, for example, that membership in "Quebec" as a quasi-state would be justified by the state's promotion of the collective identity of Québécois (understood as a linguistic-ethnic category, rather than as a category of citizenship equally applicable to anglophone or allophone citizens of Quebec). According to the third perspective, political community is a good in itself: ③
political traditions constitute living totalities that cannot be reduced to the purposes of individuals or the goals of subcommunities, and our humanity would be diminished if our lives lacked a focus for this civic dimension of existence, even if it were somehow possible to satisfy all of our individual and group purposes without participation in a larger political community. This ambitious claim is a modern (and no doubt watered-down and liberalized) version of Aristotle's ancient claim that human beings are by nature political animals, that without full membership in some kind of polis, we live a life that is less than fully human.[39]

As a kind of easily accessible shorthand, we can call the first perspective the "Pierre Trudeau" vision of citizenship (with its uncompromising appeal to individual rights).[40] In the same way, we can call the second perspective the "Jacques Parizeau" vision of citizenship (with its invocation of "old stock" Québécois). I find both of these accounts of citizenship radically deficient, but I lack confidence that I can come up with a third account that will satisfy readers or satisfy myself, a third perspective that supplies the deficiencies of the first two and retains (in a higher synthesis) the strengths of each (relative to the other). The convincing "NO" that issued forth from the citizens of our political community in the 1992 referendum, some of whom voted no for "Pierre Trudeau" reasons and some of whom voted no for "Jacques Parizeau" reasons, brings home to us in a very concrete political fashion the difficulty of conceptualizing the experience of citizenship in a way that doesn't get drawn into the unhappy either/or enforced by these polarizing alternatives.

Let us summarize our analysis by specifying three models of political community: political community in the service of individual identity (liberalism); political community in the service of communalist identity (nationalism); and political community as an expression of "civic" identity (?).The closest

I can come to filling in this question mark is Václav Havel's appeal to the idea of "Czechoslovakia" as a civic union. But of course, as we all know, both the political movement that Havel founded and the idea of Czechoslovakia to which he appealed have recently succumbed to liberalism in Bohemia and nationalism in Slovakia. The now-departed Czechoslovak federation provides one example, and our own polity provides another, of a more general syndrome whereby citizenship gets squeezed out between the opposing imperatives of liberalism and nationalism: just as Czecho-Slovak citizenship gets squeezed out between Czech liberalism and Slovak nationalism, so Canadian (Anglo-Gallic) citizenship gets squeezed out between Anglo liberalism and Gallic nationalism.[41] Needless to say, these formulas represent a gross simplification of complex societies.[42] But theory typically involves radical simplification, in the interests of sharpening our sense of fundamental alternatives in the midst of complexity.

My basic thesis is that liberalism is correct in its diagnosis of what's wrong with nationalism, and nationalism is correct in its diagnosis of what's wrong with liberalism. Therefore we are left deprived of a suitable vision of political community unless we can come up with a third possibility that is neither liberal nor nationalist, and that somehow escapes the liberal's arguments against nationalism and the nationalist's arguments against liberalism.[43] The problem, as my examples are intended to convey, is that this other possibility tends to get squeezed out between universalizing and particularizing antipodes.

Reflection on citizenship is occasioned by certain commonplace experiences – in my case, reflection on the experience of being a "rootless cosmopolitan." Being a Jewish intellectual in an economically advanced, socially liberal, culturally diverse, and politically very marginalized society, I could not avoid turning out to be a rootless cosmopolitan. The pressures toward rootless cosmopolitanism are so strong that an intellectual (a cosmopolitan intellectual!) such as Michael Walzer has to devote the full force of his energies as a theorist to showing that the moral and intellectual claims of rootless cosmopolitanism are illegitimate.[44] When Kant set out his ideal of the "world citizen," considering politics in the light of a "weltbürgerliche Absicht," he articulated something genuinely attractive, but I suspect that even Kant himself realized that there is at the same time something not entirely attractive in this point of view. (Consider, for instance, what Kant says concerning the sublimity of war in the *Critique of Judgment*.) So, cosmopolitanism is morally and intellectually deficient. But what are the alternatives? Are we to resist rootless cosmopolitanism through the vehicle of something like Canadian nationalism, with all the ludicrous parochialism that this entails? Or do we opt for, say, Québécois nationalism, which is no less ludicrously parochial? All nationalisms are driven by the urge to resist rootless cosmopolitanism, but at the price of embracing various stifling parochialisms in relation to what one might call the ideal of an open humanity. So, cosmopolitanism is unsatisfactory, and anti-cosmopolitanism is unsatisfactory. This inevitably forces upon us the question: can there be an ideal of citizenship that is neither deracinating nor parochializing, or is such an ideal nothing but a chimera?

What is meant exactly by references to the pettiness of nationalism? Of the countless examples that might be offered, let one suffice. Consider the following exchange during a conversation between Salman Rushdie and Edward Said:

> Said: A close friend of mine once came to my house and stayed over-night. In the morning we had breakfast, which included yogurt cheese with a special herb, *za'atar*. This combination probably exists all over the Arab world, and certainly in Palestine, Syria and Lebanon. But my friend said: "There, you see. It's a sign of a Palestinian home that it has *za'atar* in it." Being a poet, he then expatiated at great and tedious length on Palestinian cuisine, which is generally very much like Lebanese and Syrian cuisine, and by the end of the morning we were both convinced that we had a totally distinct national cuisine.
>
> Rushdie: So, because a Palestinian chooses to do something it becomes the Palestinian thing to do?
>
> Said: That's absolutely right.[45]

These discussions of the real or imagined uniqueness of national cuisine may seem innocent enough, but in the fevered world in which we live, there is no telling when such benign reflections may turn ugly. In a documentary film by Michael Ignatieff entitled *The Road to Nowhere*, depicting the shambles that the former Yugoslavia has become, Ignatieff suggests gently to his interlocutors, members of a Serbian paramilitary unit in a village outside Vukovar, that the wine they are drinking is Croatian wine. This draws the vehement retort, "*Serbian* wine!"

This kind of thing is inherent in all nationalisms. (Needless to say, Canadian examples would not be hard to find.) On the other side, I agree with Joseph Carens's argument, cited earlier, that there is something in the very logic of liberalism that carries one toward cosmopolitanism. If we follow this through all the way, we eventually arrive at a point where all national (civic) boundaries become meaningless; that is, where citizenship itself becomes meaningless. These strike me as not very satisfactory alternatives.

A central reason for my concern with citizenship is the feeling that there must be a third alternative beyond liberalism and nationalism, which represent two opposing extremes in the relationship between the individual and group identity. Liberalism seeks to give the individual primacy over the group, even at the price of an alienation from any and every group identity.

Nationalism seeks to give the group primacy over the individual, which – as we see with more and more stark evidence today – contains the seeds of real human evils. As one of the neo-fascist thugs in the film *My Beautiful Laundrette* (directed by Stephen Frears) says, "You have to belong to something." Extrapolating from the film, this statement about the need for belonging can be interpreted in two possible ways: either fascism is a uniquely evil expression of an otherwise benign human need for belonging, or there is a kind of latent fascism implicit in any impulse toward group belonging. I find myself unable to dismiss the element of truth expressed in the second interpretation. Again, given this choice between alienating liberalism and the latent evil in any fully consistent nationalism, my response is that there has to be a third alternative.

In his essay "Nationality," Lord Acton wrote: "The co-existence of several nations under the same State is a test ... of its freedom."[46] The fate of what was previously the state of Czechoslovakia proves how difficult it is for contemporary states to pass this test – notwithstanding the huge advances of liberal democracy that we have witnessed since 1989. Indeed, paradoxically, these advances of liberal democracy appear to have made it *more* difficult for contemporary states to pass this test! What I've been trying to suggest here is that the fate of a country like Czechoslovakia (alas, no longer a country!) – or for that matter the fate of a country like our own – constitutes a philosophical problem.

Source

This chapter was written in 1993; it was published in Spanish translation in *Revista Internacional de Filosofía Política* 10 (1997): 5-22. A revised version also appeared as the introductory essay, entitled "Why Citizenship Constitutes a Theoretical Problem in the Last Decade of the Twentieth Century," in *Theorizing Citizenship*, ed. Ronald Beiner (Albany: State University of New York Press, 1995), 1-28.

Notes

1 Cf. J.G.A. Pocock: "I recall reading, a couple of months ago, an article in the *Economist* forecasting that Canada might become the first postmodern democracy, and wondering whether this was an encouraging prospect." "The Ideal of Citizenship since Classical Times," in *Theorizing Citizenship* (hereinafter *TC*), ed. Ronald Beiner (Albany: State University of New York Press, 1995), 47.

2 Of course, this aspect of the contemporary world economy is a direct entailment of liberalism as applied to the realm of economics. For a good recent statement of the connection between political liberalism and economic liberalism, see James Fallows, "What Is an Economy For?" *Atlantic Monthly* (January 1994): 76-92. As Fallows makes clear, the Western liberal commitment to the primacy of universal markets over national borders necessarily undermines the claims of citizenship in the formation of economic policy. (Thus, Western nations typically treat their citizens as consumers first and foremost, whereas Asian societies such as Japan typically require that the welfare of consumers be subordinated to their interests as members of a distinct political community.)

3 For an account of the globalizing, and therefore implicitly anti-civic, thrust of the liberal tradition, see Joseph H. Carens, "Aliens and Citizens: The Case for Open Borders," *TC*, chapter 8.

4 Jürgen Habermas, "Citizenship and National Identity: Some Reflections on the Future of Europe," *TC*, 255-6. The crisis of immigration and the crisis concerning European integration are clearly connected. The nature of this connection is nicely summarized by Jean-Marie Colombani, editor of *Le Monde*: "Just when we need a sense of strong nationhood to help integrate and absorb a new generation of immigrants, with different races and religions, the French are asked to transfer their allegiance to some vague European idea. This contradiction is feeding an identity crisis and undermining trust in our political leadership." Cited in the *Washington Post*, 21 March 1993, A32.

5 As Michael Ignatieff lays out with great lucidity in *TC*, chapter 2, the modern welfare state was intended to embody a definite *civic* ideal, in the sense that it grew out of the conviction that the state would have to guarantee a modicum of material security in an insecure world if it were serious about giving a content to citizenship that a relentlessly market-based society would otherwise betray without limit. In this respect, the willingness of contemporary Western democracies to tolerate a much greater flux in the structures of economic life, entailing a greatly reduced security of employment, cannot help but be symptomatic of a profound crisis in the idea of citizenship (*TC*, 69). (George Armstrong Kelly's critique of what he labels "Civil II," in chapter 3 of *TC*, strikes me as failing to appreciate sufficiently this civic aspiration at the root of the expansion of the welfare state.)

6 For an elaboration of this phenomenon with respect to the European Community (viz., European federalism as a source, paradoxically, of Le Penism), see Conor Cruise O'Brien, "Pursuing a Chimera: Nationalism at Odds with the Idea of a Federal Europe," *Times Literary Supplement*, 13 March 1992, 3-4.

7 Ronald Beiner, *What's the Matter with Liberalism?* (Berkeley: University of California Press, 1992), 109.

8 Cf. Ernest Gellner, "From the Ruins of the Great Contest," *Times Literary Supplement*, 13 March 1992: "A modern society is a mass, anonymous one in which work is semantic not physical, and in which men can only claim effective economic and political citizenship if they can operate the language and culture of the bureaucracies which surround them. The socio-economic processes which helped establish a liberal and consumerist society in the West also engendered nationalism, for men can only live comfortably in political units dedicated to the maintenance of the same culture as their own. So in the West, the emergence of modernity was accompanied by the emergence of nationalism" (10).

9 On nationalism as a reaction against deracination, cf. Isaiah Berlin, "Nationalism: Past Neglect and Present Power," in *Against the Current*, ed. Henry Hardy (London: Hogarth Press, 1979), 349, 351-2.

10 See, for instance, John Keane, "The Limits of State Action," in Keane, *Democracy and Civil Society* (London: Verso, 1988), 1-30. While Keane is certainly a proponent of the "civil society argument," he fully appreciates why traditional leftists are uneasy about promoting the autonomy of civil society at the expense of the state.

11 Michael Walzer, "The Civil Society Argument," in *TC*, 169.

12 Ibid., 170.

13 See G.M. Tamás, "The Legacy of Dissent," *Times Literary Supplement*, 14 May 1993, 14-19, for a good account of the reasons for the appeal of the anti-political slogan "civil society," and of its sorry consequences in post-communist Eastern Europe. For another useful critique of the civil society argument, see Elizabeth Kiss, "Democracy without Parties?" in *Dissent* (Spring 1992): 226-31.

14 See Iris Marion Young, *Justice and the Politics of Difference* (Princeton, NJ: Princeton University Press, 1990).

15 Will Kymlicka, *Recent Work in Citizenship Theory: A Report prepared for Multiculturalism and Citizenship Canada*, September 1992, 24. (This is a fuller version of *TC*, chapter 10.)

16 A good analysis, in the Canadian context, of what the "politics of difference" does to citizenship, and of how civic solidarity becomes hopelessly fragmented when each interest group puts in its own distinct claim for recognition, is offered in an unpublished paper by Reg Whitaker entitled "What is the Problem with Democracy?" At its worst, the politics of difference is really just a new, trendier version of the old liberal interest group politics, not less cynical for all the leftist patina that accompanies it. For a fuller analysis of the Canadian

situation with respect to citizenship, see Alan C. Cairns, "The Fragmentation of Canadian Citizenship," in *Belonging: The Meaning and Future of Canadian Citizenship,* ed. William Kaplan (Montreal and Kingston: McGill-Queen's University Press, 1993), 181-220.

17 Roger Scruton, "In Defense of the Nation," in Scruton, *The Philosopher on Dover Beach* (Manchester: Carcanet, 1990), 299-337.

18 Ibid., 323.

19 Scruton insists that the communitarian ideal of such thinkers as Walzer, Sandel, and Taylor offers no remedy to the emptiness of liberalism because these theorists fail to recognize that real community entails an affirmation of "sanctity, intolerance, exclusion, and a sense that life's meaning depends upon obedience, and also on vigilance against the enemy" (ibid., 310). Relative to this exacting standard, Scruton would surely say that my efforts to map out an alternative to the liberal idea of political membership really amount to just another version of liberalism.

20 Ibid., 325, 318.

21 Parekh is the prime target in the Scruton essay cited in the preceding notes.

22 Bhikhu Parekh, "The Rushdie Affair: Research Agenda for Political Philosophy," *Political Studies* 38 (1990): 701. For a more balanced view of the reciprocal obligations of majority and minority cultures, see Parekh, "British Citizenship and Cultural Difference," in *Citizenship,* ed. Geoff Andrews (London: Lawrence and Wishart, 1991), 183-204.

23 As is alluded to in my examples, this argument is coming to a boil in France in the political debates concerning assimilation of the Muslim North African population concentrated in the absolutely wretched suburbs circling most of the major cities, especially in the South. The Front National, like Scruton, argues that this is not a matter of racism, but of "national identity." The Socialist government, with Kofi Yamgnane as Secretary of State for Integration, attempted, I believe, to move toward something like what Habermas means by "constitutional patriotism." That is, one cannot be a proper French citizen without being able to accept, for instance, the equality of women, or without being able to serve in the French army in a war against Iraq, and so on. For a good summary of these dilemmas, see *L'Express,* 31 October 1991, 74-88.

24 Does it make sense to apply the term *nationalism* to historical phenomena such as the unification of Italy during the Risorgimento and the founding of Czechoslovakia under Masaryk? This would seem confusing insofar as we tend to think of nationalism today as a separatist force seeking to subdivide existing states according to national-ethnic criteria, whereas Italy under the leadership of Mazzini and Garibaldi and Czechoslovakia under the leadership of Masaryk built up political communities that joined together national subcommunities (Czechs and Slovaks in the case of Czechoslovakia; regional subgroups in the case of Italy). For the same reason, I would hesitate to speak of chauvinistic attitudes in the United States as "American nationalism," whereas the militancy of, for instance, Black Muslim groups in the United States would easily qualify as nationalistic. Perhaps what we require here is a distinction, corresponding to my national-civic/national-ethnic distinction, that distinguishes movements of national self-determination that gather together different groups in a more encompassing political entity and those that split up larger political entities along ethnic or religious lines. This would allow us to distinguish, for instance, the "synthesizing nationalism" of Czechoslovakia in 1918 from the divisive Czech and Slovak nationalisms we are witnessing today (and a similar process of de-unification is afoot in contemporary Italy). Thus one might opt for labels such as a building-up or integrating nationalism versus a demolishing or tearing-asunder nationalism; however, as a point of terminology, I would prefer to reserve the term *nationalism* strictly for the latter. I am grateful to Clifford Orwin for pressing me to clarify this point.

25 See Jürgen Habermas, "Historical Consciousness and Post-Traditional Identity," in Habermas, *The New Conservatism,* ed. Shierry Weber Nicholsen (Cambridge, MA: MIT Press, 1989), 249-67.

26 For a somewhat similar laying out of alternatives, see William Rogers Brubaker, "Introduction," in *Immigration and the Politics of Citizenship in Europe and North America,* ed. Brubaker (Lanham, MD: University Press of America, 1989), 3-6. In saying that I find the multiculturalist alternative unsatisfactory, I don't mean to suggest that claims by cultural

minorities for special treatment are always destructive of citizenship, or that they should never be accommodated. On the contrary, I am in full agreement with Will Kymlicka and Wayne Norman's conclusion ("Return of the Citizen: A Survey of Recent Work on Citizenship Theory," in *TC*, 309) that, given the great variance in historical, cultural, and political situations in multination states, it would not be realistic to expect any generalized answer to the question of how to reconcile common citizenship identity with more particularistic group identities. One must go from case to case and from country to country, and see what actually works in different situations. Federalism is obviously a major device for trying to accommodate cultural differences while preserving common citizenship.

27 These views are typically derived from what Charles Taylor rightly calls half-baked neo-Nietzschean subjectivism. *Multiculturalism and "The Politics of Recognition,"* ed. Amy Gutmann (Princeton, NJ: Princeton University Press, 1992), 70.

28 It is more than a little ironic that Nietzsche is generally cited as the patron saint of the postmodern movement, for Nietzsche anticipated by a hundred years this aspect of postmodernism – namely its "deconstruction" of a unitary culture – and bitterly criticized what he foresaw: see his discussion of the "style of decadence" in *The Case of Wagner*, section 7 (*Basic Writings of Nietzsche*, ed. Walter Kaufmann [New York: Modern Library, 1968], 626).

29 Salman Rushdie, *Imaginary Homelands* (London: Granta Books, 1991): "*The Satanic Verses* celebrates hybridity, impurity, intermingling ... It rejoices in mongrelization ... *Mélange*, hotchpotch, a bit of this and a bit of that ... is the great possibility that mass migration gives the world, and I have tried to embrace it. *The Satanic Verses* is for change-by-fusion, change-by-conjoining. It is a love-song to our mongrel selves" (394). Cf. Edward Said: "The whole notion of crossing over, of moving from one identity to another, is extremely important to me, being as I am – as we all are – a sort of hybrid" (ibid., 182).

30 Pocock, "The Ideal of Citizenship since Classical Times," 47-8.

31 Ibid.

32 For a classic statement of this older vision of citizenship, see Sheldon S. Wolin, *Politics and Vision* (Boston: Little, Brown, 1960), 9-11. In line with Wolin's delineation of the term *political*, a society deserves to be thought of as a "polis" to the extent that it transcends groupism.

33 It is of decisive importance in this connection that one distinguish between countries such as Israel and (contemporary) Germany, where citizenship laws are based on ethnic criteria, and countries such as Canada and France, where citizenship laws avoid ethnic criteria. As is pointed out in a perceptive *Globe and Mail* editorial ("Behind Europe's Fear of the Foreigner," 21 June 1993, A10), there is a disturbing tendency, in France for example, in the direction of ethnically defined citizenship. For further discussion of this contrast between the French "state-centred" conception and the German "*Volk*-centred" conception, see Brubaker, "Introduction," 7-9; and William Rogers Brubaker, "Immigration, Citizenship, and the Nation-State in France and Germany: A Comparative Historical Analysis," *International Sociology* 5, 4 (December 1990): 379-407. See also Michael Ignatieff, *Blood and Belonging* (Toronto: Viking, 1993), 3-10. I am much indebted to Nissim Rejwan for giving me a sharper angle on these questions, particularly on the issue of how nationalism contradicts the universalistic implications of the idea of citizenship.

34 Among the forms of social cleavage that may or may not coincide with national-ethnic cleavages, religion, of course, looms extremely large. Consider, for instance, recent efforts by Hindu extremists to subvert the tradition of secularism in postcolonial India. See Amartya Sen, "The Threats to Secular India," *New York Review of Books*, 8 April 1993, 26-32.

35 I have tried to develop this reading of Rousseau in an essay entitled "Machiavelli, Hobbes, and Rousseau on Civil Religion," *Review of Politics* 55, 4 (Fall 1993): 617-38. What I draw from Book 4, chapter 8 of Rousseau's *Social Contract* is the following schema:
liberalism = Christianity = anti-civic
nationalism = the "national religions" = parochial, inhuman
citizenship = the non-existent civil religion that would combine, impossibly, the universalism of Christianity and the civic character of the national religions.

36 Jean-Jacques Rousseau, *On the Social Contract,* ed. Roger D. Masters, trans. Judith R. Masters (New York: St. Martin's Press, 1978), 162.

37 Jean-Jacques Rousseau, *The First and Second Discourses,* ed. Roger D. Masters, trans. Roger D. and Judith R. Masters (New York: St. Martin's Press, 1964), 160.

38 It strikes me that the message of *The Satanic Verses* is in this respect exactly the same as that of the *Social Contract* (both books, on my reading, are committed to the dual teaching of the soullessness of cosmopolitanism and the inhumanity of tribalism), and it is interesting that in the twentieth-century case no differently than in the eighteenth-century case, the inner ambivalence of the author in relation to the contest between tribalism and cosmopolitanism does not spare his book the fate of being burned by members of his own tribe.

39 The same applies to Hegel's idea of citizenship as combining in a higher synthesis the substantiality of pre-liberal political community with liberalism's respect for universal humanity. Hegel, however, entertained the extravagant assumption that the historical evolution of the modern state somehow guaranteed the emergence of this synthesis. I fully share Hegel's aspiration for something more robust than liberal citizenship that does not involve relinquishing liberal principles, but I see nothing in the cultural and political experience of the past two centuries that warrants Hegel's confidence that the conditions for the realization of his civic ideal are already inscribed in the historical reality of the modern state.

40 Deborah Coyne's denunciation of the collective rights of Acadians offers a good illustration of the argument by Trudeau and the Trudeauites that the major Mulroney constitutional initiatives – Meech Lake and Charlottetown – represented a betrayal of the Charter's vision of the equal citizenship of rights-bearing individuals throughout the polity.

41 It is a nice illustration of the ironies of Canadian citizenship that the leading spokesperson of "Anglo" liberalism in Canada is a French Canadian.

42 In particular, my formula makes it seem as if nationalism were absent on the Czech side of the new border. As a corrective, it is worth noting that the new citizenship law adopted in the Czech Republic reposes on an ethnic classification that has the consequence that many Gypsies who had been citizens of Czechoslovakia find themselves stripped of Czech citizenship, notwithstanding the fact that they had been born on Czech soil; in this respect, the new law appears to follow the exclusivist German model rather than the inclusivist French model (see n. 33 above).

43 I allude to this problem of why liberalism and nationalism offer unsatisfactory alternatives to each other in *What's the Matter with Liberalism?* 123 and 110 n. 33.

44 See Edward Said's defence of Palestinian nationalism in Rushdie, *Imaginary Homelands*: one cherishes national particularity because "twentieth-century mass society has destroyed identity in so powerful a way" (183). Cf. Alasdair MacIntyre, *Whose Justice? Which Rationality?* (Notre Dame, IN: University of Notre Dame Press, 1988): "Rootless cosmopolitanism ... is the fate toward which modernity moves" (388).

45 Rushdie, *Imaginary Homelands,* 175. It is striking that Said and Rushdie are so keen to unearth a distinctive Palestinian national identity, notwithstanding their remarks in celebration of hybridity and mongrelization cited elsewhere in this essay. They seem to allow themselves a little bit of irony here, but not so much irony as to upset their political purpose.

46 Lord Acton, *Essays on Freedom and Power* (Cleveland, OH: Meridian Books, 1955), 160.

2
The Fetish of Individuality: Richard Flathman's Willfully Liberal Politics

The intention that animates Richard Flathman's liberalism lacks nothing for clarity: it is to push the idea of liberalism as far as it will go in the direction of a minimalist conception of political community, short of ceasing to be liberalism and turning into an anarchist or libertarian politics. The motivation behind this theoretical project is equally clear: his political philosophy is motivated by an intense and sometimes hysterical fear of the agencies of state power, as well as a fear that a strongly politicized conception of human purposes will constrain and diminish the otherwise much more expansive range of human possibilities. I confess that when I look at the political characteristics of contemporary liberal societies, what I see is radically different from what Flathman perceives: not a hyperpoliticized experience of life that threatens to crowd out concerns beyond the boundaries of politics, but an underpoliticized existence that leaves most citizens disempowered and indifferent; not a monster state that politicizes everything, but a state that is fairly diffident in applying political power to desirable public purposes (for instance, with respect to public regulation of the economy and the amelioration of material inequalities). In one of his more apocalyptic moments Flathman writes, in *Reflections of a Would-Be Anarchist,* "the fires of state power burn hot and destructively among us" (*R*, 102). I honestly cannot square this judgment with my own perception of the ambitions of the liberal state, and when Flathman refers to "the rage to legislate and administer that is rampant in the modern state" (*R*, 175 n. 12), I wish he would specify precisely what domains of legislation and administration he would like to see expunged from liberal statecraft.

It is tempting to jump to the (unwarranted) conclusion that Flathman's real agenda is to slander the state in order to impugn its welfare functions (which is the purpose of most, though not all, contemporary enemies of state authority).[1] There are some suggestions in this direction in chapter 1 of *Reflections:* willful liberalism, according to Flathman, presupposes "a substantial number of associates who for the most part 'take care of themselves,' who do not need to be 'cared for' by others or by society. And there must be associates who, by cultivating virtuosities such as civility and especially magnanimity, care for others in the [emphatically minimalist!] sense of not inflicting themselves harmfully or destructively on the latter" (*R*, 15-16). Flathman also complains, in both *Reflections* and *Willful Liberalism*, that proponents of what he calls "virtue liberalism" place too much emphasis on the problem of social equality, at the cost of what ought to be the dominant liberal concern, namely themes of free agency and self-enactment (*R*, 9-11, 131; *WL*, 4-5). On the other hand, in *Thomas Hobbes: Skepticism, Individuality and Chastened Politics,* he concedes that "use of governmental authority and power is sometimes the least objectionable way to combat unjustifiable inequalities" (*TH*, 170; unfortunately, he fails to specify the kinds of situations for which this resort to state power is or is not appropriate); and he at least hints that he has little sympathy for neoconservative critics of the welfare state (*R*, 123-4 and 178 n. 11).

In *Willful Liberalism,* we get the same tension between, on the one hand, Flathman's reluctance to commit himself to any particular set of political-economic prescriptions, and on the other hand, his insinuation that contemporary liberalism's preoccupation with social equality and the defence of the welfare state constitutes a betrayal of what fundamentally defines the liberal vision of politics. He writes that "strong voluntarism doesn't attempt to provide, in advance and on the basis of (say) a theory of political economy, a recipe for determining what the state or other aspects of public life can and cannot, should and should not do ... Accordingly, there may be circumstances under which the measures characteristic of socialist and welfare states will be appropriate" (*WL*, 210-11), contrary to the libertarian dogma that such measures are never appropriate. Yet there are repeated hints that he disapproves strongly of the welfarist thrust of much of the most influential versions of recent liberal theory (see *WL*, 128 n. 2, where Flathman makes explicit that "welfare liberalism and the welfare state" embody a failure of nerve in relation to the robustly "voluntarist" version of liberalism that he favours and on whose behalf he argues throughout the book). Again, it is in Flathman's most Oakeshottian moments that his antipathy to the welfarist version of liberalism is most apparent. He appeals to Oakeshott in trying to clarify what he finds repellent and what he finds attractive in Nietzsche's anti-egalitarianism; Nietzsche "crystallizes resistances that I have come to have concerning liberalism as it has evolved" during the last century (*WL*, 181 n. 77). According to Oakeshott, liberalism properly understood is concerned with "the menace of 'sovereign' authority and with constitutional devices [namely institutionally embodied 'natural rights'] to reduce it ... the menace was identified as the propensity of rulers to inhibit the enjoyment of these rights by the exercise of lordship. But these 'natural rights' came to include the enjoyment of certain substantive conditions of things capable of being assured only in the exercise of lordship (e.g., employment, medical attention, education) and consequently what was menacing became, not a lordly managerial government, but a government which failed in its lordly office of assuring to subjects the enjoyment of these conditions" (*WL*, 181 n. 77).[2]

When we put this sympathetic appeal to Oakeshott together with Flathman's earlier suggestion (*WL*, 123-4, 127-8) that the authentic understanding of liberalism is the voluntarist one – social agents should make their own lives without paternalistic intervention by the state – and that recent liberals have caved in to leftist and communitarian challenges "by altering that understanding and sometimes by questioning their own commitment to it" (*WL*, 127), we can discern a definite doctrine concerning the relation between liberalism and the pursuit of social justice, however reluctant Flathman may be to profess it openly.

In fact, however, concerns about political economy and issues of distributive justice cannot be what is driving Flathman's central preoccupations as a liberal, for if they were, these topics would not be (as they are) barely present in his writings.[3] It is clear that something else lies at the core of his reflections, namely, the idea of an unbounded art of living, the self's commitment to the project of its own self-design or self-fabrication, and how this existential enterprise relates to both philosophy and politics, or how philosophy, morality, and politics might constrain or inhibit the self's joy in its own self-creation. Flathman thinks that libertarianism (with which he otherwise has so much in common) has been corrupted by its vulgar "preoccupation with truck and barter," and by its failure to see that the fundamental concern of the philosophical individualist should be "with the making and living of lives, not with 'making a living'" (*WL*, 211 n. 110; he cites the authority of Nietzsche in this context). The catchword of Flathman's political philosophy is self-making, and it is for individuals to make their individuality, not for collectivities or individuals in concert to make their collective or citizenly identity.[4] Like Michel Foucault in the last phase of his work, Flathman conceives, as the supreme end of life, an aesthetics of the self whereby self-designing individuals fashion the authentic singularity of themselves, and the chief purpose of political reflection is to identify threats that politics might pose to this extravaganza of self-making.[5]

Indeed, politics poses such a threat, from Flathman's point of view, that the very status of citizen is regarded as suspect. Citizenship, he writes, is "an office" (*R*, 157) and thus is implicitly a function of "a politically organized and governed society" (ibid.). Therefore, to assume this office is already to be "enmeshed" or "embroiled" in the state (*R*, 182-3 n. 22). "To become a citizen is to submit to political rule; it is to yield to rule that aims to make one into what the regime wants one to be" (*R*, 157). Contrary to the deluded imaginings of participatory democrats, who pretend that citizenship can involve "all citizens [ruling] all of the time," it's untrue that membership in political community can ever be free of "the sting of the submission that is involved in acquiring the office of citizenship" (*R*, 158). In fact for most individuals the reality of citizenship (obscured by "the moraline language of legitimacy and obligation") consists in more or less steady submission to an elite (ibid.). Embracing the office of citizenship therefore implicates us in a structure of authoritative rule, however much we may delude ourselves that we are partners in an enterprise of self-rule (or ruling-and-being-ruled-in-turn): "when we identify ourselves first and foremost as citizens we con-script ourselves to the state that creates that office; in making the activities of citizenship our primary commitment we risk adding the force of our thinking and acting to the authority and power of the state. To the extent that politics becomes avidly participatory and government widely popular, political rule [perniciously] extends its range and deepens its [otherwise already too deep] penetrations" (ibid.).[6] Or as Flathman puts it in "Citizenship and Authority": "citizenship is inseparable from authority ... [Authority] has a role to play only when we disagree concerning the merits of the actions we should and should not take, the policies we should and should not adopt ... either authority has no work to do or it works to give us a reason for an action that we would not otherwise (that is, in the absence of authority) take. To subscribe to authority is to commit oneself to take actions that one would not take if considered exclusively on the merits of the actions themselves [a commitment one can never make without regret] ... [Consequently,] citizenship implicates us in the perhaps necessary but nevertheless objectionable mode of relationship that is subscription to political authority" (*CA*, 143-4, 147).

Flathman's remarks concerning citizenship in *Willful Liberalism*, though brief, help a lot to elucidate just how profoundly hostile he is to what he calls our society's "morally charged and therefore onerous politicality" (*WL*, 198 n. 99; strangely, he claims that it is not just our own society that is pervaded by this onerous politicality but also Montaigne's, Hobbes's, and Nietzsche's). The discussion of citizenship occurs in the context of Flathman's important critique of Tocquevillean liberalism in *Willful Liberalism* (*WL*, 74-80). Tocqueville, like other liberals, is worried that the seeming liberty and pluralism of democratic American life masks a deeper conformism, "a new physiognomy of servitude": "Variety is disappearing from the human race; the same ways of acting, thinking, and feeling are to be met with all over the world" (*WL*, 77). Genuine independence is therefore in deep peril in this new egalitarian age, and is in need of rescue. The means of rescue, for Tocqueville, is a heightened sense of citizen engagement; a strong experience of citizenship and civic-mindedness will rebuild the cultural resources for individuality that other aspects of modern life dissolve. As Flathman sums up the Tocquevillean analysis: "independence or individuality requires *political* activity ... Tocqueville looked to politics rather than government to check these tendencies and to invigorate independence and diversity" (*WL*, 78). Flathman makes the observation here (which will turn out to be a key one) that Tocqueville is relying in this analysis on "a distinction [the politics/government distinction] that requires scrutiny." As Flathman correctly perceives, the Tocquevillean strategy is to push liberalism as far as possible in the direction of civic republicanism, to the point where Tocqueville's proposed cure for American conformism and sameness reads like a direct anticipation of Hannah Arendt's political vision (ibid.). Flathman himself, of course, wishes to push liberalism in precisely the opposite direction, hence the crucial importance of his debate with Tocqueville on the topic of citizenship.

Why does Flathman say that the politics/government distinction requires scrutiny? As a good liberal, Tocqueville is extremely anxious about the centralizing momentum of modern government and the danger that it will turn citizens into passive receptacles of state power; the more that individual citizens can retain civic power in their own hands and assume their civic responsibilities with vigour and commitment, the greater the prospect that individuality and plurality will survive the threats to which modern life exposes them. Why does Flathman resist this analysis? The answer to this question will clarify further the force intended by Flathman when he speaks of citizenship (deprecatingly) as "an office." Flathman argues against Tocqueville that political activity cannot be adequately separated from government (and therefore cannot be an adequate prophylactic against too much government) precisely because "citizenship is an office in, or rather of, government" (*WL*, 80). "Accordingly, to act as a citizen is in part to discharge the duties or fulfill the responsibilities established and defined by an entity that, in Tocqueville's view, those holding that office should be trying to act against. [This generates a] tension between acting against that which one is acting within" (ibid.). What results is a "*complicity* of citizenship and political activity" with "government and its immense and immensely dangerous authority and power" (ibid., my italics). In the next paragraph Flathman refers to the futile "reach for politics *and hence government* to protect and enhance individuality" (ibid., my italics). Flathman means this as a refutation of the Tocquevillean cure for conformity-enforcing and individuality-contracting government: since political activity puts into practice the "office" of citizenship, and since this office is a function of governmental authority, what is meant to counter centralized authority actually reinforces it; no matter how hard individuals try to direct their civic energies *against* the established regime, they cannot escape "complicity" with it. Given the concision of Flathman's account here, it is easy to miss just how paradoxical his argument is. Suppose one asserts one's sense of civic responsibility by joining with other fellow citizens in protest marches against the policies of a heavy-handed or mean-spirited government. Flathman sees this as complicity in the threat to individuality embodied in government *per se*. How so? I suppose he could reply that if the efforts of the protestors ultimately prevailed, they would simply succeed in substituting a new regime, legislating a new set of policies that would presume to install an authoritative regulation of civic life for all citizens (true!); that is, the very act of participating politically aspires to government, or to contributing to the authoritative regulation of the life of fellow citizens (true again). But this simply restates the claim that Flathman wishes to establish, which is that the real threat to individuality and plurality doesn't reside simply in oppressive or excessive government, but is implicit in civic involvement generally. Governmental constraint of individuality is coterminous with civic activity as such (which is what Flathman means by the reference to "politics and hence government").[7]

As Flathman emphasizes throughout his work, anyone who has read Wittgenstein with care and attention (as he himself certainly has) knows that language and social convention thoroughly constitute human experience, and therefore no reasonable liberal will regard "atomism" – the idea that individuals are self-sufficient units rather than products of socialization, tradition, and constitution by linguistic and historical communities – as anything other than an entirely unpersuasive myth. On the other hand, the rhetoric of self-making and the notion that it should be the ideal of liberal politics to leave individuals as much as possible to their own devices reinscribe the idea that individuals can make a life for themselves in abstraction from social relations and larger political realities. It seems almost as if the purpose of Flathman's persistent fascination with Wittgenstein is to keep reminding himself of a reality that he is constantly tempted to wish away: namely the social constitution of individual experience. It is, as the great voices of liberalism since the nineteenth century have forcefully brought to our attention, certainly true that, living in a mass society, autonomy and meaningful individuality are continually in jeopardy. And it is also undoubtedly the case that it is a leading purpose of Flathman's celebration of individuality to respond to the powerful critics of the social conformism reigning within a mass society (see *WL*, 107: Flathman cites Tocqueville, Thoreau, William James, Nietzsche, Weber, Ortega y Gasset, Arendt, Goffman, Oakeshott). But when Flathman echoes Oakeshott's indictment of the "individual manqué" created by the statist and paternalistic political culture of the modern age (*WL*, 203), he is invoking a more radically individualistic – and more emphatically anti-civic – social ideal than the conceptions of individuality appealed to by Tocqueville, or J.S. Mill in his more Tocquevillean moments, or Hannah Arendt.[8] Unlike the more civic-minded nineteenth-century liberals who shared Flathman's concerns about individuality and plurality, Flathman's preferred liberalism "would favor public arrangements and institutions exclusively to the extent that they serve private values" (*WL*, 208). This commitment to hyper-individuality and the corresponding dismissal of political life as a "self-diminishing activity" (*WL*, 205) helps to explain why Nietzsche looms so large in *Willful Liberalism* – and not just this or that aspect of Nietzsche but specifically Nietzsche in his most anti-political and hyper-individualistic guise.[9] (Flathman knows that there are dramatically different sides to Nietzsche's thought, but he deliberately highlights the side of Nietzsche that he thinks can be most suitably appropriated to his own conception of voluntaristic liberalism.) It is striking that the epigram that is quoted most frequently in the three books upon which I have focused in this essay is from Nietzsche, and it expresses a thought that is brutally individualistic: "This is what *I* am; this is what *I* want: – *you* can go to hell!" (*WL*, 177, 190; *TH*, 50 n. 15; *R*, 167 n. 9, 168 n. 3).

One might well ask: What does it mean to "favor public arrangements and institutions exclusively to the extent that they serve private values"? Which "private values"? Flathman knows that politics is inescapable (otherwise one could opt for anarchism rather than liberalism), and he surely knows that any form of politics (including liberal politics) enforces a particular ranking of ideals and aspirations, social practices and moral priorities, ways of life and human possibilities. Yet he recurrently appeals to an experience of individuality that would simply turn its back on the political realm and presume to "make itself" in a social vacuum that actually, as Flathman knows, cannot exist. As quoted earlier, Flathman conjures up the impossible dream – his exemplars here are Montaigne, Hobbes, Nietzsche – of withdrawal from "societies that are pervaded with a morally charged and therefore onerous politicality" (*WL*, 198 n. 99): one cannot fully achieve this withdrawal, Flathman concedes, but there is in the mere attempt to accomplish the impossible a genuine pathos. Flathman's political ideal is nicely encapsulated in a formulation he borrows from William James: "Hands off: ... It is enough to ask of each of us that he should be faithful to his own opportunities and make the most of his own blessings, without presuming to regulate the rest of the vast field" (*WL*, 66).[10] Whether or not we are openly presuming this, or willing or not to acknowledge this presumption, the fact is that the vast field *is* being regulated (that's what politics is, and again, Flathman concedes that politics is inescapable), and therefore the promise of a "hands off" policy that simply leaves individuals to pursue their own opportunities and develop their own blessings is one that cannot be fulfilled.

Flathman recognizes that it is not easy to carry through in a thorough-going way the voluntarist impulse that forms the essence of liberalism as he conceives it. As he writes: "The fundamental and abiding commitment of liberalism is to the most disturbing moral and political idea of all, the idea that each and every human being should be free to think and act as she sees fit. This idea is no more than barely intelligible, and the ideal of implementing it fully is manifestly impossible to achieve" (*WL*, 14). But (leaving aside the question of how to implement fully one's normative principles and sticking with the question of what those ultimate normative commitments should be), Flathman never satisfactorily answers the question his inquiry naturally generates: If unconstrained self-enactment is the core liberal ideal, if uninhibitedly free agency is what gives liberalism its normative power, why stop with liberalism? Why not carry forward right the way to libertarianism? Why not be an anarchist rather than merely a would-be anarchist? Why not scrap institutionalizations and institutionalisms rather than merely abide them grudgingly? Flathman is explicitly and deliberately reluctant to apply his principles to concrete policy questions, and I have considerable sympathy for the reasons that underlie this reluctance.[11] Nonetheless, I think it would help a lot to clarify the content of Flathman's normative vision if he allowed himself to illustrate in more detail how these theoretical commitments might translate into practical commitments. Let me offer an example of how the puzzle I've presented is left unanswered by Flathman – for reasons, I think, that go to the heart of his not-fully-coherent normative commitments. In *Reflections,* he lets it be known that he favours gun control legislation "because it might restrict somewhat the distribution of weapons among folks like you and me" (133-4), as opposed to criminals, who will manage to acquire guns in any case. If individuality and plurality are the supreme liberal goods, why allow the state to prevent individuals from expressing their individuality by purchasing a wonderful plurality of different kinds of guns? Shouldn't a strongly voluntarist liberal celebrate a liberal society where "folks like you and me" (as opposed to real criminals) exercise their powers of self-enactment through their diverse taste in guns, rather than being boringly, monotonously gun-averse? In a liberal society governed by will rather than by reason, one should be fully open to (relish the excitement of) being surprised at any moment by what one's willful and exuberantly unpredictable fellow citizens will spring on one. Again, why liberalism and not libertarianism?

Flathman's liberalism is situated at the threshold that divides liberalism from libertarianism, and he exposes his thought to the full force of the tension between the warring normative ideals that pull on individuals from one side and the other side of this threshold. Flathman's liberalism, as he openly admits, is composed within the intellectual space of the strong temptation to step outside liberalism – to come down on the anarchist or libertarian side of the threshold.[12] In order to articulate a more persuasive social philosophy, Flathman needs to spell out why, on an issue such as gun control, his appreciation of agencies of social regulation allows him to remain true to his genuinely liberal (or even "virtue liberal") impulses, to fight off the temptation to give in to his libertarian impulses. But to give such an account, he would have to start to flesh out more substantive conceptions of shared human goods, and would thus violate his "individuality-oriented," "agency-oriented," voluntarist ideal (which tries to avoid substantive teleological arguments at all costs). It seems to me that Flathman simply evades this predicament by refusing to spell out his own commitments.

It is hopeless to think that on major issues such as gun control, social welfare policies, education, or environmental policies, the outcomes can be "left for each of us to determine for ourselves" (*WL*, 13). Rather, as Flathman sometimes concedes, such issues are inescapably matters for political determination; and it makes sense to empower the broadest range of citizens so that as many of them as possible can contribute to the political determination of outcomes that will shape a public life shared by all. By urging us to settle for a minimalist conception of citizenship, Flathman's politics would have the effect of getting us to resign ourselves to less control over our collective destiny than is tolerable, given the magnitude of what is, willy-nilly, at stake in political life. By encouraging us to think that the major spheres of life-praxis can and should be largely privatized, the idea of self-enacting individuality misconstrues our existential situation and mystifies our relationship to our society.

I want to conclude with two reflections on Flathman's relationship to the discipline of political philosophy, one paying tribute to his fidelity to the vocation of the political philosopher and the other criticizing a kind of resistance on his part to the rationalist predisposition, as it were, of the political philosopher as such. Let me present the latter reflection first (which will allow me to end on a note appreciative of Flathman's substantial intellectual contribution).

The main theme of Flathman's recent work in political philosophy is the idea that political philosophers (or at least liberal political philosophers who cherish individuality as much as he does) should give less emphasis to notions of shared rationality and considerably more emphasis to the notion of incommensurable wills. In general, we think of as liberals thinkers such as Rawls and Habermas who, in their vision of politics, aspire to public reason and mutual transparency. We think of as anti-liberal, on the other hand, thinkers such as Nietzsche and Heidegger who disdain liberal democracy because it banishes the sense of mystery and quasi-religious impenetrability that gives depth to human experience. Flathman's purpose in *Willful Liberalism* is to offer a version of liberalism that embraces the opacities and impenetrabilities that liberals typically fear and anti-liberals typically relish. As he puts it, his purpose in the book is to foreground and valorize "not only difference, separation and incompatibility but indeterminacy, opacity, and incomprehensibility ... features of human affairs that have no better than an insecure place in liberal thinking [and] that are accorded much greater prominence in doctrines and outlooks widely regarded to be illiberal"

(*WL*, 119). Hence the appeal of "voluntarism": "Perhaps [liberals'] frequent insistence on the rational, reasonable, mutually intelligible character of action itself serves to make voluntary conduct vulnerable to control and to diminution? Do liberal attempts to augment these characteristics of action serve rather to enhance the possibilities for intrusion and manipulation?" (*WL*, 128). These questions are given greater urgency, for Flathman, by the rise of new versions of liberal theory – what he labels generically "virtue liberalism" – that place the idea of public reason and public deliberation at the centre of the liberal idea. Rawls offers a weak and ambiguous species of virtue liberalism; "more uncompromisingly virtue-oriented" varieties of liberal theory include the liberalisms formulated by Galston, Gutmann, and Macedo, "all of whom share Habermas's view that, ideally, no domain of thought and action would be exempt from the requirements of deliberative rationality and morality" (*R*, 10). If citizens of a liberal political community are required to be rational deliberators, then what is philosophically salient are the features of human experience that are shareable and mutually accessible; if we deliberate in common about rational norms of public life, then in principle, once those norms are rationally defined, they are binding upon all of us in common. The purpose of political philosophy, seen from this view, is to pursue a rational dialogue concerning the character of suitable public norms, desirable public goods, and the public virtues necessary to sustain this rational dialogue and secure its appointed ends.

This is the conception of liberal political philosophy that causes Flathman the most grief. He relishes opacity and diversities of experience sufficiently far removed from each other as to render the human beings who are the subjects of these experiences well-nigh mutually unintelligible to each other; and he strenuously rejects those versions of rationalist liberalism that interpret such diversities and opacities as a problem to be overcome rather than as something to be welcomed and embraced.[13] This set of ideas is nicely expressed in the following commentary on William James: "Group relationships must be, in part, relationships of mutual intelligibility or comprehension. The actions of numbers of people who are unfathomable to one another may come together to produce consequences that they severally recognize or not, intend or seek to prevent, welcome or regret, and so forth, but some measure of mutual intelligibility is a necessary condition of groups and group activity. One of the charms of James's thinking is his relish for cases in which this condition goes unsatisfied" (*WL*, 72).

Flathman's central idea is that what it means for individuality (and therefore plurality as well) to flourish is to have a form of social order that favours the emergence of individuals who are unique bundles of desire, passion, and purpose, who can be only inadequately fathomed by applying the rational categories generally available for the understanding of human beings, who vitiate general norms and rules, and who are perhaps barely intelligible.[14] The flourishing of individuality is the flourishing of existential mystery, which defeats (or at least eludes) the rational comprehension of human beings by each other.[15] To Flathman's credit, this is a radical social vision. The problem with all of this, quite apart from whether it represents a fully attractive conception of social order, is that there is something in this philosophical idea that runs against the very idea of political philosophy as an enterprise of rational understanding and public reason-giving. If the most desirable social order is one that spawns individuals who are essentially unfathomable, doesn't this undercut the possibility of political philosophy as a discipline of rational reflection on desirable human purposes and desirable social orders? If will, not reason, constitutes the core human reality, wouldn't there seem to be something misguided about the whole enterprise of political philosophy as the pursuit of rational argument and rational dialogue about the best way for human beings to live their lives, individually and collectively? Flathman's brief comments concerning postmodernism (namely, that its adherents postulate "the claim ... that every presumption of more or less definite mutual or even self-understanding can and should be exposed as illusory" [*WL*, 171]) show that he is aware of this risk. As with the postmodernists, does Flathman's celebration of will pull the rug out from under his own activity as a reason-seeking political philosopher?

I promised two reflections on Flathman's relationship to political philosophy; now for the second of these.

Political philosophy in its most ambitious sense consists in the relentless pursuit of a few favoured themes. It is a form of reflection that is uncompromisingly focused on an intellectual epicentre, and then radiates outward, extending to every dimension of social and moral life. Richard Flathman's work meets these highest standards of political philosophy, and the idea of individuality, whether it is or is not ultimately defensible as the supreme political-philosophical norm, is unlikely to find a more articulate champion or a more genuinely philosophical advocate.

Abbreviations

CA = "Citizenship and Authority: A Chastened View of Citizenship," in *Theorizing Citizenship*, ed. R. Beiner (Albany: State University of New York Press, 1995), 105-51.

R = *Reflections of a Would-Be Anarchist: Ideals and Institutions of Liberalism* (Minneapolis: University of Minnesota Press, 1998).

TH = *Thomas Hobbes: Skepticism, Individuality and Chastened Politics* (Newbury Park, CA: Sage, 1993).

WL = *Willful Liberalism: Voluntarism and Individuality in Political Theory and Practice* (Ithaca, NY: Cornell University Press, 1992).

Source

This chapter is in *Skepticism, Individuality, and Freedom: The Reluctant Liberalism of Richard Flathman*, ed. Bonnie Honig and David Mapel (Minneapolis: University of Minnesota Press, 2002), 111-26.

Notes

1 One of the notable features of Flathman's thought that prompts this suspicion is the strong sympathy for Michael Oakeshott's efforts as a political philosopher, expressed consistently throughout Flathman's work. Oakeshott, of course, was committed to what he called "the political economy of freedom," that is, a laissez-faire understanding of the relation between state and economy. That Oakeshott is the major intellectual influence upon Flathman's notions of individuality and self-enactment, and that Oakeshott hugely shapes Flathman's reading of Hobbes (*TH*, 174; *WL*, 2), are incontestable; what impact Oakeshott has on Flathman's thinking concerning the relation between liberty and social justice is much less clear.

2 Quoting Michael Oakeshott, *On Human Conduct* (London: Oxford University Press, 1975), 245 n. 2.

3 In *WL*, 9 n. 3, Flathman recognizes that his readers will be curious where he stands on these issues, but he does little to satisfy their curiosity. What we get are tortuous equivocations: on the one hand, welfarist liberalism diminishes the voluntarist aspect of liberalism that Flathman desires to augment; on the other hand, anti-welfarist doctrines are distinct from Flathman's preferred version of liberalism because libertarianism is by definition a nonliberal doctrine. The most that Flathman can say by way of clarification is that his willful liberalism "partly overlaps with, but in fundamental respects is in opposition to, libertarianism," which falls well short of being sufficiently helpful.

4 "Self-making and self-command wherever possible; mutual, collective, and above all governmental and political disciplines only as necessary or manifestly contributive to the former" (*WL*, 14).

5 For Flathman's strong endorsement of Foucault's "persuasively advanced" critique of "pervasive social control ... abetted and intensified by democratic government," cf. *WL*, 79.

6 My interpolations make explicit the judgments that are implicit throughout Flathman's text.

7 Cf. "that species of state official called a citizen" (*R*, 150)!

8 Contrary to liberalism's critics, "my inclination is increasingly to think that liberalism is *insufficiently* individualistic" (*WL*, 50).

9 Cf. the following: "A liberalism that appropriated something like Nietzsche's affirmation of 'the will' would be less avid for commonality, transparency, and cooperation; it would be more appreciative and celebratory of diversity, disagreement, and mutual indifference. Perhaps it would even diminish somewhat liberalism's notorious ambivalence concerning politics, the state, and the rule of some over others that politics and the state invariably involve" – that is, resolve this ambiguity in the direction of greater hostility toward politics (*WL*, 166).

10 Flathman rebukes Tocqueville, Arendt, and participationist democrats generally for violating the "hands off" rule (*WL*, 79).

11 "This analysis doesn't settle any of the questions concerning public policy that are debated between liberals and libertarians" (*WL*, 9 n. 3), nor does a suitable understanding of the relationship between theory and practice oblige the theorist to settle these questions; "strong voluntarism leaves open most of the issues of public policy ... the particular ways in which [ourselves and our lives, our affairs and activities] will change [as a result of embracing a more voluntarist liberalism], the shapes and characters they will acquire and assume, are left indeterminate – that is, are left for each of us to determine for ourselves" (*WL*, 13); "If a theorist claims that her theory answers [questions of policy] she becomes, in Oakeshott's derisive sense, a 'theoretician,' an 'impudent mountebank'" (*R*, 133).

12 The best liberal thinking is haunted by the thoughts of antinomians and individualist anarchists (*R*, 79); "liberal political theory at its best is enticed by but cannot fully embrace anarchist or antinomian thinking" (*R*, 161); the best proponents of moral and political liberalism are haunted by libertarianism, anarchism, and antinomianism (*R*, 180 n. 9). Cf., anarchism and antinomianism "haunt all forms of liberalism and particularly its strongly voluntarist formulations" (*WL*, 208 n. 106). In *CA*, 151 n. 45, Flathman refers to "the immense attractiveness" of philosophical anarchism.

13 The problem with virtue liberalism, as Flathman sees it, is that it puts too much emphasis on what is public (and therefore general, shareable, and implicitly oriented to the demands of citizenship) and fails to put enough emphasis on what is private (therefore unique and inaccessible to shared experience). Cf., "Claims on behalf of the private realm typically valorize will and spontaneity, independence and autonomy, individuality and diversity, and are accompanied by skepticism concerning the reach of rationality, reasoning, and the principles and rules, duties, and responsibilities that those human abilities sometimes allow us to delineate and to justify to one another. In contrast, argumentation concerning the public domain stresses already-established commonalities as well as the possibilities for extending them through knowing, judging, mutually convincing justification, and the like" (*WL*, 173).

14 Flathman cites three main exemplars of this philosophical ideal: Jamesian zest, Nietzschean free-spiritedness, Oakeshottian self-enactment (*R*, 153).

15 Just as theological voluntarists "sought to restore the majesty of God" by emphasizing the inscrutability of divine will, so secular voluntarists attempt to elevate human self-regard by emphasizing the inscrutability of human volition ("insisting that we human beings are – or could become – what each of us chooses to make ourselves by our own acts of will") (*WL*, 130). See also: the "conception of human action as wonder-ful," as involving a miracle of creativity analogous to divine action, is "the single most important idea in strong voluntarism, the idea – and ideal – in strong voluntarism that is most valuable to a liberalism with a heightened sense of and commitment to individuality" (*WL*, 158 n. 46).

3
Civic Resources in a Liberal Society: "Thick" and "Thin" Versions of Liberalism

The publication of Stephen Macedo's important new book, *Diversity and Distrust,* offers an opportune moment to take stock of some of the major debates that have unfolded in political theory in the past decade or two.[1] In 1999 I heard a talk given in Toronto by a leading American political theorist, Nancy Fraser, in which, in response to a question from the audience, she offered with evident glee her view that the debate between communitarians and liberals had ended in a decisive outcome: the trouncing by liberals of their communitarian adversaries. This judgment is highly debatable. At the very least, Macedo's book demonstrates the extent to which the best in contemporary liberal theory incorporates communitarian insights; more than this, we see that the preoccupations that animate liberal theorizing have actually been reshaped by communitarian themes.

Reflection on Macedo's book gives us the opportunity to pose once again one of the crucial questions that arose from the communitarian challenge to liberalism, namely: How can liberal political philosophy offer a sufficiently rich account of the civic virtues necessary to a good society if the dominant version of liberalism proscribes the weighing of ultimate human ends and the philosophical adjudication between alternative visions of a good human life? Can political philosophy do justice to the experience of full-bodied citizenship without engaging "comprehensive doctrines" about the good for human beings?

Opposing Challenges to Liberalism
During the past ten to fifteen years there have been two kinds of critics of liberalism, more or less. On the one hand, communitarians of different descriptions have complained that liberalism is morally anemic and not concerned enough with defining and pursuing a shared civic good, thereby attenuating the moral resources upon which a good society must draw. On the other hand are postmodernists and proponents of the politics of difference who reject the adequacy of liberalism as a political philosophy. These

critics agree with communitarians that the neutralist aspirations professed by liberals are a sham: even if liberals are genuinely sincere in their desire for neutrality, the liberal social order instantiates a distinctly non-neutral ranking of social priorities (in fact, the difference theorists claim, the liberals represent the interests and point of view of a male/white/middle-class hegemony). The postmodern critic of liberalism differs from the communitarian, however, in thinking that what is needed is not a more robust shared civic good that unites the community of citizens, but, rather, a much more ambitious embrace of diversity that regards even liberal social norms as homogenizing and exclusionary. *Liberal* claims to fairmindedness may be a sham (because insufficient power and voice are given within its public space to those who don't belong to whatever race, ethnicity, class, culture, gender, or sexual orientation happens to be hegemonic); but a non- or anti-liberal regime of difference or diversity *is* both possible and desirable.

Confronted with this dual challenge, liberals, of course, must decide which of these two sets of critics to try to satisfy. (Clearly, satisfying both is impossible, for the more one beefs up the civic core of liberalism, the more the postmodern critics will scream, Marginalization of difference! – and the more one waters down the civic definition of liberalism to appease the difference theorists, the more communitarian critics will repeat their original complaint.)

As Macedo notes in the book, a liberal like Richard Flathman sides with the postmodern critics: the worst sin that liberalism can commit is suppression of difference, and therefore, the thinner and more void of substance liberalism can be made the better.[2] Macedo, on the other hand, sides with the communitarians. Communitarian and civic-republican critics of liberalism, he observes, "have been on to something, [although] not quite what they think [they have been on to]."[3] Communitarian depictions of the neutralist aspirations of liberalism, he concedes, are "not entirely unearned."[4] Macedo basically accepts the communitarian thesis that in any intergenerationally viable society, there will be a "shared civic project," requiring that citizens be educated to this project, and motivated to participate in it (although the liberal project is considerably more modest than the civic project postulated by communitarians and civic republicans).[5] The problem is that liberalism, in recent centuries (at least in certain lucky societies), has been sufficiently successful that its civic project (building tolerance, abating religious and ethnic hatreds, fighting racism, and so on) has been largely forgotten and taken for granted. The main purpose of Macedo's historical narrative in the middle of the book is to remind us of the mammoth cultural struggle involved (and not yet completed) in making public schools an important site of this liberalizing project (what Macedo calls the "transformative ambitions" of a liberal constitutional order). Macedo presents the public school system as a "transformational project" intended to serve "specifically *civic* ends"[6]

– to promote a trans-sectarian *civic agenda*.[7] The purpose of public schools is: "forging a public life."[8]

The mistake made by difference theorists, and their liberal fellow travellers (such as Flathman), is that they too presuppose a civic project, requiring the assimilation of a set of liberal virtues, but this is so much taken for granted that they can focus on the slogan of difference without any attention to the problem of fostering the kind of civic community that could sustain their (tacit) social ideal. There is a nice demonstration by Macedo of how, for instance in Iris Young's work, we encounter another (more ambitious) version of the sham neutrality in liberal neutralism. Young suggests that unlike the limited openness and constrained diversity present in liberal society, in her own preferred social order there would be openness to *all* difference, leaving *no one* voiceless, excluded, or marginalized. But Macedo shows that this cannot be so (nor would we want it to be so). He writes: "A politics that does not, as Young puts it, 'devalue or exclude any particular culture or way of life' is neither plausible nor attractive."[9] Difference theorists, no less than liberals, are committed to a civic regime where freedom, equality, and diversity (but not indiscriminate diversity) are promoted; therefore, "racists, nativists, sexists, homophobes, the corrupt, the violent, and no doubt many others, will be marginalized in their [Young and Flathman's] favored regime. We must all hope that certain groups become and remain marginalized."[10] "There are groups that thrive on ignorance and the demonization of outsiders. Surely, a world in which such groups are marginalized is exactly what we want."[11]

Rawls's Thin Liberalism

One of the key aspects of what is at stake in Macedo's "civicized" version of liberalism is the old question of whether a stance of philosophical neutrality in regard to fundamental conceptions of human good defines contemporary liberalism, which was at the heart of the liberal-communitarian quarrels of the 1980s and 1990s. And if we look at the crucial discussion of liberal neutrality in John Rawls's *Political Liberalism,* we see that a claim about philosophical neutrality continues to be central to the Rawlsian idea of liberalism.

Macedo presents himself as a Rawlsian liberal. Yet Macedo's version of liberalism involves more of a departure from Rawls's political philosophy than Macedo wishes to concede. (I say this as a friend of Macedo's liberalism and as a critic of Rawls's liberalism.) In fact, Macedo lists Rawls among those recent liberals, along with himself and William Galston, who have repudiated the neutralist ambitions of liberalism.[12] Rawls's quite dubious distinction between neutrality of aim and neutrality of effect, developed not in his early work but in *Political Liberalism,* shows that this is not the case.[13] He concedes that neutrality of effect is impractical because any state policies will, willy-nilly, end up affecting the choice of different conceptions of the good on the part of members of the political community. Rawls also renounces a notion of neutrality that gives equal encouragement to "*any* conception of the good" freely affirmed by citizens, since political liberalism enables the pursuit "only [of] permissible conceptions," namely "those that respect the principles of justice."[14] Rawls goes on: "The state is not to do anything intended to favor or promote any particular comprehensive doctrine rather than another."[15] This, Rawls points out, is the Dworkinian meaning of neutrality, and it is precisely this notion of liberal neutrality that the neutrality of aim/neutrality of effect distinction leaves intact (or safeguards).[16]

It is true enough that Rawls, in the same section, insists, Macedo-like, that "political liberalism ... may still [viz., without running afoul of neutrality of aim] affirm the superiority of certain forms of moral character and encourage certain moral virtues," namely, "the virtues of fair social cooperation such as the virtues of civility and tolerance, of reasonableness and the sense of fairness."[17] The crucial point is that – or so, at least, Rawls claims – these virtues are intended to sustain liberalism as a *political conception,* and so, don't draw one into perfectionism, located in the realm of comprehensive doctrines. In fact, one readily suspects that Rawls constructs this whole distinction between political conceptions and comprehensive doctrines (a kind of metaphysical hocus-pocus!) just so that he can allow space for the civic virtues that liberalism needs without upsetting the neutrality of aim that, for him no less than Dworkin, continues to define a liberal regime. Throughout this section, the idea of neutrality of aim depends entirely on the notion of segregating political conceptions from comprehensive doctrines, so that virtues that are manifestly non-neutral politically can be asserted to be somehow neutral in relation to comprehensive doctrines ("the political virtues [which can be embraced without violating neutrality of aim – R.B.] must be distinguished from the virtues that characterize ways of life belonging to comprehensive religious and philosophical doctrines"[18]). In other words, Rawls props up one very shaky theoretical distinction (between neutrality of aim and neutrality of effect) by having it rest upon another very shaky theoretical distinction (between political conceptions and com- prehensive doctrines).[19] The fact that Rawls does this amount of bobbing and weaving in order to salvage the idea of neutrality of aim conveys to us very clearly that Rawls is fully determined to retain the neutralist thrust of his liberalism. What Rawls's neutrality of aim/neutrality of effect distinc- tion implies is that a liberal order *aims* to be neutral, but it can't fully live up to this aspiration because, as it were, non-neutral effects inadvertently ooze out of its norms and policies. Macedo himself pulls the rug out from under this conception when he (quite rightly) refers to "the pattern of life that is promoted by ... political liberalism" – or any other social-political order, for that matter.[20]

Macedo's "Liberalism with Spine"

I don't see any of this hocus-pocus in Macedo's robust account of liberal citizenship in the first five chapters of the book. There are a few passages in this section in which he employs deliberately Rawlsian formulations, echoing the neutrality of aim/neutrality of effect distinction.[21] However, there is no indication here that Macedo is hung up on upholding the neutralist pretensions of liberalism; nor is there any of the fastidiousness with which Rawls denies that any (permissible) comprehensive doctrines are being favoured or disfavoured by his political conception. Later, of course (particularly chapters 7-9), Macedo buys into the basic Rawlsian framework – to be sure, offering an eloquently articulated version of it. In fact, I think the central conception underlying Macedo's book, that of the "transformative constitutionalism" implicit in civic liberalism, makes more sense if one makes a much sharper break with the residual neutralism of Rawls's political liberalism. I don't think Macedo would have a great problem swallowing the proposition that citizenship in a self-governing republic is a substantive good, and that virtues, social practices, and public agencies that fortify this good are to be welcomed, whereas habits of behaviour or conceptions of life that hinder this good are to be resisted. Public education is a good because it furthers the good of common civic identity. This is "perfectionism," in Rawls's vocabulary, not "neutrality of aim." The fact that Rawls *does* have a problem swallowing anything that smacks of perfectionism tells us something important about the limits (or one might say, the highly deliberate self-limiting character) of his philosophical horizons.

Unless we are willing to invest the idea of citizenship with some perfectionist credentials, we won't be able to give our liberalism a sufficiently civic dimension (as Macedo does and Rawls doesn't). Consider another important passage from *Political Liberalism,* this one directly addressing the problem of civic education: "justice as fairness does not seek to cultivate the distinctive virtues and values of the liberalisms of autonomy and individuality, or indeed of any other comprehensive doctrine. For in that case it ceases to be a form of political liberalism."[22] Macedo says he wants to articulate "a liberalism with spine" (10). But I have trouble seeing how we can have a liberalism with spine if, bound by Rawls's philosophical strictures, political liberals are prohibited from endorsing "virtues and values" tied to any particular comprehensive doctrine, such as the promotion of autonomy as a morally desirable attribute.[23] Indeed, why should virtues such as loyalty to civic community, or toleration for that matter, be considered less philosophically controversial than autonomy? As Macedo says, "We should acknowledge [liberalism's partisanship], lest it appear that political liberalism is a Trojan horse for a more comprehensive conception."[24] But if the partisanship is on behalf of a substantive civic order, as it clearly is, then it's hard to see how far-reaching philosophical views of social life can fail to be at stake. Despite

Macedo's efforts in chapter 9 to defend Rawls against Joseph Raz's challenge, Raz's conclusion still stands: "the 'epistemic abstinence' on which political liberalism rests is impossible and, moreover, unnecessary" (this is Macedo's summary of Raz's argument in "Facing Diversity: The Case of Epistemic Abstinence").[25]

Let me go out on a limb and restate the above analysis in a way that Rawlsian liberals may find somewhat provocative: I'd be inclined to say that *Diversity and Distrust,* if we look at the substance of the themes and concerns in chapters 1-5 of the book rather than the Rawlsian account it gives of itself in chapters 7-9, is closer in spirit to *Democracy's Discontent* than it is to *Political Liberalism.*[26] (And, needless to say, Macedo could beef up even further the Sandelian civic side of his civic liberalism if he were willing to shelve his Rawlsian meta-theory.)

Given the differences we've already traced between Macedo's and Rawls's versions of liberalism, we are left asking why Macedo is nonetheless so anxious to present his "civic liberalism" within a standard Rawlsian theoretical framework. An expanded account of the philosophical motivation that is common to these two kinds of liberalism should help us to understand this more clearly. In particular, getting a better idea of how Macedo interprets his own Rawlsianism should illuminate *why* Macedo presents himself as a Rawlsian.

In chapter 7, Macedo gives an account of his own "civic liberalism" that presents itself as orthodoxly Rawlsian. Civic liberalism, like political liberalism, according to his account, is a response to radical pluralism in modern democratic societies. The Rawlsian question is: How does one share a political order with those whose fundamental philosophical and religious views differ radically from one's own? How can the political order be made to embody mutual respect between these divergent conceptions of life? The answer is: public reason – the attempt to justify political and legal norms in a way that doesn't presuppose a singular comprehensive doctrine, but rather cuts across a wide range of divergent comprehensive doctrines. "Citizens honor a duty of civility to one another" by bearing in mind that their fellow citizens cherish radically different religious and philosophical ultimate commitments.[27] Hence there is what one might call an ethos of public reason that seeks to unite citizens on a civic or political plane without trying to harmonize or adjudicate their private convictions. We might interpret this duty of civility by saying that to claim moral truth for the ultimate commitments of some – with political sanction – would cause embarrassment to the ultimate commitments of the rest, so the political principles of a liberal society are to be set up so as to avoid this. Those who disagree radically can agree to settle on legal and social norms *for political purposes* without attempting to settle the philosophical differences that divide them. Since any particular philosophical account of liberal principles (for instance, an autonomy-based account) will be highly contentious, the strategy is to maximize civic agreement within a liberal political community by presenting social and legal norms as a *political* settlement, rather than resting the political community on controversial philosophical principles that will have the appearance of defining a sectarian regime. "We should focus on shared civic virtues and values, and keep the liberal door open to those who reject the wider philosophical ideals of Kant, Mill, or Dewey."[28] If Protestants, Catholics, and Jews are to share a political community, they'll have to do so on the basis of public reasons that highlight what they share as citizens while abstracting from their differences on ultimate conceptions of life. Hence the advantage of defining liberalism in terms that emphasize the civic common ground, while de-emphasizing questions of the truth of this or that "comprehensive doctrine."

My reply to all of this is that, public reason or no public reason, the political order will embody a set of *outcomes* concerning how public life is organized, and these outcomes will express ultimate judgments about what is morally and philosophically desirable. In the penultimate draft of the book, Macedo wrote: "it is illegitimate to fashion basic principles of justice on the basis of religious reasons – or reasons whose force requires that one accept a particular view of human flourishing."[29] But *all* politics involves judgments about securing the conditions for human flourishing, and the contestability of these judgments doesn't alter the unavoidability of this dimension of political life. Part of the problem is giving undue weight to the problem of *religion* within a liberal civic order; as I've argued elsewhere (*What's the Matter with Liberalism?* chapter 3), we get a skewed picture of both the possibility and desirability of neutrality if we see the problem of conflict between irreconcilable religious commitments as offering a general model of how to deal with moral diversity. If we switch to the problem of class, for instance, Rawls's neutrality of aim looks much less plausible. Contrast the civic aspiration embodied in US public schools with the very different civic attitudes embodied in British-style "public schools," that is, highly elitist, class-based private schools. How can a preference for the former not rest upon a comprehensive doctrine? How can one deny the substantive egalitarianism built into the *civic* ideal, intended to embrace all citizens of the republic? A political liberal who defends public schools, as opposed to elitist private schools, cannot do so on the grounds that the latter violate the constitutional requirements of a liberal democracy as such, for the public culture of the United Kingdom is, no less than the United States, the public culture of a liberal democracy. What this shows is that what is at stake in partisanship on behalf of an ideal of civicism, of shared citizenship, is the choice between competing comprehensive conceptions, that is, competing understandings of individual and social good. We *could* say that it's not for a political philosopher to judge between the comprehensive philosophies that these two institutions express, but if that were Macedo's view, I don't see how he could have written *Diversity and Distrust*. As Macedo puts it, public education is part and parcel of "our shared civic project," and affirmation of this shared civic project is itself tied directly to a "perfectionist" ideal: sharing a civic community with all one's fellow citizens.[30]

In the case of religion, for reasons that don't have to be spelled out at great length, the liberal state might well have good reason to do its utmost to display evenhandedness toward the various religious denominations, which one might go so far as to call neutrality of aim – and political liberalism can then be seen as the theoretical encapsulation of this state policy.[31] But if we think, instead, of the problem of class in civic education, there is nothing comparable here to what had motivated upholding an ideal of neutrality of aim with respect to different religious denominations. If civic integration of classes is a social good, the aim, not just the effect, is non-neutral. Any regime of public education – in its robustness, in its command of social resources, in the priority it has among other public priorities – will express a certain way of thinking about citizenship, and this civic conception, in turn, will be grounded in an ultimate ranking of the human good (what Aristotle called an "architectonic" ordering of social purposes, which is what politics is). *All* politics involves ultimate judgments about human flourishing. For instance, why would we ask citizens to set aside (for political purposes) their deeply felt religious commitments for the sake of a shared civic commitment unless we were convinced that citizenship itself embodied a substantive conception of human flourishing? Relative to a context of radical religious disagreement, commitment to citizenship may look "uncontroversial," but the fact is that there is nothing philosophically uncontroversial about the notion that citizenship is a sufficient human good to warrant trumping (for certain purposes) other nonpolitical commitments.[32] If someone is of the view that the key to their human flourishing is to withdraw from the civic sphere and join a monastic order (or for that matter, to agitate on behalf of a sectarian theocratic regime), the claim about the importance of civic community is bound to appear as controversial as any other important claim about what's important in human life. (The Rawlsian strategy, which is to brand such moral-philosophical challenges as "unreasonable," is simply to beg the philosophical question.) The valorization of citizenship itself can only be established on a perfectionist basis; this is where Rawlsian liberalism refuses to tread.

To illustrate the inadequacy of the distinction between political and comprehensive conceptions, let us discuss one example of a particularly dramatic "transformative project" that, precisely on account of the astonishing speed with which the cultural transformation was wrought, gives striking insight into the scale of what is at stake: the liberalization of Quebec society spearheaded by the liberalizing political regime of Jean Lesage in the early 1960s. This involved not just a different kind of politics, but a remaking of the culture of Quebec, a wholesale transformation of the Québécois identity, and a redistribution of political-cultural authority throughout the society, with colossal consequences for the place of religion in the civic life of Quebec. The notion of a "political conception" simply doesn't capture the magnitude of what was transformed politically with respect to culture, identity, and conceptions of life as a whole (precisely what a "comprehensive conception" signifies). Must one consider this liberalizing project illegitimate from the point of view of Rawlsian liberalism? It would seem that this kind of civic project is too morally and culturally ambitious to be consistent with what *Rawls* associates with a political conception of liberalism. Yet it is not at all clear that *Macedo* would deem it too ambitious: this is precisely the sort of thing he is pointing toward with his conception of a liberal transformative project – though usually the transformative project is not conducted with such speed and intensity, and therefore doesn't offer such a dramatic contrast to the modest intentions of a liberalism that tries to steer clear of comprehensive claims.

The basic problem with political liberalism lies, I think, in its very starting point, namely the postulate of radical pluralism. The presumption is that individuals or groups are more or less locked into incommensurable moral-religious commitments, and the political challenge is to get them to share a political order on the basis of whatever aspect of their life ideals is not incommensurable. But any social order qua social order itself embodies deep conceptions of human good (it is for reasons of this kind that Macedo rightly criticizes Niklas Luhmann's views on the "differentiation of society");[33] and political liberalism, with its "epistemic abstinence" and its preoccupation with (especially religious) convictions that set citizens in a liberal polity apart from one another, is handicapped from giving an account of what we can call these civically shared comprehensive commitments. As Macedo himself says, there is a "pattern of life" promoted by political liberalism,[34] which belies Rawls's distinction between neutrality of effect and neutrality of aim. As I suggested earlier, Macedo's central idea of the educative or "transformative" dimension of a liberal constitutional order isn't merely the source of non-neutral effects but is incompatible with neutrality of aim. If Macedo really wants fully to repudiate the neutralist pretensions of liberalism and to offer a thicker account of the "civic project" of liberal society, he would be well advised to jettison his allegiance to Rawlsian political liberalism.

Beefing Up the Civic Dimension

The theoretical distinctions that define Rawlsian liberalism (between neutrality of aim and neutrality of effect, between liberalism as a political conception and liberalism as a comprehensive conception) are a kind of metaphysical sleight of hand by which Rawls tries to smuggle more civic content into liberalism than his embargo on comprehensive doctrines officially allows. Yet the minimalist account of liberalism offered by Rawls inevitably has the effect of stifling the moral and cultural resources that give liberal society civic depth. We get a better idea of how the claim about neutrality handcuffs modern liberalism if we consider how a liberalism like that of John Rawls deals with the relationship between civic life in a liberal society and the religious commitments of its citizens. To take a dramatic example, consider the civil rights movement. It's hard to conceive Martin Luther King Jr. mobilizing political energies as successfully as he did without his religious faith and the moral and rhetorical resources supplied by that faith. Rawls knows this yet he cannot straightforwardly embrace this fact. In *Political Liberalism,* Rawls revealingly confesses that he needed to be talked out of what he calls the "exclusive view" of public reason by two of his followers (namely, the view that "on fundamental political matters, reasons given explicitly in terms of comprehensive doctrines are never to be introduced into public reason. The public reasons such a doctrine supports may, of course, be given but not the supporting [comprehensive] doctrine itself" such as a religious commitment).[35] Yes, Martin Luther King is permitted to appeal to particularistic (or less than fully general) religious commitments in the public realm. But consider what a tortured account Rawls has to give in order to reconcile himself to the appeal to anything other than public reason alone: "the leaders of the civil rights movement did not go against the ideal of public reason ... *provided* they thought, or on reflection would have thought (as they certainly could have thought), that the comprehensive reasons they appealed to were required to give sufficient strength to the political conception to be subsequently realized."[36] In other words, King is permitted to make religious appeals only if it's the *only way* to see his political ideals prevail, as a necessary substitute for what really *ought to be* appeals to public reason! This is, to say the least, a rather convoluted way to think about how we exercise our citizenship, and it offers a telling symptom of how civic resources are diminished by the thin version of liberalism.

Macedo makes the following fair point about critiques of liberalism: "In choosing to criticize neutralist liberalism, ... critics of liberalism [Macedo cites Sandel] [choose] a particularly vulnerable rather than a particularly powerful target."[37] In summarizing this chapter in my Introduction I offered a *mea culpa,* and I'll offer another one here. I certainly accept the conclusion that Macedo's version of liberalism is a lot more powerful than the influential versions of liberalism developed in the 1970s and 1980s; and I also more or less accept the conclusion that critics of liberalism like me made their job of criticism rather easier for themselves by targeting less plausible varieties of liberalism. By way of partial excuse, I can point out that precisely by hammering away at issues of more robust civicism, civic virtue, character formation, and habituation to worthy civic purposes, the critics of liberalism helped to highlight what was woefully missing in an earlier generation of liberal political philosophy, and thereby helped to generate the richer civic themes in a liberalism like Macedo's. In this respect, the communitarian and civic-republican critics of liberalism did liberal theory a big favour. But I won't go so far as to concede that one can do full and adequate justice to civic concerns while remaining within the theoretical horizon of liberalism (certainly not within the horizon of Rawlsian liberalism). If citizenship as a central theme of theoretical concern is now present to a much greater degree in books defending liberalism than it was ten or twenty years ago, then I think communitarian critics of liberalism can claim at least some of the credit; and if communitarians and civic republicans keep the pressure on (rather than proclaim themselves now satisfied), they may also be able to claim credit for pushing the boundaries of liberalism somewhat further in the direction of forms of civic life that are socially and civically more ambitious than liberalism.

Source
This chapter is a revised and expanded version of an essay originally published in *Responsive Community*, 10, 2 (2000): 16-27. Macedo published a response to the essay in *Responsive Community*, 10, 3 (2000): 91-5.

Notes
1   Stephen Macedo, *Diversity and Distrust: Civic Education in a Multicultural Democracy* (Cambridge, MA: Harvard University Press, 2000). In a couple of instances I have quoted phrases or passages from the pre-copyedited manuscript of the book, and have indicated that I have done so.
2   For a critique of Flathman's views concerning citizenship (really, the anti-citizenship implicit in his minimalist version of liberalism), see chapter 2 above. There is a short but sharp Flathman-Macedo debate in *Political Theory* 26, 1 (1998): 81-9.
3   *Diversity and Distrust* manuscript, vii; deleted during the editing process.
4   *Diversity and Distrust*, 8.
5   Ibid., 119.
6   Ibid., 66.
7   Ibid., 53.
8   Ibid., 6.
9   Ibid., 24.
10   Ibid., 26.
11   Ibid.
12   Ibid., 282 n. 13.
13   John Rawls, *Political Liberalism* (New York: Columbia University Press, 1996), 192-5.
14   Ibid., 192 (my italics), 193.
15   Ibid., 193.
16   Ibid., 193 n. 25.
17   Ibid., 194.
18   Ibid., 195.
19   As Macedo concedes, "some of the distinctions that separate a civic [i.e., Rawlsian] liberalism from a comprehensive liberalism are fairly subtle" (*Diversity and Distrust*, 239) – though the concession doesn't deter him from endorsing these distinctions. The motivation behind Rawlsian liberalism is supposed to be a political one, namely, that citizens would balk at being subject to politically enforced norms based on comprehensive conceptions that they don't necessarily share; but this is strange, since one would have to have a fairly sophisticated

grasp of Rawlsian political philosophy in order to sift out comprehensive conceptions from civic ones.

20 *Diversity and Distrust,* 181.

21 Ibid., 12. See also 31 and 121.

22 Rawls, *Political Liberalism,* 200. The claimed neutrality of aim here is again suspect. The passage continues: "Justice as fairness honors, as far as it can, the claims of those who wish to withdraw from the modern world in accordance with the injunctions of their religion, provided only that they acknowledge the principles of the political conception." Rawls's purpose here is to defend political liberalism against the charge that it is "unjustly biased" against, for instance, "religious sects [that] oppose the culture of the modern world and wish to lead their common life apart from its unwanted influences" by insisting that the *intention* governing civic education is limited to the political conception, even if the *effects* spill over into the competition between comprehensive conceptions (ibid., 199). "Society's concern with [the education of children whose parents adhere to such religions] lies in their role of future citizens, and so in such essential things as their acquiring the capacity to understand the public culture and to participate in its institutions" (ibid., 200). But this is puzzling: if what defines the comprehensive conception of the religionists is withdrawal from the modern world, how can political liberalism honour their claims by schooling their children in a way intended to cultivate virtues that will equip them for participation in modern citizenship? This Rawlsian doctrine of civic education (in *Political Liberalism,* section V, 6) also receives scrutiny in Eamonn Callan, "Self-Defeating Political Education," in *Canadian Political Philosophy: Contemporary Reflections,* ed. Ronald Beiner and Wayne Norman (Toronto: Oxford University Press, 2001), 92-104; Callan argues that what is implied is a more ambitious doctrine of civic education than Rawls asserts it to be.

23 Cf. *Diversity and Distrust,* 328-9 n. 34, where Macedo reformulates his own position concerning autonomy in order to bring it into line with Rawls's views. On the other hand, Macedo concedes that "a broad (not comprehensive) commitment to critical thinking is inseparable from the core civic capacities of good liberal citizens" (ibid., 239). This registers his awareness that an "emphasis on equal liberty, critical independence, an awareness of the world and its options, and the ability to reflect on one's particular convictions and aims for the sake of doing justice come[s] very close to a comprehensive philosophical ideal of individuality or autonomy" (ibid.). (Cf., "While I have ... argued for the value of casting liberalism as something less than a fully comprehensive philosophical system, there is no question that the civic liberalism I have defended has broad implications for the shape of people's lives as a whole" [274].)

24 Ibid., 227.

25 Ibid., 212.

26 In conversation, Macedo offered the following response to this challenge: he said that, in his view, there is no necessary conflict between the civic ideals articulated by Sandel and those articulated by Rawls. Macedo thinks that Sandel exaggerates the differences between himself and Rawls, and has failed to demonstrate any intrinsic incompatibility between Sandelian and Rawlsian civic aspirations. This nicely highlights, I think, just how expansive is Macedo's reading of Rawls's political liberalism.

27 *Diversity and Distrust,* 172.

28 Ibid., 175-6.

29 *Diversity and Distrust* manuscript, 349; during the editing process, the phrase "view of human flourishing" was changed to "religious or philosophical framework" (*Diversity and Distrust,* 177-8).

30 *Diversity and Distrust,* 119.

31 Speaking from a Canadian perspective: another important part of the story here is the fixation of Americans on the Supreme Court. Public reason is to be thought of on the model of how a Supreme Court justice would frame his or her arguments, as Rawls himself makes explicit (*Political Liberalism,* lv). Think of how much of politics this leaves out. As Michael Walzer points out in a recent unpublished essay, "Drawing the Line: Religion and Politics," one shouldn't overstate the reason-giving character of political agency, and modelling political

life on Supreme Court judgments does just that: "Politics isn't only a matter of argument, and it's not always the case, perhaps it's only rarely the case, that the best arguments win. Passion and power are also determinative" (14). Cf. John Gray, "The Light of Other Minds," *Times Literary Supplement,* 11 February 2000: "The core institution of recent liberalism is not a parliament, or any other sort of deliberative assembly, but a Supreme Court. Though it describes itself as 'political liberalism,' Rawls's doctrine is in fact a species of anti-political legalism" (12).

32   "A liberal polity does not rest on diversity, but on shared political commitments weighty enough to *override* competing values" (*Diversity and Distrust,* 146, my italics). Given the philosophical depth of the "competing values" that are being overridden, what gives the civic conception the kind of weight sufficient to dictate this deference to itself? The answer must be that citizens (not all of them, but the majority) glimpse something in the idea of citizenship itself of sufficient philosophical depth to warrant this deference.

33   *Diversity and Distrust,* 181.

34   Ibid.

35   Rawls, *Political Liberalism,* 247 n. 36, and 247.

36   Ibid., 251, my italics.

37   *Diversity and Distrust,* 308 n. 52.

4

From Community to Citizenship: The Quest for a Post-Liberal Public Philosophy

Michael Sandel's *Democracy's Discontent* is by far the most ambitious recent attempt to make the civic-republican tradition relevant to current dilemmas.[1] Sandel's argument has two main strands. Part 1 of *Democracy's Discontent* offers a root-and-branch challenge to the grip exercised by procedural liberalism over American constitutionalism in recent decades.[2] Following a general characterization, by Sandel, of the meaning of contemporary liberalism, the main topics of chapter 3 are freedom of religion, free speech, and the regulation of pornography; the main topics of chapter 4 are abortion, homosexuality, and no-fault divorce laws. As one would expect, Sandel's claims in this area are vigorously contested by legal scholars committed to the basic tenets of liberal jurisprudence. Part 2 of Sandel's book lays out a history of civic-republican politics in the United States (and its progressive eclipse) from Thomas Jefferson to Ronald Reagan. Here, too, Sandel's provocative claims have been scrutinized and challenged by thinkers who are more skeptical of the attractions of civic republicanism, and the encounter between Sandel and his critics opens up a full-blown philosophical dialogue on issues of the greatest theoretical and political moment.[3]

A number of intelligent and sophisticated liberal political philosophers have sought to reintegrate the two visions of political life that get opposed to each other in the "liberal-communitarian debate" (which is more accurately depicted as a debate between liberalism and civic republicanism).[4] The liberal vision, concerned with institutional safeguards for human rights, rule-governed civil freedom, and the promotion of individual autonomy, is, these theorists argue, compatible with the republican vision, with its emphasis on collective self-rule, civic virtues, and immersion in shared social practices that build civic character. Why settle for one or other of these visions if we can effect a theoretical synthesis – republican liberalism or liberal republicanism – that gives us the best of both worlds? Yet it's not clear that, while marrying the themes of republican political thought to the liberal vision of politics, one can do full justice to the radicalism of the philosophical claims inhering in the republican tradition (Aristotle's conception of the human being as by nature a "political animal," a creature of the polis; Machiavelli's idea of salvation of one's city trumping salvation of one's own soul; Rousseau's claim that only collective self-rule can redeem the notion of autonomy in a postnatural condition; and so on). In my view, it's not a weakness but rather an important intellectual strength of Sandel's theorizing that he keeps alive a keen sense of the tension between liberal and civic-republican preoccupations. But this very strength of Sandel's theorizing poses a problem in regard to how theory relates to the world of political practice that Sandel doesn't own up to sufficiently, and that he tends to skirt over. As I try to spell out in the last section of this essay, the more faithful we are to the republican tradition in all its philosophical radicalism, the more we are obliged to present our theorizing as an ultimate critical standard (which is what republican political philosophy was for Rousseau) rather than as a practicable political project. As liberal critics of Sandel never fail to point out, the sociology of the modern world renders the republican ideal (at best) a distant dream.[5] This opens up a gulf between theory and practice that is by no means fatal to republican theorizing, but which Sandel, with his hope for a post-liberal public philosophy, is reluctant to acknowledge.

The "Communitarian" Critique of Liberalism

In 1982, Sandel published *Liberalism and the Limits of Justice,* a penetrating theoretical challenge to Rawlsian liberalism. This major work soon came to be associated with an important current within contemporary theory that was subsumed, not necessarily by its proponents, under the label "communitarianism." This had the happy effect of organizing theoretical discussion along what appeared to be clear lines of debate; it had the unhappy effect of lumping together theorists with overlapping but still importantly distinguishable intellectual and moral concerns. More to the point, making "community" in the abstract the point of contention between liberals and their critics often caused considerable confusion about the real basis of the theoretical challenge, by Sandel and others, to the 1970s and '80s style of the political philosophy of liberalism, as I'll now try to go on to explain.[6]

There are real perils in using "community" as the banner under which to rally critics of procedural liberalism. There are, of course, all kinds of communities: big and small, national and local, liberal and illiberal. It's not terribly helpful to be told that community is a good, and that a philosophy that diminishes the importance of community is deficient, until we have more information about the kinds of communities that we are supposed to be defending.[7] Just as a quick antidote to abstract theorizing about the attractions of community as such, consider a few instantiations of community in its concrete diversity: an Amish village, a suburban bridge club, a local chapter of the "Nation of Islam," a skinhead youth gang, a clandestine organization of Irish Americans constituted for the purpose of fund-raising for the Irish Republican Army. Each of these in some respect confers a sense of belonging that allows its members to transcend their bare individuality. Is it therefore true that they all offer commensurable experiences of something – "community" – that, for the very reason that it involves a mode of belonging, is morally superior to individuality? The problem of community was put on the theoretical agenda by critics of liberal individualism such as Sandel, Charles Taylor, Michael Walzer, Robert Bellah, and Christopher Lasch, and they did so by addressing questions both to liberalism as a social philosophy and to the kind of society we think of as a liberal society. They asked whether liberalism as a basically individualistic creed could do justice to the richly textured narrative histories and socially constituted practices by which individuals in any society come to acquire meaningful selves. And they asked, quite properly, whether liberal societies, which basically define and understand themselves within a framework of individualistic categories, can offer the rich experiences of co-involvement and communal solidarity that make for a meaningful human life. The chief point that these critics of liberalism were trying to make is that if we are restricted in our thinking about social and political life to an exclusively individualist moral language (e.g., the moral language employed in the work of John Rawls, Ronald Dworkin, Bruce Ackerman, to say nothing of Robert Nozick), we find ourselves confined within an unacceptably narrow horizon of moral and social experience. It's true that we need a richer and more encompassing moral-political vocabulary than the one we get from procedural liberalism, but this surely doesn't entail the notion that any and all experiences of "community" elevate us to a higher plane of moral experience.

Sandel is well aware of these perils of appealing to community in the abstract. In an important review essay on Rawls's *Political Liberalism* published in the *Harvard Law Review* in 1994, Sandel goes out of his way to insist that it was not at all the intention of so-called communitarians like himself to sanctify community as such as the ultimate standard of right; rather, the intention was to highlight issues of substantive good, present or absent in liberal societies, that were shunned on principle by proponents of neutralist liberalism such as Rawls and Dworkin and their followers.[8] The real issue in the debate with Rawls and his followers, as Sandel rightly says, is whether a liberal theory of justice can be vindicated while avoiding appeal to one among a set of rival and controversial conceptions of the good.[9] Again, what is unfortunate about the term *communitarian* is that it suggests that the ultimate standard of theoretical judgment is community as an indiscriminate good. It's true that some of the writings of so-called communitarians gave some encouragement to this notion.[10] None of these theorists were prepared to hold fast to the banner of community expressed as a full-blown principle of ultimate philosophical judgment, however, and all of them more or less renounced the communitarian label as a helpful or illuminating description of their thought.[11]

If the appeal to community is meaningless in advance of a clear specification of the community being celebrated, which community does Sandel mean to champion: is it the immediate locality, friends, and neighbours one knows personally, or some much larger nationwide community of citizens, the vast majority of whom are in any literal sense strangers? Is it one's family, in the literal sense, or a metaphorical "family" of citizens stretching from coast to coast? In his works prior to *Democracy's Discontent,* Sandel has always been reluctant to specify which of these communities should be privileged, and in his new book, that reluctance to opt for one kind of community or the other is still very much present.[12] In order to dramatize the issue, let's contrast Sandel with one of his putative allies in the assault upon procedural liberalism, namely Alasdair MacIntyre. There is no such ambivalence in MacIntyre: he opts decisively for the local – "schools, farms, other workplaces, clinics, parishes" – as the privileged locus of communal goods.[13] MacIntyre writes:

> When practice-based forms of Aristotelian community are generated in the modern world, they are always, and could not but be, small-scale and local ... modern nation-states which masquerade as embodiments of community are always to be resisted. The modern nation-state, in whatever guise, is a dangerous and unmanageable institution, presenting itself on the one hand as a bureaucratic supplier of goods and services, which is always about to but never actually does, give its clients value for money, and on the other hand as a repository of sacred values, which from time to time invites one to lay down one's life on its behalf ... it is like being asked to die for the telephone company. [So] the liberal critique of those nation-states which pretend to embody the values of community has little to say to those Aristotelians, such as myself, for whom the nation-state is not and cannot be the locus of community.[14]

Sandel is obviously not a pure communitarian localist like MacIntyre, for his project, a revival of civic republicanism, must in some quite large measure involve community in a pan-national sense. Moreover, Sandel, notwithstanding his criticisms of distributive justice as the dominant liberal preoccupation, is a strong supporter of the welfare state, which he would prefer to "beef up" or make more robustly egalitarian rather than diminish. In this sense, Sandel's difference with welfare liberals such as Rawls and Dworkin concerns only the *grounds* of one's egalitarian commitment (or perhaps the rhetoric in which one would like to see it enveloped), not its substance. For MacIntyre, the modern state, far from being redeemed by its redistributive function or its provisions for social welfare, is a monstrosity of liberal-bureaucratic impersonality, Nietzsche's "coldest of all cold monsters." For Sandel, on the other hand, the issue is not whether to accept or reject the welfare state, but whether to mobilize support for it in a language of distributive justice and the entitlements of rights-bearing individuals (which Sandel sees as having proved ineffective) or in a language of civic solidarity and the pursuit of a common good (which he sees as more promising).[15]

Admittedly, there are some significant tensions in Sandel's argument. Sandel, like Charles Taylor, is keen to present himself as a "Tocquevillean decentralist" (this is Taylor's self-description), but, as Clifford Orwin remarks in his critique of Sandel, it is hard to see how one can argue for state decentralization and at the same time expect public authority to be equal to the task of resisting corporate power and combating social inequality.[16] More generally, as Michael Walzer points out, Sandel never really comes to terms with the *tension* between local communities on the one side and national community on the other.[17] Clearly, what Sandel is hoping for is that experiences of local allegiance and experiences of nationwide civic allegiance will work together, reinforcing each other, as they did in nineteenth-century America as depicted by Tocqueville.[18] But as Walzer again persuasively argues, the contemporary United States, with all its ethnic and racial heterogeneity, is vastly different from the social conditions that characterized Tocqueville's America.[19] As Sandel's critics have highlighted in different ways, there is no way of guaranteeing that different kinds of community won't make contradictory rather than complementary claims upon their members.[20] My point here isn't that one ought to rule out the possibility of a harmony between allegiance to local communities and allegiance to a larger civic community; the point is that there is no guarantee that in appealing to community one is appealing to a singular good, and no guarantee even that any particular community embodies a good at all. As Orwin rightly puts it: "Community ... cannot serve as a moral principle; rather our moral principles must furnish the basis of our community."[21] In fact, it's quite clear that one of Sandel's deliberate intentions in writing *Democracy's Discontent* is to move discreetly away from the language of community – presumably in order to avoid the confusions introduced by treating community as an ultimate philosophical standard.[22] In *The New Golden Rule*, Amitai Etzioni has remarked that the term *communitarian* is not to be found in the index of Sandel's book; this is obviously no accident.[23] But switching from the language of community to a language of civicism and republican virtue doesn't necessarily by itself banish the tensions that were previously expressed in the appeal to different kinds of communal embeddedness.

Civic Republicanism and American History

The theoretical armature upon which *Democracy's Discontent* is built is a remarkably simple one. The entire work revolves around a sharply drawn contrast (much *too* sharply drawn, critics contend) between two rival conceptions of political association, corresponding to two rival conceptions of political freedom. The first conception, liberal-proceduralist, is centrally defined by a vision of moral agency, of rational individuals as autonomous choosers of their own ends; with this goes an understanding of politics that leaves maximal space for the exercise of moral autonomy, and that tries to maximize possibilities of practical consensus in a radically pluralist society by steering away as much as possible from the political endorsement of morally and philosophically controversial notions of the good.[24] The rival conception, civic-republican, is preoccupied with problems of character formation and the fostering of virtues conducive to deliberative self-rule. Because civic republicanism involves a much more ambitious idea of politics than what we associate with liberal politics, it also requires, so to speak, a much more ambitious cultural infrastructure, supplied by citizens with deep identities rather than shallow identities. Again, this way of characterizing the moral alternatives will be strongly contested by Sandel's liberal critics. In any case, on the basis of this theoretical contrast, Sandel develops basically two ambitious historical narratives: first, an account of a global shift, over the course of the middle decades of this century, of jurisprudential norms (with respect to family life, religious affiliations, sexual identity, patriotism, and so on) in the direction of the liberal conception of moral autonomy; then, on a larger canvas, an account of the transformation of the social and economic structures of American life, played out in political debates stretching across the whole history of the republic. Here too, the story is one of an inexorable waning of the civic-republican vision, culminating in a near-total eclipse, in recent decades, of civic-republican aspirations, in favour of an idea of politics that privileges the individual's autonomous choice of ends. Sandel tries hard to hold out hope that the candle of the civic-republican ideal continues to flicker, but when we run through the various episodes of his story, we are left, irresistibly, with a considerably grimmer picture of the fate of republican ideals.

In one important sense, at least, *Democracy's Discontent* is more faithful to the communitarian ideal than *Liberalism and the Limits of Justice* was. Sandel's first book pursued the argument about the strengths and weaknesses of liberalism at the level of general (i.e., universalist) principles, whereas *Democracy's Discontent* analyzes the liberal legacy in one particular society. It is, as Michael Walzer says, an exercise in "immanent social criticism" – in Walzer's view, "social criticism as it ought to be written."[25] But whereas the earlier book had assured us that, whatever certain philosophers may presuppose, selves have deep attachments and are rooted in constitutive communities because that is what a coherent theory of the self requires, we learn from Sandel's more recent book that the living of a certain kind of history can do much to loosen our attachments and uproot us from our constitutive communities. What are the major episodes in Sandel's history of liberal America? The central story in chapter 5 is the eclipse of Jefferson's vision of the virtue and independence of yeoman farmers and the move toward large-scale manufacturing within the political economy of the early republic. The central story in chapter 6 is the eclipse of "the artisanal republican tradition" and the failed struggle of the Knights of Labor against the wage system.[26] The central story of chapter 7 is the contest between the decentralist vision of Louis Brandeis and Woodrow Wilson and the nationalizing impulse of Theodore Roosevelt and Herbert Croly during the Progressive era. Chapter 8 continues chapter 7's story of the displacement of the "political economy of citizenship" by the "political economy of growth and distributive justice" as this unfolded in the Keynesian regime of F.D.R.[27] In the final two chapters, we get a few glimmers of the vanquished republican tradition (notably, in the civil rights movement of Martin Luther King Jr.), but Sandel leaves no doubt that the past few decades have seen the more or less total triumph of the procedural republic, with almost every aspect of economic, legal, and cultural life helping to consolidate it. According to Sandel, throughout this whole series of continuous debate across American history, right up until the most recent decades, both sides in each debate appealed to civic considerations (what organization of economic and political life will form better citizens?), but the clear implication of his narrative is that the outcome of these debates has pushed the civic impulse right outside the bounds of contemporary American political life.

In every one of these stories, the bad guys win and the goods guys lose. My impression is that Sandel wants more than anything to write a hopeful book; but the tale he tells is a woeful one. The book is the story of how people in modern America progressively lose the sense that they have meaningful control over their own affairs. The world of *Democracy's Discontent* is a bit like the anti-world of Tocqueville's America – that is, a world where the basic institutions that structure the lives of citizens do not lay a foundation for meaningful self-government, but render that very thing impossible or nearly so. Does Sandel offer solutions? One gets the sense in reading the book that he does very much *want* to.[28] If "public philosophy" got us into this mess, then public philosophy can somehow show us the way out of it. Overall, the narrative of the book, the rather discouraging story it tells about the social and economic process whereby American life has been relentlessly "modernified," seems to me a lot more persuasive than the book's implicit promise that political theory can offer a source of civic edification. This is not to say that modern citizenship is necessarily doomed. People can find modest ways (and very occasionally, quite spectacular ways) of regenerating the civic resources of their lives. As Sandel rightly reminds us, this was – in its essential meaning – the achievement of the civil rights movement in the United States.[29] And it is also the aspiration that now animates the valiant efforts of Ernesto Cortes Jr. and others in the IAF (Industrial Areas Foundation) – again, precisely a movement of civic regeneration.[30] Sandel sees signs of hope in a few other places – the heartening response to the final moments of Bobby Kennedy's career; new initiatives in urban theory; anti-Wal-Mart campaigns – but, let's face it, these intimations of a renewed civicism offer a slender basis upon which to challenge (politically rather than intellectually) the overwhelmingly dominant public philosophy described in Sandel's book.

Is Sandel's story just one big lament? Is the whole thing just the construction of an anti-liberal mythology that has little relevance to the economic and political realities that we face today? Even if one entirely accepts the historiographical accuracy of Sandel's history of the United States, the civic-republican dream is, surely, irrecoverable. Each of the battles in the Sandelian cosmic war between liberalism and republicanism was decisively won by the liberal side, and the losers in these battles (Jeffersonian yeomen, civic-minded artisans, Knights of Labor, corner-store pharmacists) have no sociological or political basis for resuming the fight. Taking Sandel's narrative at face value, we are tempted to concede the point to one of his critics who writes: "Are you a communitarian who is sick and tired of hearing that you see the past through rose-tinted glasses? Is it irksome for you to waste so much time denying claims that communitarians sigh nostalgically for a past that never existed? Then stay away from *Democracy's Discontent,* in which Michael Sandel unwittingly vindicates the charges levelled by communitarianism's critics."[31] But here we must fill in more of the theoretical background in order to have a more subtle appreciation of what Sandel is up to.

A decisive moment in the articulation of contemporary liberalism occurred when Ronald Dworkin wrote that liberal equality demands that "political decisions must be, so far as is possible, independent of any particular conception of the good life, or of what gives value to life. Since the citizens of a society differ in their conceptions, the government does not treat them as equals if it prefers one conception to another."[32] From Sandel's point of view, this articulation of neo-Kantian liberalism has dramatic moral and political consequences that actually shape in crucial ways the contemporary political landscape. Although Sandel never comes right out and says so explicitly, I think he believes that the political discrediting of American liberalism in the 1980s must be interpreted in conjunction with this philosophical endorsement, by Dworkin and others, of "official neutrality amongst theories of what is valuable in life."[33] Rightly or wrongly, liberalism came to be seen as indifferent to moral concerns and cultural anxieties that were, not unreasonably, widespread among American citizens following the turbulent decades of the

1960s and '70s. Reaganite conservatism succeeded in thoroughly discrediting American liberalism by portraying it as the ideology of a morally indifferent and non-judgmental culture (think of John Travolta's brilliant parody, near the beginning of *Pulp Fiction*, of the anything-goes philosophy of liberal Amsterdam – a society where the legal order exists in order to encourage maximum self-indulgence). This association between liberalism and non-judgmentalism destroyed the political credibility of the Democratic Party for a whole generation, until Bill Clinton put it back on the political map by returning to moral themes that earlier Democrats had failed to address. As Sandel rightly points out: "A politics that brackets morality and religion too completely soon generates its own disenchantment. Where political discourse lacks moral resonance, the yearning for a public life of larger meaning finds undesirable expression. Groups like the Moral Majority seek to clothe the naked public square with narrow, intolerant moralisms. Fundamentalists rush in where liberals fear to tread."[34] Sandel puts the point even more directly in a column in the *New Republic:* "Democrats ... resisted the politics of virtue, not by disputing conservatives' particular moral judgments but by rejecting the idea that moral judgments have a place in the public realm ... the Democrats' rejection of the politics of virtue carried a high price, for it left conservatives with a monopoly on moral discourse in politics."[35] So a great deal is at stake, politically, in Sandel's quarrel with neutralist liberalism: nothing less than the political redemption of egalitarian politics in the United States. If egalitarians and centre-leftists come to present themselves in terms closer to Sandel's vocabulary of civic virtue and more remote from the procedural-neutralist vocabulary of his liberal adversaries, this will have real political advantages in re-equipping the American left.[36] *This*, it seems clear, is the real point of Sandel's grand narrative of republican virtues and deep identities.

Sandel tends to postulate Dworkinian liberalism as the telos of American life, and therefore he projects Dworkin and Rawls back into key episodes in American political history, reading these historical turning points as anticipations of the telos: the Rawlsian-Dworkinian procedural liberalism of the 1970s. Sandel makes such ambitious use of this interpretive grid that it begins to sound like a full-blown "philosophy of history," or what postmodernists call a "meta-narrative." One shouldn't be surprised if all of this makes Sandel easier prey for critics in the historical profession. Yet his historical claims are rather peripheral to his primary theoretical project, as I understand it; the real project is to reorient the terms by which the contemporary American left defines itself. Even if the civic-republican vision as a global political possibility isn't recoverable (and everything in Sandel's own narrative suggests it isn't), it will do liberals and social democrats a lot of good to engage with Sandel's anti-liberal narrative (a narrative of virtues, character building, and civic agency rather than a narrative of rights, autonomy, and self-chosen identity). Indeed, some of these good effects have already been apparent in the new (post-neo-Kantian) generation of liberal theory in the past decade or so. The sketching of the relevant political context should help us to understand the central preoccupation of Sandel's work, namely, the need to open up more space for moral deliberation and civic character building as a way of refuting the long-unchallenged presumption that only the New Right in the United States upholds moral standards and takes seriously the moral commitments (of faith, patriotism, devotion to family and neighbourhood) that are central to the identity of most Americans.[37]

Sandel and His Critics

Democracy's Discontent has already elicited lively critical responses, and there is no doubt that Sandel's book will continue to generate fruitful controversies. Liberals, of course, will complain that Sandel attributes to them theoretical vices that they actually avoid, or the avoidance of which is consistent with the liberal tradition at its best.[38] Liberal theorists will also complain that Sandel highlights the virtues of the civic-republican tradition and plays down its vices in a way that obscures why liberal politics came to be seen as more attractive than the politics of republican virtue.[39] Feminists will charge that Sandel romanticizes the traditional family, and that he gives insufficient attention to the patriarchalism of a male-dominated history that is even more deeply inscribed in the civic republican tradition than it is in the liberalism criticized by Sandel.[40] Aristocratic conservatives will argue that Sandel fails to go far enough in his philosophical interrogation of liberalism, and will accuse him of failing to acknowledge to what extent the cultural pathologies he rightly traces in contemporary society are intimately related to modern egalitarianism.[41] Historians of American political thought will challenge the historical accuracy of the liberal/republican dichotomy upon which Sandel structures his narrative.[42] Analysts of public policy and American law will question his interpretations of the American legal tradition as well as the feasibility and coherence of his prescriptions.[43] Finally, even those broadly sympathetic to Sandel's project may find themselves wishing for less reliance upon historical narrative, which merely whets their appetite for a more direct political-philosophical grounding of Sandel's substantive political vision.

This is a formidable array of critical responses; most of these challenges arose in response to Sandel's first book, and it would have been unreasonable to expect that the narrative presented in his second book would satisfy or silence all of these various critics. I don't have the space here to address each of these sets of critics or to evaluate the justice or injustice of their critical challenges (although I will just mention, in support of Sandel, that it's not clear to me why, in order to avail himself of a civic-republican vocabulary, he's obliged to take responsibility for all the sins of the republican tradition

ON 'PUBLIC PHILOSOPHY'

going back to Aristotle – which is what some of his liberal and feminist critics imply). In any case, whether we are persuaded by Sandel or by his critics, we cannot help concluding that only a radical interpretation of our moral and political condition could spawn debates of this scope and depth.

Rather than trying to engage in these multifaceted debates, either on Sandel's side or on that of his critics, I want to limit myself to highlighting one key aspect of Sandel's theoretical approach, and to discuss briefly why I think its centrality to his thought poses an important problem for those, like myself, who are sympathetic to his project. If there is one notion that, more than any other, defines the Sandelian enterprise, it is the one announced in the subtitle of his book: public philosophy. But the notion is not exactly free of ambiguity. Notably, we need to ask: What is the relationship between the Rawlsian political philosophy challenged in chapter 1 of the book, and the "public philosophy" disclosed in the central chapters of Sandel's narrative? It may help to distinguish two possible ways of thinking about public philosophy: (1) an implicit but nonetheless cohering set of conceptions associated with the reigning social, economic, and political practices of a society;[44] (2) an explicit articulation of theoretical principles that has some significant causal role in the evolution of such practices. I'm not sure whether Sandel would be eager to embrace a fully ambitious version of this second rendering of the public philosophy idea (indeed, I'm pretty sure he would prefer to disavow it), but the way in which he talks about the battle of public philosophies, and the fact that it figures so centrally in his historical narrative, suggests that Sandel's conception of public philosophy is closer to the second of these two accounts than he sometimes professes. Sandel would deny, I think, that he attributes any particularly strong causal agency to "official" philosophical articulations of the public philosophy. Still, his narrative reads *as if* the key actors in American history had already read Rawls's philosophy of procedural liberalism, and were guided by it in shaping the American polity in a Rawlsian direction.[45]

Elements of *both* of the conceptions I've distinguished are to be found in Sandel's explicit account of public philosophy in his preface to the book. He writes:

Philosophy inhabits the world from the start; our practices and institutions are embodiments of theory. We could hardly describe our political life, much less engage in it, without recourse to a language laden with theory – of rights and obligations, citizenship and freedom, democracy and law. Political institutions are not simply instruments that implement ideas independently conceived; they are themselves embodiments of ideas ... My aim is to identify the public philosophy implicit in our practices and institutions and to show how tensions in the philosophy show up in the practice. If theory never

is SANDEL LOOKING for AN IDENTITY HERE?

keeps its distance but inhabits the world from the start, we may find a clue to our condition in the theory that we live. Attending to the theory implicit in our public life may help us diagnose our political condition.[46] ⟶ WHAT FOR ?

This important passage doesn't quite resolve the ambiguities that trouble me. If Sandel really means to put the principal stress in this account on the quasi-philosophy "implicit in our practices and institutions," then in principle it would be possible for one to tell exactly the same story about the American public philosophy even if philosophers like John Rawls and Ronald Dworkin had never written their books or were entirely unknown to a larger lay citizenry outside the academy. On the other hand, when Sandel talks about "theory embodied in practice" and "philosophy inhabiting the world," he unmistakably implies that academic political philosophy makes a big difference to the shape of practices and institutions crystallized in a particular public philosophy. Reading *Democracy's Discontent,* it is difficult not to get the impression that Sandel thinks that the American polity would not be in the sorry shape it's in if it weren't the case that John Rawls is the United States' leading contemporary public philosopher. The fact that his account of public philosophy in chapter 1 focuses on Rawls and Richard Rorty reinforces the sense one has that contests within philosophy in the ordinary sense guide his subsequent chronicle of the unfolding of the American *Geist.*[47]

Therefore, while it's not Sandel's intention to inflate the causal efficacy of ideas having their source in the realm of philosophy, the way in which he tells his story (as prestructured by one all-important quarrel between philosophers) smacks of idealism.[48] Consider once again all the liberal-republican battles that Sandel narrates, and whose loss by the republican side he laments: an agrarian versus commercial political economy; a political economy of free labour versus a political economy of wage labour; industrial democracy versus big government; the political economy of citizenship versus the Keynesian preoccupation with growth and consumerism. In each of these cases, it seems to me that one can tell a story that has much less to do with competing public philosophies and much more to do with the all-too-tangible evolution of economic and sociological realities. There is in each case a more-or-less materialist explanation for why the winners won and the losers lost, and the attempt to tell the story at the level of self-interpretations that could have been otherwise (and are therefore in principle reversible) tends to put an overly idealist gloss on social and economic history. This problem is particularly well illustrated in a striking passage in the book where Sandel writes: "The problems in the theory of procedural liberalism show up *in the practice it inspires.* Over the past half-century, American politics has come to embody the version of liberalism that renounces the formative ambition and insists government should be neutral toward competing conceptions

[right margin handwritten notes:] DUE TO REPUBLICAN IDEALISM OF U.S.

[left margin handwritten notes:] OVER TIME, THESE CHANGE; THEY CAN BE BETTER RESPONDED BY A PROJECT THAN BY A REPUBLICAN OR LIBERAL CONCEPTION OF STATE. USE WARRANT CASE REBUTTAL Osama/crisis GOVT/Priv. ETC.

of the good life."[49] One feels compelled to ask: How can a theory articulated in *1971* "inspire" a half-century of political practice?[50]

It strikes me that Sandel faces a problem whichever way he goes with his concept of public philosophy. If he really wants to make the deficiencies of Rawlsian and Dworkinian political philosophy central to the story that he wants to tell about American history, then he is lumbered with a rather implausible view of the causal efficacy of ideas vis-à-vis social reality – which is something he clearly wants to avoid. On the other hand, Sandel could – and should – stick with the notion that a public philosophy is *implicit in social practices* (economic practices, norms of constitutional law, the character of political relationships), waiting to be teased out by an activity of social interpretation, or self-interpretation (precisely what defines Sandel's enterprise). But thinking this through, it turns out that the promise of a Sandelian public philosophy is less than it appears to be at first glance. For it then follows that the consciously or philosophically articulated version of the public philosophy (for instance, Rawls's political philosophy) is more the *expression of* than the *source of* what is embodied in social practices (i.e., the philosophy doesn't "inspire" but merely crystallizes what's already implicit in the practices). This has rather deflating consequences for the enterprise of a renewed contest of public philosophies. Even if we persuade philosophers of the deficiencies of the reigning public philosophy, what reason is there to believe that the practices themselves will change? And if the practices don't change, then neither does the public philosophy. If we reject an idealist account of the causal efficacy of philosophical theories (as Sandel says he does), there isn't much reason to hope that the mere articulation of new philosophical ideals will change the existing public philosophy. Writing a book such as *Democracy's Discontent* surely won't by itself transform apathetic, disconnected, politically alienated quasi-citizens of the contemporary United States into Sparta-like paragons of republican virtue, nor will it turn hyper-individualistic consumers into whole-hearted citizens preoccupied with the common good.[51] This of course certainly doesn't mean that telling the kind of civic narrative that Sandel offers is a pointless endeavour. If we lower our expectations to more modest proportions, Sandel's book does precisely what any good work of social criticism ought to do: it helps those who find themselves unsatisfied or unfulfilled by existing social arrangements articulate or clarify to themselves some of the sources of their dissatisfaction. *Democracy's Discontent*, rightly understood, does not magically transport us into a new public philosophy; rather, it provides us with theoretical insights and historical terms of comparison by which we can submit to critical analysis and judgment the public philosophy we now have and will continue to have for the foreseeable future.

Those who expect social theorists such as Sandel to present us with the redesign of an entire social order are asking too much. What we need most urgently from political theory are the philosophical resources to be fearlessly self-critical as a society. For this purpose, we need alternative vocabularies that pose a radical challenge to the reigning vocabulary of our society – intellectual equipment for thinking outside the boundaries of our present condition. *This* is what Sandel and other critics of liberal theory and liberal practice try to furnish: certainly not some miraculous cure for the "dysphoria" of citizens in our "joyless polity,"[52] but at least a set of theoretical categories that will help us articulate what it means for a society to be deprived of public happiness.

Source

This chapter is a revised version of an essay that originally appeared as the Introduction to *Debating Democracy's Discontent: Essays on American Politics, Law, and Public Philosophy*, ed. Anita L. Allen and Milton C. Regan Jr. (Oxford: Oxford University Press, 1998). The revised version has also been published in French translation in *Politique et Sociétés* 20, 1 (2001): 45-67.

Notes

1   Michael J. Sandel, *Democracy's Discontent: America in Search of a Public Philosophy* (Cambridge, MA: Harvard University Press, 1996). Hereinafter, *DD*.

2   Sandel tends to suggest that liberal public philosophy shapes liberal jurisprudence. But it is not implausible to think that the causal arrow could go the other way. Consider, for instance, the following claim in Brian Barry, "How Not to Defend Liberal Institutions," in Barry, *Liberty and Justice: Essays in Political Theory 2* (Oxford: Clarendon Press, 1991): "The best way of looking at the principle of neutrality [that defines liberal political philosophy *à la* Rawls, Dworkin, and Ackerman] is to see it as a generalization of the line of postwar Supreme Court cases that interpreted with increasing stringency the constitutional requirement that Congress shall make no law establishing a religion" (30).

3   An excellent selection of both jurisprudential and philosophical challenges to Sandel by leading political and constitutional theorists is assembled in *Debating Democracy's Discontent: Essays on American Politics, Law, and Public Philosophy*, ed. Anita L. Allen and Milton C. Regan Jr. (Oxford: Oxford University Press, 1998). Hereinafter, *DDD*. The book also contains a concluding "Reply to Critics" by Sandel (*DDD*, chapter 24). The subtitle of the book is a little misleading: no fewer than five contributors to the book are Canadian, so themes deriving from Canadian political reflection are not entirely absent.

4   For a good recent example, see Richard Dagger, *Civic Virtues: Rights, Citizenship, and Republican Liberalism* (New York: Oxford University Press, 1997). See also Cass R. Sunstein, "Beyond the Republican Revival," *Yale Law Journal* 97 (1988): 1539-89; and Lawrence B. Solum, "Virtues and Voices," *Chicago-Kent Law Review* 66, 1 (1990): 111-40, followed by my "Comment on Solum," 141-3.

5   See, for example, Jeremy Waldron (*DDD*, chapter 2).

6   For a fuller elaboration, see Ronald Beiner, *What's the Matter with Liberalism?* (Berkeley: University of California Press, 1992), chapter 2; and Ronald Beiner, *Philosophy in a Time of Lost Spirit: Essays on Contemporary Theory* (Toronto: University of Toronto Press, 1997), chapter 1.

7   For an excellent discussion of the clash between different kinds of community, different kinds of "encumbrance," see Michael Walzer (*DDD*, chapter 13). Similar dilemmas also run through Nancy Rosenblum's essay (*DDD*, chapter 21). Cf. Mark Tushnet, "A Public Philosophy for the Professional-Managerial Class," *Yale Law Journal* 106, 5 (March 1997): "Sandel wants our public philosophy to acknowledge ... that we are embedded rather than 'free and independent selves.' But in what community or communities are we embedded? And when the selves these communities attempt to shape conflict, how is our public

philosophy to resolve such conflicts?" (1601); Tushnet argues persuasively in this context that Sandel welcomes the civic advantages of American federalism but makes things too easy for himself by tacitly assuming that giving more authority to local communities won't yield illiberal outcomes.

8 One shouldn't be misled by this into thinking that neutralist or proceduralist accounts of liberalism exhaust contemporary liberal thought. Therefore one can sympathize with critics who complain that Sandel, in *Democracy's Discontent*, fails to address the more virtue-oriented or perfectionist versions of liberalism that arose subsequent to the initial liberal-communitarian debate: see, for instance, Daniel A. Bell, "Liberal Neutrality and Its Role in American Political Life," *Responsive Community* 7, 2 (1997): 62. But the attempt to show that the liberal tradition has the intellectual resources to generate more ambitious kinds of social theory than the proceduralist versions of liberalism that were dominant in the 1970s and early '80s somewhat misses the point of Sandel's new book. In *Democracy's Discontent*, the central issue is not the limits or potentialities of political philosophies as such, but rather, their symptomatic character in relation to *public* philosophies. Hence what concerns Sandel in Rawls's thought is not its (perhaps inadequate) character as a political philosophy but rather the way it reflects (*accurately*) the reigning public philosophy.

9 Michael J. Sandel, "Political Liberalism," *Harvard Law Review* 107, 7 (1994): 1767. In his presentation at the McDonough Symposium, William Galston suggested that the supposed contest between appeals to "the right" and appeals to "the good" is in fact a contest between two competing conceptions of the good. According to Galston's wonderful formulation, "the right" is really the liberal conception of the good "that dare not speak its name." (Most of the papers in *DDD* were originally presented at the McDonough Symposium, held at the Georgetown University Law Center on 21-22 April 1997.)

10 Cf. Sandel, "Political Liberalism," 1767 n. 12.

11 I can report from personal experience how difficult it can be to shake off this annoying label. Even though one of the sections of my book on liberalism carries the subtitle "Why I Am Not a Communitarian," Brenda Almond, in a review essay on that book in *Critical Review* 8, 2 (1994), is not deterred from classifying me as a communitarian (236); Jeffrey Friedman, in an article in the same issue (328), softens this somewhat by calling me a "quasicommunitarian." Cf. Alasdair MacIntyre, "The Spectre of Communitarianism," *Radical Philosophy* 70 (1995): "I have myself strenuously disowned this label, but to little effect" (34). For a statement of Sandel's own uneasiness with the label, see *Liberalism and the Limits of Justice*, 2nd ed. (Cambridge: Cambridge University Press, 1998), ix-xi (Preface to the Second Edition: The Limits of Communitarianism).

12 As Nancy Rosenblum wrote in an earlier draft of chapter 21 of *DDD*, "The public philosophy Sandel prescribes ... is sympathetic to decentralization and to the inadequacies of national community, but exhibits reservations in its commitment to local autonomy."

13 Alasdair MacIntyre, "I'm Not a Communitarian, But ...," *Responsive Community* 1, 3 (1991): 91.

14 Alasdair MacIntyre, "A Partial Response to My Critics," in *After MacIntyre: Critical Perspectives on the Work of Alasdair MacIntyre*, ed. John Horton and Susan Mendus (Notre Dame, IN: University of Notre Dame Press, 1994), 302-3. Cf. MacIntyre, "Nietzsche or Aristotle?" in Giovanna Borradori, *The American Philosopher* (Chicago: University of Chicago Press, 1994): "Large-scale politics has become barren. Attempts to reform the political systems of modernity from within are always transformed into collaborations with them. Attempts to overthrow them always degenerate into terrorism or quasi terrorism. What is not thus barren is the politics involved in constructing and sustaining small-scale local communities, at the level of the family, the neighborhood, the workplace, the parish, the school, or clinic, communities within which the needs of the hungry and the homeless can be met" (151). See also MacIntyre, "Poetry As Political Philosophy: Notes on Burke and Yeats," in *On Modern Poetry: Essays Presented to Donald Davie*, ed. Vereen Bell and Laurence Lerner (Nashville, TN: Vanderbilt University Press, 1988), 149, 152-4, 156-7. For the most recent statement of his position, see MacIntyre, *Dependent Rational Animals: Why Human Beings Need the Virtues* (Chicago: Open Court, 1999), chapter 11.

15 This is the crux of the Sandel-Kymlicka debate. With the debate cast in these terms, Sandel's view seems to me the more persuasive one.

16 *DDD*, 88.
17 *DDD*, chapter 13. Cf. Galston, *DDD*: "Sandel cannot escape a tension between the authority of the state to shape character and the kinds of 'encumbrances' on which he dwells. To the extent that we take seriously particularist duties (for example, to family members) or group identification (for example, with faith communities), we may be inclined to resist rather than embrace public direction of civic character formation" (81); also: "the extent to which the power of the national state should be deployed against local communities and civil associations in the name of shared citizenship raises moral and prudential considerations that do not always favor enhanced localism" (84).
18 See *DD*, 314, 320-1, 347-8. A key notion in this context is Sandel's idea of a "dispersal of sovereignty" (345, 347).
19 *DDD*, 179.
20 Cf. Orwin, *DDD*: "It is because we are claimed to be constituted by our communities that loyalty to communities overrides any broader patriotism ... The teaching that our identities are communal from the ground up has thus proved every bit as corrosive of the bond of common citizenship as the individualism blamed by Sandel" (89).
21 *DDD*, 90.
22 Here one can point out a remarkable reversal in the Sandel-Rawls confrontation. The following is Sandel's rebuttal of Rawls's strategy, in *Political Liberalism*, pbk ed. (New York: Columbia University Press, 1996), of neutralizing the communitarian challenge by "communitarianizing" his own liberalism (i.e., by construing it as an interpretation of the American tradition): "The liberal conception of the person ... has only recently come to inform our constitutional practice. Whatever its appeal, it does not underlie the American political tradition as a whole, much less 'the public culture of a democratic society' as such. Any role it may play in the justification of liberalism *must therefore depend on moral argument, not cultural interpretation or appeals to tradition alone*" (*DD*, 103, my italics). In other words, Sandel rebukes Rawls for being too communitarian!
23 Amitai Etzioni, *The New Golden Rule* (New York: Basic Books, 1996), 269 n. 20.
24 For an instructive account of what is morally attractive about this liberal conception, see Richard Rorty (*DDD*, chapter 8).
25 *DDD*, 175.
26 *DD*, 193.
27 Ibid., 231, 242, 250.
28 It's not the case that all critics of liberalism are committed to coming up with remedies for the disabilities of a liberal social order. MacIntyre, for instance, writes: "I am not a communitarian. I do not believe in ideals or forms of community as a nostrum for contemporary social ills. I give my political loyalty to no program" (Borradori, *The American Philosopher*, 151). I strongly agree with MacIntyre here: as I've tried to argue in various places, the business of social criticism shouldn't oblige one to legislate an alternative for the social order one is criticizing (see, for instance, *What's the Matter with Liberalism?* chapter 7).
29 *DD*, 348-9. Cf. Rorty, *DDD*, 123.
30 See *DD*, 336-7.
31 Mark Hulliung, "The Use and Abuse of History," *Responsive Community* 7, 2 (1997): 68. Cf. R. Bruce Douglass, "A House Built on Sandel," *Commonweal*, 22 November 1996, 27. Jeremy Waldron (*DDD*, chapter 2) mounts a vigorous case against Sandel on a charge of aggravated nostalgia.
32 Ronald Dworkin, *A Matter of Principle* (Cambridge, MA: Harvard University Press, 1985), 191.
33 Ibid., 203. Kymlicka offers a very clear restatement of this view: "The state should be neutral amongst conceptions of the good, in the sense that it should not justify its legislation by appeal to some ranking of the intrinsic worth of particular conceptions of the good" (*DDD*, 133); also, "The state should leave judgments about the good life to individuals, and should seek instead to ensure a free and fair context for individuals to make these judgments" (ibid., 138-9).
34 *DD*, 322.
35 Michael J. Sandel, "Easy Virtue," *New Republic*, 2 September 1996, 23. Cf *DDD*, 328.

36 Although Sandel wouldn't necessarily want to align himself with Clinton's politics, I think the proven appeal of Clinton's political rhetoric, with its unmistakable communitarian resonance, offers some evidence that Sandel's project may be a quite promising one for those concerned with rebuilding an egalitarian or social-democratic politics in the United States and elsewhere. Cf. Charles Taylor, *DDD*, 223; Michael Walzer, *DDD*, 181; Robin West, *DDD*, 267-8; Joan Chalmers Williams (*DDD*, chapter 7); each of these, in various ways, presents Sandel's book as an attempt to remedy the deficiencies of procedural liberalism as a basis for egalitarian politics. [Added in 1998: Since I first wrote this, President Clinton has become enmeshed in a quite considerable sex scandal, from which one can draw two further relevant observations. First, Clinton's own personal irresponsibility has clearly disabled him from continuing to deploy a stirring communitarian rhetoric of family obligations and moral responsibility. On the other hand, the fact that Clinton has politically survived a scandal of such large proportions reconfirms just how much in tune with the American public was the public rhetoric that helped to get him elected (and re-elected) in the first place.]

37 Although Christopher Lasch presents a rather different "meta-narrative" of American history, I interpret the essential thrust of Lasch's enterprise in a very similar way: for elaboration of Lasch's social theory, and its affinities to Sandel's project, see my essay "Left-Wing Conservatism: The Legacy of Christopher Lasch," in Beiner, *Philosophy in a Time of Lost Spirit*, 139-50.

38 See, for instance, William Galston, Richard Rorty, and Will Kymlicka (*DDD*, chapters 4, 8, and 10), who offer powerful restatements of the central liberal idea, as each of them conceives it. Again, one certainly shouldn't make the mistake of assuming that procedural liberalism of the Rawls-Dworkin variety is the only available version of liberal theory (*Democracy's Discontent* perhaps tends to encourage this false assumption). Neither should one think that contemporary liberalism has been left untouched by the communitarian critique. On the contrary: communitarianism has been very good for liberalism. It has elicited a much more robust engagement with issues of civic virtue and character-formation in the work of, for instance, Galston, Stephen Macedo, Stephen Salkever, and Peter Berkowitz; and it has helped to provoke Kymlicka's interesting work exploring how liberal theory ought to deal with problems of group membership for minority cultures.

39 See, especially, Nancy Rosenblum (*DDD*, chapter 21).

40 See, for instance, the interesting dialogue between Mary Lyndon Shanley and Robin West: Shanley's critique of Sandel in *DDD*, chapter 18 (see, especially, 362 n. 27, where Shanley complains about Sandel's failure to address feminist criticisms of his first book), and West's partial critique and partial defence of Sandel in *DDD*, 260-6, 268-9. In her oral presentation at the McDonough Symposium, Shanley mentioned Christopher Lasch's *Haven in a Heartless World,* and recalled the critical response when that book was published: "haven *for whom*?" Along with many other feminist critics, Shanley clearly sees Lasch and Sandel as sharing a presumed communitarian nostalgia for the patriarchal family. Equally clearly, Sandel sees this as a bum rap.

41 See, for instance, the fine essays by Thomas Pangle and Clifford Orwin in *DDD* (chapters 1 and 5).

42 See, for instance, Eric Foner, "Liberalism's Discontents," *Nation*, 6 May 1996, 36-7. See also Rogers M. Smith, "America's Contents and Discontents: Reflections on Michael Sandel's *America*," *Critical Review* 13, 1-2: 73-96, which exposes glaring omissions in Sandel's account of American history that, according to Smith, stem from the fact that Sandel's liberal/republican dichotomy fails to capture crucial political traditions historically constitutive of American civic experience.

43 See, for instance, Shanley on family law (*DDD*, chapter 18); Andrew Siegel on the abortion issue (*DDD*, chapter 11); James E. Fleming and Linda C. McClain on constitutional issues concerning privacy or autonomy (*DDD*, chapter 19); discussions, by West and by Fleming and McClain, of the moral analysis of homosexuality offered by Sandel (*DDD*, chapters 20 and 19); Joan Chalmers Williams on Sandel's treatment of religion (*DDD*, chapter 7); Milton Regan on how the modern corporation fits into Sandel's civic-republican narrative (*DDD*, chapter 22); and challenges to Sandel's championing of American federalism by Clifford

Orwin (*DDD*, 88), Mark Tushnet (*DDD*, chapter 23), and Rogers Smith (see the critique of Sandel cited in the preceding note).

44 This is more or less the way William Galston presents the idea of public philosophy: *DDD*, chapter 4.

45 In the "Reply to Critics" published at the end of *DDD* (319-21), Sandel makes explicit that his preferred conception of public philosophy is public philosophy as the crystallization of pre-philosophic social practices rather than as the causality that calls forth those practices; but he brushes off the broader challenge to the Sandelian idea of public philosophy posed in this essay (the original version of which was published in *DDD*).

46 *DD*, ix-x.

47 See *DD*, 354 n. 28. It's worth noting that Rawls seems more or less to share Sandel's idea of public philosophy. In a recent text, Rawls writes: "Debates about general philosophical questions cannot be the daily stuff of politics, but that does not make these questions without significance, since what we [i.e., we philosophers – R.B.] think their answers are will shape the underlying attitudes of the public culture and the conduct of politics" (*Political Liberalism*, lxi). It would seem to follow fairly directly from this statement that philosophers are the ones who "shape" public culture, and non-philosophical ordinary citizens enact in their political conduct the attitudes thus shaped.

48 Cf. Galston, *DDD*, 81-2. The issue of Sandel's idealism was also highlighted in exchanges between Galston and Sandel at the McDonough Symposium. (Galston: "I am not a materialist, but reading Sandel's book is almost enough to turn me into one.") See also Rorty, *DDD*, 122-4.

49 *DD*, 322, my italics.

50 Cf. Susan Okin's review of *Democracy's Discontent* in *American Political Science Review* 91, 2 (1997): 441, explaining why one can hardly blame "the teenaged John Rawls or the infant Dworkin" for the arrival of the procedural republic *in 1943* (she cites *DD*, 54).

51 As Michael Walzer forcefully argued in a dialogue with Sandel at the McDonough Symposium, precisely if Sandel's diagnosis of the pervasive atomization and consumerization of contemporary American life is *correct*, Americans today are grossly ill fitted for the duties and responsibilities of citizens. Hence Walzer's own preferred response: building up a kind of surrogate citizenship founded on existing ethnic and class allegiances that define the reality of American pluralism. Cf. Walzer, *What It Means to Be an American* (New York: Marsilio, 1996), 37-8, 47, emphasizing the tension between republican and cultural-pluralist notions of citizenship; but see also pages 10-12, 17, on how the two kinds of politics can work together.

52 Nancy Rosenblum, *DDD*, 277; Rosenblum borrows these phrases from Robert Lane.

5
Is There Such a Thing As a Communitarian Political Philosophy?

It's frequently said that the debate between liberalism and communitarianism that was so charged up in the 1980s has now run out of steam – that either those labelled communitarians (usually by others, not by themselves) have failed to sustain interesting critiques of the kind of politics that now prevails, or communitarian criticisms have been sufficiently incorporated in new, more capacious versions of liberalism – and I suppose one should concede a reasonable measure of truth to this conventional wisdom. Still, it may be worthwhile to take one last look at the communitarian challenge before closing the book on this interesting chapter in late-twentieth-century political philosophy.

As every political philosopher in the Western world knows, the standard liberal rejoinder to the communitarian challenge – articulated most feistily by Stephen Holmes – is that communitarians have no interesting positive political vision to offer as an alternative to liberal politics.[1] Either supposed communitarian critics of liberalism are much closer in their political thinking to liberalism than they profess, or they offer not really a political theory but rather a political rhetoric of cultural lament: can one base a politics on lament? I propose to consider, by a process of elimination, how various influential communitarians fare in the light of this counterchallenge.

For purposes of convenience rather than exhaustiveness, I'm going to focus on four thinkers generally associated with the communitarian critique of liberalism, namely Michael Sandel, Charles Taylor, Michael Walzer, and Alasdair MacIntyre (really, I'm focusing on only one of these thinkers, but that will become clear soon enough). These four thinkers share more or less the following theoretical tendencies. All of them embrace as a crucial task of social theory the need to develop a rich account – richer, at least, than that available either in standard liberalism or in standard leftist analyses – of how individual identity is constituted by membership in families, in churches and in other voluntary associations, by local and society-wide solidarities, by bonds of nationhood, and by cultural traditions. All of them seek to highlight the inadequacy of strictly liberal-individualist categories for understanding how we actually experience our moral and civic life, and try to give more attention to the social resources that build meaningful character. Finally, all of them attempt to be more sensitive to the limits of liberal individualism (notwithstanding its moral advantages in relation to pre-liberal cultures), and seek to explore possibilities of social experience beyond the horizon of a parochially liberal social universe (what Walzer has recently called a culture promoting the "entrepreneurship of the self"[2]).

Sandel's book *Liberalism and the Limits of Justice* offered a powerful critique of Rawlsian liberalism. Sandel tried to show that the version of liberalism articulated in Rawls's *A Theory of Justice* was based on an incoherent theory of the self (a moral self only contingently related to its ends and its bases of identity), thus prompting Rawls and other liberal political philosophers to articulate alternative versions of liberalism less vulnerable to these criticisms. However, if one asks (as many of Sandel's readers did) how politics would look different under a communitarian regime, *Liberalism and the Limits of Justice* does not provide much of an answer. Sandel's later book, *Democracy's Discontent,* goes much further in laying out a positive counter-image to liberal politics. But Sandel probably does as good a job as any of his critics could have done in showing how the communitarian/civic republican opts for a succession of lost causes and why a "procedural-liberal" vision of politics enjoys a decisive sociological advantage over Sandel's preferred alternative. One reviewer of the book unkindly but not unjustly suggested that Sandel had unwittingly vindicated charges that communitarians are hopelessly nostalgic about "a past that never existed."[3] Despite Sandel's own attempt to present the book strictly on the plane of competing public philosophies, *Democracy's Discontent* is more than anything a lament for how modern economic and sociological realities (and not just a mistaken public philosophy) have defeated republican possibilities, leaving at best just flickering republican moments in an overwhelmingly liberal-procedural political universe to remind us of what we've lost. This doesn't by itself invalidate Sandel's political ideal, but it does show that realization of the ideal requires a much more radical break with modern social and economic circumstances than Sandel generally acknowledges.

As David Miller has correctly observed, if one looks at Taylor's and Walzer's explicit discussions of the liberal-communitarian debate, neither of these supposed communitarians presents himself as a resolute partisan of the communitarian cause.[4] As far as Taylor is concerned, it suffices to think of his great debt as a theorist to the pluralistic liberalism of a classic liberal such as Isaiah Berlin, who was at the same time very anxious to accommodate cultural particularism, in order to realize that the main purpose of Taylor's "communitarianism" is to challenge overly one-sided or "monistic" versions of liberalism; and a similar observation could clearly be applied to Walzer's theorizing. In a response to Taylor's essay "The Politics of Recognition," Walzer suggests that what he and Taylor offer is not an alternative *to* liberalism but a more collectivized, more pluralized version *of* liberalism; it is easy to imagine Taylor consenting to this characterization of his political theory.[5] And in the article cited by Miller, Walzer presents contemporary communitarianism as a corrective for versions of liberalism that have swung too far to the individualist end of the spectrum.[6]

So we turn to MacIntyre. No one could fairly complain that MacIntyre's challenges to liberal politics and liberal theory are insufficiently robust. At least on the rhetorical plane, MacIntyre is as stringent a critic of the liberal view of social order as one could hope to encounter. The problem again is that when it comes to specifying a viable alternative, it is hard to see what new institutions or succeeding political structures MacIntyre means to propose. *After Virtue* of course famously concluded with a stunning call for a retreat to the monasteries: "What matters at this stage is the construction of local forms of community within which civility and the intellectual and moral life can be sustained through the new dark ages which are already upon us. And if the tradition of the virtues was able to survive the horrors of the last dark ages, we are not entirely without grounds for hope. This time however the barbarians are not waiting beyond the frontiers; they have already been governing us for quite some time."[7]

Whatever MacIntyre's politics turn out to be (and as we shall discuss, this is something that has only come fully to light in recent writings of his), one thing at least is clear: his politics are a bracingly radical alternative to liberalism. He says in "An Interview for *Cogito*," published in *The MacIntyre Reader*, that he learned from Marxism early in his intellectual career "how to identify the moral impoverishment and the ideological function of liberalism" (*MR*-IC, 267), and this is one conviction or set of convictions that remains immovably constant through all the twists and turns and transformations of MacIntyre's intellectual development.

MacIntyre's view in *After Virtue* is clearly that the mode of moral-political association available in liberal society compares very poorly with the kind of rich, ethos-inculcating shared life encountered in the ancient polis. But is MacIntyre willing to go so far as to propose a revivification or reinstatement of the Greek polis (or some modern equivalent)? Such a notion would certainly violate the historicist strain in MacIntyre's moral thinking, as well as his emphatic insistence, throughout his work, on the inseparability of sociology and moral theory. MacIntyre may be of the view that ancient forms of moral and political life furnish a critical standard for judging the deficiencies of contemporary ethical life, but nothing in his work suggests that he welcomes the project of re-creating the polis.

So is there a politics in MacIntyre's classic work? What's clear in *After Virtue* is that the standard for judging contemporary liberal society is shared goods, virtues, and the practices that embody and engender these shared goods and virtues. (A virtue is a dispositional excellence in realizing some communal good, and a practice is a historically evolved form of life that provides a social site for the enactment of virtues.) What's also clear is that liberal society appears less than impressive in the light of this standard. What's significantly less clear (at least in this key book) is MacIntyre's picture of a nonliberal way of structuring political life (under contemporary conditions) that would more adequately meet this standard.

Kelvin Knight has labelled MacIntyre's position "revolutionary Aristotelianism" in order to emphasize the point that MacIntyre's politics, whatever they turn out to be, are hardly conservative; but what Knight treats under the heading of "Politics" still doesn't seem very political.[8] Knight seems to oppose free-floating "practices" to the inevitably oppressive "institutions" of the modern world, and to say, as he does on MacIntyre's behalf, that we need institutions that are subordinate to practices rather than practices that are subordinate to institutions, doesn't appear to yield a very determinate conception of politics.[9] In "An Interview with Giovanna Borradori," MacIntyre himself insists: "I do not believe in ideals or forms of community as a nostrum for contemporary social ills. I give my political loyalty to no program" (*MR*-IGB, 265).[10] Fair enough: I have full sympathy with the view of theory as an enterprise of ambitious social criticism, and agree with MacIntyre that one can practise this critical theorizing without being obligated to supply nostrums for society-wide reform of existing institutions. Still, it should be said that one can't offer coherent criticism of existing society without definite standards of judgment, and this requires some vision of desirable political possibilities, even if current circumstances rule out a direct realization of these ideals.

MacIntyre complains that his political philosophy has been widely misunderstood, but the fact is that he does little in his most influential works to clarify how his philosophical views bear on politics. One could read MacIntyre for many years (as I have) and yet still be fundamentally puzzled about where he stands politically. I offer the following account (drawing on more recent clarifications of his politics) in the hope that it will dispel the puzzlement.

MacIntyre is not the only one of our four thinkers to disown the communitarian label, but his denials have been more robust and more fleshed-out than those of the other three. So a good place to start our consideration of MacIntyre's politics may be with a careful examination of his explanations of why he doesn't consider himself a communitarian. Basically, there are two reasons behind his insistence that his philosophy is not a communitarian one. The first, articulated in *Dependent Rational Animals*, is that he considers it a "mistake to suppose that there is anything good about local community as such" (*DRA*, 142). "Local communities are always open to corruption by narrowness, by complacency, by prejudice against outsiders and by a whole range of other deformities, including those that arise from a cult of local community" (ibid.).[11] This is a perfectly good reason not to enshrine community as such as a normative standard: the standard, rather, is the quality of social practices that various communities enable us to realize. What concerns MacIntyre is the flourishing of humanly worthwhile practices and the virtues and excellences that they bring into play, and he is interested in communities insofar as communities provide sites for these practices and virtues (and for no other reason). Again, this is a good reason for rejecting the communitarian label, but other communitarians such as Sandel and Taylor would be in full agreement with MacIntyre on this point.

The second reason is that MacIntyre associates communitarianism with the project of applying the language of common good to the modern nation-state, and he thoroughly and wholeheartedly rejects this project. As he puts it: "the communitarian mistake [is] to attempt to infuse the politics of the state with the values and modes of participation in local community" (*DRA*, 142). For anyone who takes the basic structures of modern political life as a given, it is not easy to fathom the depth of MacIntyre's hostility to the state as a mode of organizing political activity. His essay "Poetry As Political Philosophy" probably conveys the tenor of his anti-statist rhetoric as well as any of his writings.[12] The purpose of the essay is to investigate a thesis that MacIntyre attributes to W.B. Yeats, namely "that no coherent political imagination is any longer possible for those condemned to inhabit, and to think and act in terms of the modernity of the twentieth-century nation-state," and there is no question but that MacIntyre affirms the truth of what he takes to be Yeats's insight.[13] MacIntyre highlights Yeats's image of the modern nation-state "as a tree dead from half-way up."[14] Insofar as Yeats himself intends to apply this image specifically to the Irish state of the 1920s and '30s, he mistakes the generality of his insight: what Yeats sees and condemns in the Irish state "belong[s] to it not as Irish, but as state. They are features of the modern state as such ... [expressing] the imaginative poverty not of a particular regime or type of regime, but of the structure of every modern state."[15] To overcome the "imaginative sterility of the modern state" and to engage "a less barren politics," we must seek out other forms of institutionalized community, beyond the boundaries of "the conventional politics of the contemporary state."[16]

It's not obvious where MacIntyre gets his view that what defines communitarianism is a commitment to the nation-state as the primary location for community (and that therefore he's not a communitarian). To be sure, other communitarians don't necessarily rule out the nation-state as a possible location for community, but neither do they necessarily privilege the nation-state as the preferred location for community. In truth, Sandel, Taylor, and Walzer tend to be ambivalent about whether they want enhanced community at the level of the polity as a whole or whether they want decentralized politics that would enhance community in more local settings at the expense of the national political arena, and they sometimes fudge this question rather than state a clear preference. It seems implausible to say that a preference for the nation-state is what defines their communitarianism; rather, the most that one can say is that they stand closer to the commonsensical mainstream view that certain important forms of human community *are* realized (or can be realized) at the national level, whereas MacIntyre embraces the quite radical view according to which genuine community and the goods that a genuine community subserves are entirely ruled out within the horizon of the modern state.

MacIntyre's attitude to the state can be summed up in the simple injunction: "Have no truck with the Devil!" In place of state-related politics, he substitutes something that, in the essay "Politics, Philosophy and the Common Good," he calls "the politics of local community" (*MR*-PPCG, 246-50). MacIntyre is very clear about the sorts of communities that qualify as communities of common good; in *Dependent Rational Animals* he lists "fishing communities in New England over the past hundred and fifty years ... Welsh mining communities [instantiating] a way of life informed by the ethics of work at the coal face, by a passion for the goods of choral singing and of rugby football and by the virtues of trade union struggle against first coal-owners and then the state ... farming cooperatives in Donegal, Mayan towns in Guatemala and Mexico, some city-states from a more distant past" (*DRA*, 143). Communities of this sort qualify as possible sites for common good. It is equally clear, for MacIntyre, that the politics of the national state doesn't come anywhere near qualifying as a possible site of common good. Why not?

> Modern nation-states are governed through a series of compromises between a range of more or less conflicting economic and social interests. What weight is given to different interests varies with the political and economic bargaining power of each and with its ability to ensure that the voices of its protagonists are heard at the relevant bargaining tables. What determines both bargaining power and such ability is in key part money, money used to provide the resources to sustain political power: electoral resources, media resources, relationships to corporations. This use of money procures very different degrees and kinds of political influence for different interests. And the outcome is that although most citizens share, although to greatly varying extents, in such public goods as those of a minimally secure order, the distribution of goods by government in no way reflects a common mind arrived at through widespread shared deliberation governed by norms of

rational enquiry. Indeed the size of modern states would itself preclude this. It does not follow that relationships to the nation-state, or rather to the various agencies of government that collectively compose it, are unimportant to those who practice the politics of the virtues of acknowledged dependence. No one can avoid having some significant interest in her or his relationships to the nation-state just because of its massive resources, its coercive legal powers, and the threats that its blundering and distorted benevolence presents. But any rational relationship of the governed to the government of modern states requires individuals and groups to weigh any benefits to be derived from it against the costs of entanglement with it (*DRA*, 131-2).[17]

Our formulation above should probably be qualified somewhat, as follows: "To the extent that you must have truck with the Devil, in order to avail yourself of the necessary benefits that it confers, you should not fool yourself into thinking that receiving these benefits joins you in a relationship to the Devil expressive of a common good."

Central to this conception is an understanding of rational deliberation. Members of a community can join in a politics of common good *only* when it is possible for them "to come through rational deliberation to a common mind" (*DRA*, 129). Clearly, political association on the modern scale cannot imaginably meet this standard:

[According to] the conception of political activity embodied in the modern state, ... there is a small minority of the population who are to make politics their active occupation and preoccupation, professional and semiprofessional politicians, and a huge largely passive majority who are to be mobilized only at periodic intervals, for elections or national crises. Between the political elites on the one hand and the larger population on the other there are important differences, as in, for example, how much or how little information is required and provided for each. A modern electorate can only function as it does, so long as it has only a highly simplified and impoverished account of the issues that are presented to it. And the modes of presentation through which elites address electorates are designed to conceal as much as to reveal. These are not accidental features of the politics of modern states any more than is the part that money plays in affording influence upon the decision-making process (*DRA*, 141-2).

Given the theoretical standards by which MacIntyre defines a genuine deliberative community, it would be ludicrous to characterize this general system as a process of shared rational deliberation. Without moral-political deliberation there is no possibility of arriving at "a common mind," and without a common mind shaped by shared rational deliberation, there is no common good. The conclusion, following inescapably from MacIntyre's premises, is that politics as we know it in the modern world cannot be characterized as anything other than "fragmentation through the conflicts of group interests and individual preferences, defined without reference to a common good" (*MR*-IC, 269).

Two responses seem called for. The first is to recognize the theoretical force and philosophical stringency of the notion of common good that MacIntyre here applies. Only very special kinds of communities and very particular types of social situations permit one to speak of a common good ("a common mind arrived at through widespread shared deliberation governed by norms of rational enquiry"[18]); one can pretty much define modernity as that constellation of social life that rules out, or at least drives to the margins, precisely those kinds of communities and types of social situations that warrant the language of common good. Our second response is to note just how harsh a picture this account gives us of the politics of the modern state. It more or less has the effect of disqualifying any concept of political community within the boundaries of modern social life. It's true that the goods provided by the modern state are not products of communal deliberation in any rigorous sense, but they are still goods, and expressive surely of *some* mode of political community, however attenuated (and capable, in principle, of building up more of a sense of political community in proportion to its goods being perceived as real ones). In Canada there is more or less a national consensus, shared in even by political parties on the right end of the political spectrum, that a nationally funded public health system is a shared civic good. The state, in providing this good, is seen as the agent of national consensus. This doesn't mean that there aren't controversies about the adequacy and efficiency of the medicare system; but it does seem to suggest that the state can provide civic goods, and that there is, in this respect, a civic community on behalf of which such goods are provided.

There is no question that MacIntyre's political commitments remain those of a radical egalitarian, and that his revulsion against capitalism has not diminished at all from what it was at the start of his intellectual career.[19] (As John Haldane has remarked, "In certain respects MacIntyre's position is like that of old-style Christian socialists: at once critical of society for its failure to attend to the needs of the weak, the dispossessed, the overlooked and the socially marginalised, yet also firm in defence of traditional morality."[20]) This makes his root-and-branch rejection of state-based politics all the more startling, since so much of twentieth-century left-wing politics revolved around hopes to make the state the agent of egalitarian transformations of the political community as a whole. In a discussion on 10 May 1997, I asked MacIntyre how he squares residual Marxism with antipathy to the state, since, in our situation – in the political world in which we live – the state offers the only restraint upon the capitalist market, both in its provision of regulatory mechanisms and in its capacity as an agent of distributive justice. Here is the gist of his interesting reply. MacIntyre said that what we've had since 1945 is the state-cum-market. The welfare state was invented by Bismarck, as well as Disraeli, Lloyd George, and Balfour – that is, not social democrats but conservatives trying to preserve an orderly capitalist society. Operation of this state/market produces a certain amount of disorder, which in turn needs to be corrected by welfare state policies. Welfare is therefore bound to a cycle: the state promotes growth, regulates the market with welfare, and then needs to cut back. It issues promissory notes that have to be paid for (in the context of US politics) by Republican policies. So Democrats and Republicans are simply occupying different positions within this cycle, yet they are bound to the same process. What MacIntyre therefore rejects is the whole package, namely a growth economy managed by the state, with occasional corrections with welfare, and so on. Consequently the welfare state is not an alternative to the state/market; it is, on the contrary, part and parcel of the kind of state entirely implicated in the operation of market capitalism. Most political contests in the contemporary West revolve around competing views of what constitutes the right balance between state and market (the power of the market versus the authority of the state). For MacIntyre, by contrast, market and state are two sides of the same coin, and rather than choosing between them, or deciding how to give greater weight to one or the other, we should toss away the whole coin.[21] MacIntyre doesn't go so far as to assert that there are *no* goods associated with state-based politics; what he does assert is that the basic structures of the modern state, and the form of political community it makes available, are *essentially* and not just incidentally inimical to a politics based on the common good (and it is precisely this insight into our prevailing political reality that, on his view, communitarians in the proper sense have failed to grasp).

These views lead MacIntyre into an extremely paradoxical relationship to the debates about liberalism that put communitarianism on the political-philosophical map in the 1980s:

Contemporary communitarians, from whom I have strongly disassociated myself whenever I have had the occasion to do so, advance their proposals as a contribution to the politics of the nation-state. Where liberals have characteristically insisted that government within a nation-state should remain neutral between rival conceptions of the human good, contemporary communitarians have urged that such government should give expression to some shared vision of the human good, a vision defining some type of community. Where liberals have characteristically urged that it is in the activities of subordinate voluntary associations, such as those constituted by religious groups, that shared visions of the good should be articulated, communitarians have insisted that the nation itself through the institutions of the nation-state ought to be constituted to some significant degree as a community. In the United States this has become a debate within the Democratic Party, a debate in which from my own point of view communitarians have attacked liberals on one issue on which liberals have been consistently in the right.[22]

Come again? Communitarians have attacked liberals on the one issue on which liberals have been consistently in the right? Government should remain neutral between rival conceptions of the human good? Although MacIntyre presents himself as a root-and-branch critic of liberalism in all its dimensions (moral, economic, cultural, political), he now tells us that on the very issue that decisively defines the debate between liberals and communitarians, he sides with liberal political philosophers.[23] (Here one can fairly easily imagine Stephen Holmes crowing in the background: "Press an anti-liberal to pass judgment at the level of political institutions, and he or she will immediately retreat to being a good liberal!")

Although the passage quoted above appears to suggest otherwise, in actual fact MacIntyre, like a good communitarian, does *not* concede the liberal thesis of government neutrality in relation to rival conceptions of the good. For instance, he writes: "Questions about the value of ways of life ... are [officially] excluded from the arenas of political debate and decision-making, even though answers to them are delivered by default, since among the effects of modern governmental decisions is their impact upon different ways of life, an impact that promotes some – the way of life of the fashionably hedonistic consumer, for example – and undermines others" (*MR-PPCG*, 238). The clearest statement of MacIntyre's position is in "Toleration and the Goods of Conflict," where he denounces the doctrine of the neutrality of the liberal state as a fiction and a sham; still, he clearly thinks it would be very desirable if the state could approximate more closely to its pretended neutrality than it actually does. He writes: "The state must not be allowed to impose any one particular conception of the human good or identify some one such conception with its own interests and causes ... [Although] the contemporary state is not and cannot be evaluatively neutral, ... it is just because of the ways in which the state is not evaluatively neutral that it cannot generally be trusted to promote any worthwhile set of values."[24] He also writes: "interventions by the state [in the debates between protagonists of rival conceptions of the human good] are bound to be pernicious."[25] These passages make clear that it is MacIntyre's view that while the liberal state is not in fact neutral, he would prefer it if the state could be more neutral than it actually is. One could interpret this important aspect of the liberal-communitarian debate as follows: liberals desire the state to be neutral between rival conceptions of the human good, whereas communitarians prefer that the political community openly acknowledge that it embodies certain conceptions of the good, since non-neutrality is inescapable. Seen in this light, MacIntyre is clearly on the liberal side of the debate.

Returning to the discussion in *After MacIntyre* in which MacIntyre appears to switch sides in the liberal-communitarian debate, we see that he proceeds to offer the following account of what distinguishes him from liberals:

> Liberals ... mistakenly suppose that [totalitarian and other] evils arise from any form of political community which embodies substantive practical agreement upon some strong conception of the human good. I by contrast take them to arise from the specific character of the modern nation-state, thus agreeing with liberals in this, at least, that modern nation-states which masquerade as embodiments of community are always to be resisted. The modern nation-state, in whatever guise, is a dangerous and unmanageable institution, presenting itself on the one hand as a bureaucratic supplier of goods and services, which is always about to, but never actually does, give its clients value for money, and on the other as a repository of sacred values, which from time to time invites one to lay down one's life on its behalf. As I have remarked elsewhere ["Poetry As Political Philosophy"], it is like being asked to die for the telephone company.[26]

MacIntyre sees nothing but barrenness and sterility in a politics associated with "the modern state as such": services from a giant utility company, plus the incompatible claim that its citizens lay down their lives for it – that is, a form of society in which the idiom of common good is either incoherent or meaningless.[27] An adjacent reason for MacIntyre's rejection of what he associates with communitarianism, as the above passage expresses, is that he believes that conceiving the nation-state as acting on behalf of an integral community necessarily entails conjuring up an imaginary *Volk*, which is a recipe for the most dangerous kind of politics.[28] This is certainly a legitimate anxiety, especially when one considers the vociferousness of modern nationalism. But it is surely possible for the state to present itself as acting on behalf of some kind of civic community without appealing to the idea of a *Volk*.

According to MacIntyre, the moral claims that the state makes upon its citizens should have no greater weight than if they were obligations issued by "giant utility companies."[29] (And to the extent that citizens rightly allow themselves to be enlisted by the state in resisting evils such as Nazism and Stalinism, these are to be characterized as nothing more than *"ad hoc* participation in some particular enterprises of some nation-state.")[30] But this seems mistaken. If what MacIntyre means to suggest is that the state is in no less complicity with the bureaucratism and instrumental rationality typical of late modernity than any other large-scale institution, he is surely correct. But it doesn't follow from this that the state is on the same moral plane as any other corporate bureaucracy. Indeed, unless our view of the state is as cynical as MacIntyre's seems to be, it seems obvious that the state is a more directly moral association than the telephone company. When members of the Canadian Armed Forces consent to risk their lives serving in Kosovo at the behest of the Canadian state, they don't do so because they are deluded into falsely thinking that the state is qualitatively different from other bureaucratic organizations; they do so because they rightly perceive that the Canadian state represents an association of citizens defined by certain shared purposes. The citizen-state relation (or the relation between citizens mediated by the state) involves a mode of moral association or moral community because the state doesn't just impose its own ends but in some measure reflects those of its citizens (which of course may be worthy ends or unworthy ends), and politics is the process by which we try to influence the set of purposes that the state will pursue and promote on behalf of all citizens.

Kelvin Knight, in a spirited defence of MacIntyre's views, offers the following explanation for why MacIntyre sides with *neither* liberal nor communitarian accounts of political community: "On the one hand, the state is justified as the guarantor of individuals' rights to pursue their own self-chosen goals. On the other hand, it is justified as the expression of a form of social life for which its subjects may, whenever necessary, be required to risk their lives. There cannot be a rational legitimation of the state that satisfies both of these criteria. As both criteria represent necessary aspects of the state, there cannot be any coherent solution to the modern problem of political obligation."[31] But there is a ready answer to this supposed contradiction: put less emphasis on the political community as the guarantor of self-chosen goals, and put more emphasis upon it as the site of shared purposes, whether desirable or undesirable. Practices at the level of the political community as a whole then become subject to the same standard of judgment as moral practices within MacIntyre's philosophy of the virtues: the question to be answered is whether the goods that the practices instantiate are genuine human goods. If a state mobilizes energies on behalf of its citizens to fight just wars; to combat poverty, suffering, and oppression; and to promote high standards of civic culture, then the state makes legitimate claims on its members (up to and including civic duties involving risk of one's life). If, on the other hand, the state wastes human life fighting stupid and pointless wars, reinforces the worst aspects of existing social relations, and is mainly preoccupied with augmenting its own power, then the claims it makes upon its citizens possess correspondingly less validity. The contradiction dissolves. (MacIntyre seems to exempt himself from the task of assessing the quality of different civic purposes by assuming that we can expect the worst: since modern political community involves relations between citizens and a state, and since the state *as such* is ineligible as a virtue-based community of moral agents, the project of envisioning modern political community as a location for goods-engendering moral practices is a hopeless one.)

None of the above criticisms are intended to deny that there is a great deal of truth in MacIntyre's characterization of the existing reality of modern liberal states. He has a strong case when he says that these states "are oligarchies disguised as liberal democracies" (*MR*-PPCG, 237) and that they are very far removed indeed from a politics of the common good. But this doesn't seem sufficient reason to reject communitarian aspirations toward a more ambitious vision of civic community, offering more robust civic goods than liberal society presently offers. Is it impossible to imagine ways of reconstituting the state so as to incorporate greater opportunities for democratic deliberation among its citizens, or to render citizenship more meaningful? According to MacIntyre, the problem is not just the moral barrenness or sterility of particular political orders within modernity; rather, the problem is disabling features of "the modern state as such."[32] Here one needs to weigh very seriously the force of MacIntyre's *as such*.

One can say this much for MacIntyre's statement of his position vis-à-vis the liberal-communitarian debate: unlike other communitarians, MacIntyre at least leaves no room for any possible ambiguity about where he means to situate possibilities of community.[33] Families, neighbourhoods, workplaces, local parishes, fishing villages, farming communities, schools, and clinics are generators of virtues and a common good; national political communities certainly are not. The problem here, of course, is that MacIntyre is left with no possible site for overarching *political* community compatible with the basic conditions of modernity – we are left with Aristotelianism without a polis.[34] So it looks as though (as in the conclusion to *After Virtue*) it's back to the monasteries, which will shelter us from the barbarisms of the modern world.[35]

When MacIntyre insists that he is not a communitarian, this is really just an idiosyncratic way of saying that he believes that the modern state is (along with the other dominant structures of modern life) too compromised a form of human association to be capable of being the bearer of legitimate shared purposes. Turning this around, one can say that communitarianism will generate a distinct political philosophy when it can offer a more compelling doctrine of citizenship than standard versions of liberalism provide, and when it can offer a more robust account of the kinds of desirable civic goods that would define such a doctrine of citizenship.[36] To the extent that liberal theorists join communitarians in pursuing this desideratum, the division between liberals and communitarians will indeed lose salience.

Abbreviations

DRA =   Alasdair MacIntyre, *Dependent Rational Animals: Why Human Beings Need the Virtues* (Chicago: Open Court, 1999).

MR =   *The MacIntyre Reader,* ed. Kelvin Knight (Notre Dame, IN: University of Notre Dame Press, 1998).

MR-IC =   "An Interview for *Cogito,*" in *MR.*

MR-IGB =   "An Interview with Giovanna Borradori," in *MR.*

MR-PPCG =   "Politics, Philosophy and the Common Good," in *MR.*

MR-TF =   "The *Theses on Feuerbach:* A Road Not Taken," in *MR.*

Source

This essay is forthcoming in *Critical Review* 14, 4. In it, I have drawn on exchanges with Alasdair MacIntyre during the Fourth Annual Ohio University Philosophy Forum (Athens, OH), which was devoted to MacIntyre's work and took place 8-10 May 1997.

Notes

1 Stephen Holmes, *The Anatomy of Antiliberalism* (Cambridge, MA: Harvard University Press, 1993).

2 Michael Walzer, "What Rights for Cultural Communities?" Europa Mundi – Compostela 2000: The Construction of Europe, Democracy and Globalization, Session IV, "Democracy and Multicultural Citizenship," Conference Proceedings, 7.

3 Mark Hulliung, "The Use and Abuse of History," *Responsive Community* 7, 2 (1997): 68. Cf. Jeremy Waldron, "Virtue *en Masse,*" in *Debating Democracy's Discontent: Essays on American Politics, Law and Public Philosophy,* ed. Anita L. Allen and Milton C. Regan Jr. (Oxford: Oxford University Press, 1998), 32-9.

4 David Miller, "Communitarianism: Left, Right and Centre," in *Liberalism and Its Practice,* ed. Dan Avnon and Avner de-Shalit (London: Routledge, 1999), 171. See Charles Taylor, "Cross-Purposes: The Liberal-Communitarian Debate," in *Liberalism and the Moral Life,* ed. Nancy L. Rosenblum (Cambridge, MA: Harvard University Press, 1989), 159-82; and Michael Walzer, "The Communitarian Critique of Liberalism," *Political Theory* 18, 1 (1990): 6-23.

5 Michael Walzer, "Comment," in *Multiculturalism: Examining the Politics of Recognition,* ed. Amy Gutmann (Princeton, NJ: Princeton University Press, 1994), 99-103. Walzer's argument is that one needs to distinguish between two forms of liberalism, one that places normative weight exclusively on equal individual rights and the other prepared to qualify such rights somewhat for the sake of considerations of cultural survival. According to Walzer, he and Taylor waver between these two liberalisms, depending upon the circumstances of different societies.

6 Walzer, in "The Communitarian Critique of Liberalism," says that communitarianism "is a consistently intermittent feature of liberal politics and social organization. No liberal success will make it permanently unattractive. At the same time, no communitarian critique, however penetrating, will ever be anything more than an inconstant feature of liberalism" (6). Walzer's presentation of communitarianism as merely a remedial version of liberalism is no doubt MacIntyre's view as well (which is why he prefers not to be associated with communitarianism!). Cf., "There are certainly some versions of liberal theory and some formulations of communitarian positions which are such that the two are not only not in opposition to each other, but neatly complement one another. Communitarianism from this latter point of view is a diagnosis of certain weaknesses in liberalism, not a rejection of it" (*MR*-PPCG, 244).

7 Alasdair MacIntyre, *After Virtue: A Study in Moral Theory,* 2nd ed. (Notre Dame, IN: University of Notre Dame Press, 1984), 263.

8 Kelvin Knight, "Revolutionary Aristotelianism," in *Contemporary Political Studies 1996,* vol. 2, ed. I. Hampsher-Monk and J. Stanyer (Nottingham: Political Studies Association of the United Kingdom, 1996), 885-96. In *MR*-PPCG, 235, MacIntyre endorses Knight's account of his political thought.

9 Knight, "Revolutionary Aristotelianism," 895-6. Cf. *MR,* 11 (Editor's Introduction).

10 Cf. Alasdair MacIntyre, "The Spectre of Communitarianism," *Radical Philosophy* 70 (1995): "Not only have I never offered remedies for the condition of liberal modernity, it has been part of my case that there are no remedies" (35).

11 See also Alasdair MacIntyre, "A Partial Response to My Critics," in *After MacIntyre: Critical Perspectives on the Work of Alasdair MacIntyre,* ed. John Horton and Susan Mendus (Notre Dame, IN: University of Notre Dame Press, 1994): "From an Aristotelian standpoint small communities as such have no particular merit" (302).

12 MacIntyre, "Poetry As Political Philosophy: Notes on Burke and Yeats," in *On Modern Poetry: Essays Presented to Donald Davie,* ed. Vereen Bell and Laurence Lerner (Nashville, TN: Vanderbilt University Press, 1988), 145-57.

13 Ibid., 145.

14 Ibid., 156.

15 Ibid., 157.

16 Ibid.

17 For another important articulation of MacIntyre's indictment of the modern state, see "Toleration and the Goods of Conflict," in *The Politics of Toleration: Tolerance and Intolerance in Modern Life,* ed. Susan Mendus (Edinburgh: Edinburgh University Press, 1999), 139-40.

18 Cf., "the idiom of the common good" requires the notion of "a rationally well-founded common mind" (*MR-PPCG,* 239).

19 See MacIntyre, "1953, 1968, 1995: Three Perspectives," Introduction to *Marxism and Christianity,* 2nd ed. (London: Duckworth, 1995), v-xxxi. For MacIntyre, as for Christopher Lasch, the only possibility for meaningful resistance to a capitalist social order rests with supposedly outmoded forms of production (see the discussion of independent small producers in *MR-TF,* 231-2; cf. *MR-PPCG,* 249-50). The institutions of the contemporary state, in his view, never fail to co-opt revolutionary energies, and in that sense the state is a natural ally of capitalism. Compare MacIntyre's appeal to eighteenth-century hand-loom weavers in *MR-TF* with Lasch's argument in *The True and Only Heaven: Progress and Its Critics* (New York: W.W. Norton, 1991).

20 Review of *Dependent Rational Animals: Mind* (January 2001): 228.

21 For further discussion of MacIntyre's understanding of state-market complicity, see "Toleration and the Goods of Conflict," 139-42. Alex Callinicos has made the point to me that this response is not very different from the traditional Marxist critique of the welfare state.

22 MacIntyre, "A Partial Response to My Critics," 302. As regards MacIntyre's claim that he has strongly dissociated himself from communitarianism whenever he has had the opportunity to do so, see MacIntyre, "I'm Not a Communitarian, But ...," *Responsive Community* 1, 3 (1991): 91-2; and MacIntyre, "The Spectre of Communitarianism."

23 In a discussion with MacIntyre on 9 May 1997, I asked him the following questions, and received the following answers:

RB: If you hold that the state can't be the locus for conceptions of the good, why isn't this view the same as liberalism? (Not just that you agree with liberalism on some *marginal* issue, but that you appear to agree with it on the issue that *defines* liberalism.)

AM: Liberalism is a doctrine about the legitimate use of state power. So it's concerned with the state.

RB: So you are a more radical anti-statist than liberals are?

AM: Yes.

RB: So you think this whole business about communitarianism is a giant plague?

AM: Yes.

I omitted to ask MacIntyre the question that this exchange should naturally have prompted: If one views the state as a terrible demon, why *wouldn't* one want to make available a doctrine concerning the limitation of state power?

24 MacIntyre, "Toleration and the Goods of Conflict," 143.

25 Ibid., 150.

26 MacIntyre, "A Partial Response to My Critics," 303.

27 *DRA,* 132; cf. *MR-PPCG,* 236; *MR-TF,* 227. The laying down of lives means not only as soldiers but also as police officers and firefighters: *MR-PPCG,* 242.

28 "A Partial Response to My Critics," 302-3; *MR*-PPCG, 241; *DRA*, 132-3.
29 Cf., "Modern states cannot advance any justifiable claim to the allegiance of their members, and this because they are the political expression of societies of deformed and fragmented practical rationality" (*MR*-PPCG, 243).
30 "A Partial Response to My Critics," 303. This doesn't mean that there are *no* just political obligations for MacIntyre. After all, if we receive services from the telephone company, there are corresponding obligations to pay our bills. But it might be reasonable to associate a deeper sort of obligation with citizenship as a moral bond (which is precisely what MacIntyre is impugning).
31 Knight, "Revolutionary Aristotelianism," 892. Cf. MacIntyre, "Poetry As Political Philosophy," 149; *MR*-TF, 226-7. Many readers of MacIntyre's essay "Is Patriotism a Virtue?" (in *Theorizing Citizenship*, ed. Ronald Beiner [Albany: State University of New York Press, 1995], 209-28) have taken it to be a *defence* of patriotism. Given the reading of MacIntyre's political thought offered in this chapter, that can't possibly be a correct interpretation. Rather, the purpose of MacIntyre's essay is to highlight the *contradiction* (embodied in modern political communities) between liberal universalism and national particularism. The purpose, then, is not to vindicate a patriotic morality but to expose the incoherence of modern conceptions of political community (which try to do the impossible, namely to synthesize liberal and patriotic moralities). Cf. *MR*, 285 (Guide to Further Reading).
32 "Poetry As Political Philosophy," 157.
33 "The liberal critique of those nation-states which pretend to embody the values of community has little to say to those Aristotelians, such as myself, for whom the nation-state is not and cannot be the locus of community" ("A Partial Response to My Critics," 303); "local arenas are now the only places where political community can be constructed, a political community very much at odds with the politics of the nation-state" (*MR*-PPCG, 248). For Sandel's clearest statement of how he views the advantages and disadvantages of local community in relation to national community, see his response to Nancy Rosenblum in *Debating Democracy's Discontent*, ed. Allen and Regan Jr., 330.
34 The unavoidable question is: What's political about MacIntyre's "politics of local community"? In *MR*-PPCG, he writes that a community is "political" insofar as "it is constituted by a type of practice through which other types of practice are ordered" (241). He calls this a polis. But the polis embodied concepts of law, authority, and citizenship – notions seemingly absent from the local communities that MacIntyre is calling political. (One suspects – and the discussions at the Ohio University Philosophy Forum lent weight to this suspicion – that the politics of MacIntyre's "politics of local community" have a tacitly clerical dimension: the kind of "political" office-holder that he has in mind tends to be the parish priest of a farming community.)
      Of course it may indeed be true that in denying that the modern state describes a genuine political community, MacIntyre is proving himself to be a strict Aristotelian. Aristotle himself, if he were presented with the political institutions of the modern world, might well conclude that there is nothing remotely close to a polis to be found in that world. (Cf., "The differences between political community conceived in Aristotelian terms and any modern nation-state is just too great" ["A Partial Response to My Critics," 302].) But then I don't think that Aristotle would claim that there is a "politics of local community."
35 Here, the project of trying to draw a political philosophy from MacIntyre's philosophy seems to me to reach a final impasse. At this stage of the inquiry, I'm inclined to say that of our four theorists, Sandel is the only one to offer a robustly counter-liberal *political* philosophy. However, this is still not a *communitarian* political philosophy, for the standard of judgment appealed to in *Democracy's Discontent* is not community as such (whatever one might imagine "community as such" to mean), but republican self-government. See Michael J. Sandel, "Preface to the Second Edition: The Limits of Communitarianism," *Liberalism and the Limits of Justice*, 2nd ed. (Cambridge: Cambridge University Press, 1998), ix-xi. For discussion of how, in Sandel's more recent work, the appeal to community becomes less salient and the appeal to republican citizenship becomes more so, see chapter 4 above.

When one rereads MacIntyre's "new dark ages" passage in the light of the later writings surveyed in this essay, one can see in retrospect that his political philosophy is already packed into that passage (but needing to be "unpacked"): "the construction of local forms of community" versus the barbarians who are already governing us, that is, the functionaries and politicians of the contemporary state and the managers of the capitalist economy.

36 Cf. Miller's suggestion that an essential component of "left communitarianism" is the commitment to "a doctrine of strong citizenship" ("Communitarianism: Left, Right and Centre," 178).

Part 2:
Citizenship versus Nationalism

6
Nationalism's Challenge to Political Philosophy

– Try to be one of us, repeated Davin. In your heart you are an Irishman but your pride is too powerful.

– My ancestors threw off their language and took another, Stephen said. They allowed a handful of foreigners to subject them. Do you fancy I am going to pay in my own life and person debts they made? What for?

– For our freedom, said Davin.

– No honourable and sincere man, said Stephen, has given up to you his life and his youth and his affections from the days of Tone to those of Parnell but you sold him to the enemy or failed him in need or reviled him and left him for another. And you invite me to be one of you. I'd see you damned first.

– They died for their ideals, Stevie, said Davin. Our day will come yet, believe me.

Stephen, following his own thought, was silent for an instant.

– The soul is born, he said vaguely, first in those moments I told you of. It has a slow and dark birth, more mysterious than the birth of the body. When the soul of a man is born in this country there are nets flung at it to hold it back from flight. You talk to me of nationality, language, religion. I shall try to fly by those nets.

James Joyce[1]

Both of these points of view are in some respect humanly attractive. The problem, philosophically, is that they are *radically incompatible*. The challenge that nationalism poses to political philosophy is to retain a sensitivity toward the power of these two ideals of life, those of Davin and of Stephen, without in any way diminishing the radicalism of their philosophical opposition.

Theoretical commentators on nationalism occupy different positions along the spectrum ranged between these two poles, Davin's nationalism and Stephen's anti-nationalism. Not a few contemporary theorists believe that it is possible to mediate the debate over nationalism versus anti-nationalism in a way that allows one to preserve the best of both worlds. My own sympathies tend more in the direction of Stephen Daedalus's impulse to "fly by those nets." But I am far from thinking that the human desire for a sense of belonging, rootedness, loyalty, and collective memory, as well as the desire to seek political support and protection for these feelings, can be easily dismissed. Moreover, I appreciate the efforts of liberal theorists to give full weight to these human desires, and to try to defend the nationalist impulse in a way that is entirely faithful to liberal principles. These arguments, too, need to be taken very seriously. The liberal-nationalist debate remains an open-ended dialogue (as do all living debates in political philosophy).

Why has it taken philosophers so long to rise to the normative challenges posed by nationalism? As many students of nationalism have remarked, there is an amazing disproportion between nationalism's political importance as one of the leading social phenomena of the modern world and the virtual lack of intellectual endeavour at the highest level either to vindicate or to rebut its normative claims.[2] There have, of course, been lively and intellectually challenging debates about the history and sociology of nationalism that have been unfolding for several decades, and show no sign of abatement; these have not been matched, however, by an equally serious engagement with the philosophy of nationalism, at least until very recently. Nor has nationalism been a prominent topic within the established tradition of grand theorizing that defines the history of political philosophy. As Benedict Anderson has observed: "unlike most other isms, nationalism has never produced its own grand thinkers: no Hobbeses, Tocquevilles, Marxes, or Webers."[3] Bernard Yack puts the same point even more bluntly: "there are no great theoretical texts outlining and defending nationalism. No Marx, no Mill, no Machiavelli. Only minor texts by first rate thinkers, like Fichte, or major texts by second rate thinkers, like Mazzini."[4] This absence of master theorists of nationalism may explain why nationalism has been largely neglected by philosophers and theorists, for political philosophy and theory are to a large extent tradition-bound disciplines. But this really isn't an answer, since it simply raises in turn the question: why *hasn't* the tradition of political thought generated towering philosophers who could do for nationalism what Locke did for liberalism and Marx did for socialism? It may be that the business of nationalist politics involves too much local myth-making to be conducive to the kind of more panoramic and universalistic reflection that yields a comprehensive articulation of a coherent political philosophy; this is more or less the view of critics of nationalism such as Eric Hobsbawm and Ernest

Gellner.[5] As Conor Cruise O'Brien has noted, there is something peculiar about the very idea of "theorizing" nationalism, since theory aims at what is general, namely universal conceptions of moral and political validity, whereas nationalism exalts the particular: its practitioners are invariably preoccupied with satisfying the grievances of this or that national group, not with vindicating the legitimacy of national aspirations as a matter of general principle.[6]

We should not overstate the point. There are, of course, significant texts in the history of modern political thought that we must read in order to think normatively about nationalism: the writings of Herder;[7] Fichte's *Addresses to the German Nation*;[8] the Mill-Acton debate;[9] Renan's famous lecture;[10] Julien Benda's *The Treason of the Intellectuals*;[11] and perhaps a few others.[12] In any case, even if there were no such intellectual landmarks in the history of modern thought, this would certainly not relieve contemporary intellectuals of the responsibility to engage in normatively serious reflection on the philosophical meaning of nationalism. Historians and sociologists have already made notable contributions, and continue to do so; the question now is what philosophers and political theorists can contribute to clarifying the political appeal and normative status of nationalist claims.

No one can, in a single essay, hope to do any kind of justice to the vast range of interesting and important normative questions that arise in considering the philosophical problem of nationalism. Let us propose five problem areas, simply as a way of highlighting the kinds of issues that have begun to attract the attention of leading contemporary theorists and philosophers of nationalism. I'll list them here, and then comment briefly on each of them in the remainder of this essay:

1   Do nations have a theoretically demonstrable "right" to collective self-determination?
2   What is the relationship between nationalism and "modernity" (comprising our experience of modern social life and the political principles by which that experience has been theoretically articulated), and what is the normative significance of debates concerning the modern or pre-modern character of nationalism?
3   Can nationalism and liberalism be reconciled, at least at the level of theoretical principles, or are they, in their very essence, conflicting visions of the human good?
4   Is there a theoretically legitimate distinction between so-called civic and ethnic versions of nationalism, or is such a distinction, as Bernard Yack among others charges, merely the product of (unwarranted) liberal self-congratulation?[13]
5   Is nationalism "existentially" attractive, that is, as a choice of how to live one's life?

National Self-Determination

I think it is beyond question that the legacy of European colonialism, and by consequence, the process of decolonization as one of the major political phenomena of this century, has done much to legitimize nationalist principles. When one reflects on the great movement of postcolonial independence in the middle of the twentieth century, it is impossible to think of nationalism as an ideology of the right, for left-nationalisms have been no less conspicuous, perhaps more conspicuous, in the past century; just as the movements of national liberation from the dominant empires of nineteenth-century Europe make clear why liberal nationalism was a coherent and attractive creed for nineteenth-century figures like Mazzini (and Mill). To make no concessions to the normative force of nationalist thought would entail not only embracing the nineteenth-century empires within Europe (as Lord Acton seems to do), but also denying the moral legitimacy of the politics of anti-colonialism in the twentieth century.[14] For this reason, one can applaud Elie Kedourie for the theoretical consistency of his critique of nationalism, for Kedourie suggests, at least implicitly, that anti-colonialism is theoretically dubious, to the extent that it rests upon nationalist principles. As he puts it in a crucial formulation, in judging whether a change of rulers is to be welcomed or regretted, "the only criterion capable of public defence is whether the new rulers are less corrupt and grasping, or more just and merciful, or whether there is no change at all, but the corruption, the greed, and the tyranny merely find victims other than those of the departed rulers."[15] By this he means: the nationality of the new rulers is not a legitimate criterion of moral-political judgment. Again, this way of thinking cannot be faulted for theoretical inconsistency, but I think it can be faulted for failing to take sufficient account of the kinds of moral intuition that have bestowed on this century's movements of postcolonial independence more-or-less-universal approbation.[16] The kind of moral intuition to which I'm referring has been nicely expressed by Isaiah Berlin as follows: "men prefer to be ordered about, even if this entails ill-treatment, by members of their own faith or nation or class, to tutelage, however benevolent, on the part of ultimately patronising superiors from a foreign land or alien class or milieu."[17]

So I presume that we can agree with Berlin rather than Kedourie that in a world of colonial empires, the principle of self-determination has an undeniable normative force.[18] But what happens when we leave the world of empires behind?[19] Is it theoretically coherent to try to apply the self-determination principle to *all* multinational or multiethnic states? (Admittedly, any national-secessionist movement will portray its relation to the majority culture as quasi-colonial, and will therefore present its claims as being on a moral par with those of postcolonial independence movements.) Carried to the logical limit, the theoretical consequences are somewhat catastrophic; for hardly any states today would be immune from having their legitimacy normatively subverted. As many students of nationalism have highlighted, the "nation-state" in any rigorous sense is not the norm today; the norm is multinationality.[20] As Gellner has put the point: we live in a world that "has only space for something of the order of 200 or 300 national states."[21] That leaves a vast number of potential nations, certainly many thousands, that could in principle claim statehood according to an ambitious application of self-determination principles.[22] If each of these potential nations put in its bid for full self-determination, only Iceland, South Korea, Japan, and perhaps a few others would be politically secure. Think of what a "right" of national self-determination, rigorously applied, would do to states such as India, China, and Russia (to say nothing of the various African states, with their colossal ethnic-tribal heterogeneity and arbitrary state boundaries). We immediately conjure up the vision of a hundredfold multiplication of the kind of interethnic chaos we witnessed with the fragmentation of the Soviet Union.[23]

Perhaps this problem would not be so intractable if we could at least determine clear criteria for establishing in principle the range of legitimate claimants to statehood. But this is impossible, as Eric Hobsbawm explains: "To assume that the multiplication of independent states has an end is to assume that 1. the world can be subdivided into a finite number of homogeneous potential 'nation-states' immune to further subdivision – i.e., 2. that these can be specified in advance. This is plainly not the case."[24] The problem is further compounded by the fact that the open-ended character of national self-determination as a moral-political principle does nothing to constrain ambitious political elites, provided they have a sufficient degree of political creativity, from contriving new national identities (on the contrary, it virtually invites them to do so, by promising moral sanction): "'ethnic' identities which had no political or even existential significance until yesterday (for instance being a 'Lombard,' which is now the title of the xenophobic leagues in North Italy) can acquire a genuine hold as badges of group identity overnight."[25] There is little reason to think that Umberto Bossi's dream of a republic of Padania is anything other than a cynical fabrication. But nothing prevents Mr. Bossi from invoking the morality of self-determination in pursuing his state-busting and state-inventing designs: all that needs to be done is to invent a previously imaginary "people," give it a flag, and stir it up with a suitable amount of demagoguery until it starts to believe that its national rights have been violated, and presto, a new "nation" is born. In any case, even if we leave aside the most extreme cases of far-fetched appeals to and abuse of the idea of self-determination, it seems a strange kind of normative principle that relies for its coherence on the willingness of most national groups not to cash in the moral voucher that the principle gives them.

Nationalism and Modernity

The question of whether nationalism is a radically modern construct or whether it draws upon authentically premodern experiences of nationhood has been hotly contested by historians and sociologists of nationalism, and there is no reason to anticipate an early resolution of these debates.[26] A related though somewhat different question is: Does the sense of nationhood precede, or is it the product of, nationalist *politics,* and what hangs, normatively speaking, on one's answer to this question? Kenneth Minogue offers one very forceful answer to the latter question: "Nationalist theory accords with the famous remark by Péguy: *Tout commence en mystique et finit en politique.* In the beginning is the nation, an unselfconscious cultural and linguistic nature waiting like Sleeping Beauty to be aroused by the kiss of politics."[27] Minogue very clearly regards this Sleeping Beauty conception of nationhood as an utter mystification. A radically opposed view is formulated by Roger Scruton: "To suppose that we [Englishmen] could have enjoyed [our] territorial, legal, and linguistic hereditaments, and yet refrained from becoming a nation, representing itself to itself as entitled to these things, and defining even its religion in terms of them, is to give way to fantasy. In no way can the emergence of the English nation, as a form of membership, be regarded as a product of Enlightenment universalism, or the Industrial Revolution, or the administrative needs of a modern bureaucracy. It existed before those things, and also shaped them into powerful instruments of its own."[28] It should be obvious that Scruton is responding here not just to Minogue but to all those modernist sociologists, such as Gellner, who see nations as mythic entities fashioned by nationalist intelligentsia.[29] Anderson, for instance, quotes from a history of Hungarian nationalism an extremely blunt formulation of this latter view: "A nation is born when a few people decide that it should be."[30]

In the debates we have just quickly reviewed, a radically modernist view of nations serves to debunk nationalist mythmaking, whereas the view that national sentiment is linked to authentically premodern cultural resources helps to legitimize these sentiments of national belonging. But the normative argument can go the other way: portraying nationalism as a fully modern political phenomenon can help in *vindicating* nationalist ideas over against the cruder depictions of nationalism as sheer atavism.[31] Charles Taylor offers an excellent example of how nationalism can be vindicated by stressing the emphatically modern character of nationalist consciousness.[32] For a liberal defender of nationalism like Taylor, it is essential to show nationalism's inextricable dependence on modern notions of popular will and popular sovereignty because this will at least serve to demolish the most unflattering images of nationalism, as a relic of primitive forms of social life, or as a reversion to ancient tribalism.[33] Taylor's basic idea is that once we come to see how central the quest for identity is within characteristically modern experience, and what frustration is generated if the various identities are not given public recognition at the political level, we will have a much better appreciation of the reason for the prominence of nationalism (and much else in contemporary political life) in the modern political world.[34]

I don't think one can get as much normative mileage out of this idea of identity as Taylor thinks one can. No one can deny that struggles over identity are central to modern politics. But the sheer possession of a given identity confers no normative authority on the kind of politics that goes with that identity. To answer the normative questions that interest us, it doesn't suffice to recognize the centrality of identity; we have to go on to ask *which* identities survive normative scrutiny. To dramatize this point, let me refer to a terrific 1991 film directed by Mira Nair called *Mississippi Masala*. The film is basically a love story about an interracial romance set in Mississippi. But the central pathos of the film revolves not around the clash of identities in the United States but rather the clash of identities in Uganda two decades earlier. The heroine of the film is an East Indian named Mina who falls in love with a black carpet-cleaner, but the romance is a scandal because of the trauma suffered by her family at the hands of Idi Amin's thuggish nationalism. The film opens with a passionate exchange involving Mina's father on the day of Amin's expulsion of the Ugandan Asians in 1972, and it defines the central drama of the whole film. He says, "Uganda is my home," to which he gets the plaintive response (offered not as a political affirmation but simply as an acknowledgment of the prevailing realities), "Africa is for Africans ... black Africans." The question for a political philosopher here is not the relevance of identity, but how to assess the normative claims embodied in conflicting visions of identity – in this case, the claims of African-nationalist identity on the one side and the claims of trans-ethnic Ugandan identity on the other. The appeal to identity by itself gives us no reason to favour the distinctively nationalist way of conferring identity, as opposed to other possibilities, such as a determinedly non-nationalist civic identity.

Liberal Nationalism

It is not hard to see what motivates the political-philosophical project, shared by Yael Tamir, Charles Taylor, Michael Walzer, Will Kymlicka, and others, of vindicating a liberal-nationalist vision of politics. This project offers a dual attraction: first, the prospect of taking the illiberal sting out of nationalism, by liberalizing it; and second, helping to combat unthinking and dogmatic rejections of nationalist politics *tout court,* thereby facilitating (sometimes necessary) accommodation with nationalism.[35] On the one hand, it is clear that there is no shortage in the world of poisonous versions of nationalism for which no good normative case can or ought to be made. On the other hand, it seems to many that liberalism, especially in its more individualist versions, allows too little place for legitimate expressions of group identity, and moreover, that its attenuated conception of communal membership weakens the cultural resources necessary for a sustainable political community. It would be unreasonable, however, to imagine that liberal ideas of membership allow no place for collective identity, since every significant liberal political philosopher that we can think of presupposes a world of discrete states that claim the allegiance of their members. Rather, the liberal ideal is to get as far from ideas of national exclusivity as would be consistent with the continued existence of these states. This universalistic aspiration of the liberal idea of citizenship is nicely summarized by Stephen Holmes in an essay commending "Liberalism for a World of Ethnic Passions and Decaying States." Classical liberals, he writes, were not driven by Enlightenment universalism to reject the pluralism of modern nation-states and to embrace the unrealistic dream of a single, worldwide liberal community. But it did lead them "to support the definition of exclusive citizenship which most closely approximates universalism. Citizenship, in the pluralistic world of nation-states, can never be universalistic. But it can be based on accidental territorial coexistence rather than ethnic homogeneity or ascriptive community. The *jus soli* is a liberal principle of state-formation, which allocates citizenship according to birthplace, and it stands in sharp contrast to the *jus sanguinis,* which identifies co-nationals by bloodline and 'constitutive attachments' rather than by historically accidental coexistence on the same (arbitrarily demarcated) piece of land."[36] Is it possible to "beef up" liberal conceptions of citizenship short of embracing nationalism? This is clearly Jürgen Habermas's aim in developing his notion of "constitutional patriotism" (which is basically a Habermasian synonym for what others have labelled civic nationalism).[37] But as critics of Habermas have complained, it is not clear how Habermas's conception, with its strong aversion to more robust appeals to cultural identity, can offer much beyond a new name for liberalism.[38] Hence the attraction of trying to liberalize nationalism.

How well does the liberal-nationalist project succeed? Since Yael Tamir has done the most to put this on the agenda of contemporary political philosophy, let me start with a few comments on her version of the project.[39] My main response is that in Tamir's statement of the liberal-nationalist case, the nationalist side of the equation is so watered down that the nationalism in her political theory is barely detectable.[40] What nationalists want, typically, is not a vaguely defined "public space" for the display of their national identity, but rather, control over a *state* as the vehicle for the furtherance of national self-expression.[41] No real nationalist would say what Tamir does, namely, that the "ideal of the nation-state should ... be abandoned."[42] She refers to the idea of the homogeneous national state as "a pipedream," and she anticipates that new options, neither conventionally liberal nor conventionally nationalist, will present themselves once the obsolete nation-state ideal has been renounced: "Liberal nationalism advocates taking cultural and national differences into account."[43] It seems to me quite misleading to call this a version of nationalism; a more accurate description of her position is: liberalism, with an attention to the ways in which people care about national identity and wish to see it expressed in some fashion. To be sure, Tamir sees allegiance to national community as intrinsically valuable. This may at least distinguish her liberalism from that of an ardent liberal individualist such as George Kateb. Even Kateb concedes that strong group identity and membership should not be condemned "when the cultural group has been or is now being victimized and is struggling to overcome its victimization or the remains of it. Solidarity is needed"; but he immediately goes on to insist that "cultural group solidarity is not intrinsically valuable, only provisionally and tactically and instrumentally so."[44] One can see group membership as intrinsically valuable, however, without embracing any of the tenets of characteristically nationalist politics. And it seems that this is true of Tamir's position: what it is, really, is not any kind of nationalism, but rather, a form of liberalism that is not indifferent to concerns about national identity.

In pursuing my critique of nationalism as an alternative to liberalism, let me focus on what I see as the decisive problem; if this problem is as intractable as I think it is, then any attempt to synthesize liberalism and nationalism theoretically will be forced to drop either the liberalism or the nationalism when it comes to the crunch (or at least a serious philosophical wedge will be placed between one's liberalism and one's nationalism). The problem, in a nutshell, is how to privilege the majority cultural identity in defining civic membership without consigning cultural minorities to second-class citizenship. To simplify the argument, let us limit ourselves to discussion of Zionist nationalism, though the same analysis could be applied to any state conceived in nationalist categories. Let us leave aside Palestinians in the West Bank and Gaza and what justice toward them might require, and think only about Arabs who aspire to be citizens within a state that defines itself officially as a "Jewish state." What qualifies Zionism as a classic form of nationalism is not that it involves a celebration of Israeli nationality or Israeli citizenship, but rather, that it provides an ideology that specifies the properly nationalist *content* of this citizenship, namely Jewish national belonging (notwithstanding the fact that who counts as a Jew for this purpose is far from uncontroversial – so that eligibility or ineligibility under the Law of Return is sometimes hotly contested).[45]

Consider the following descriptions of Jewish statehood and what it means for the content of Israeli citizenship:

> Israel's founders dreamed of, and its people have fought for, the creation of a Jewish state in the Holy Land. The blue and white Israeli flag features the quintessentially Jewish symbol, the Star of David, and the national anthem proclaims that for 2,000 years its people have longed to return to and be free

in Zion. None of this includes or even makes much sense to Israeli Arabs, most of whom are Muslim and have family histories on this land extending back hundreds of years. Moreover, while Israeli Arabs exercise many of the rights enjoyed by the Jewish majority, no one suggests all Israelis are equal. A small minority of Israeli Arabs focus their demands on achieving individual equality, but most demand collective or national rights, and by equality they mean that Israel should become either binational or declare itself the state of all its people.[46]

All of the state's symbols, national holidays, holy days, language, myths, and a great deal more, are drawn from Jewish history and experience. Israel was conceived in specifically Jewish memory.[47]

"Hatikva" ... is exclusively Jewish. The national anthem of the state of Israel is one that 18 percent of Israeli citizens do not and cannot share.[48]

Similar issues are debated in a very lively exchange between Michael Walzer and James Rule.[49] Rule argues for the unmitigated anti-nationalist position that Israel's self-conception as an officially Zionist state is morally intolerable. In response, Walzer writes: "There can't be a political community of any sort that doesn't favor some particular people, members of the community over all others. This is what it means to share a common life."[50] This is beyond dispute, but it doesn't address the crucial issue here, which is whether it is morally proper for the state to favour one tribe over another *within* the boundaries of a shared civic life. To the latter challenge, Walzer answers: "There are also, obviously, internal discriminations – as when we choose what language to privilege, what history and civics to teach in the public schools, what holidays to celebrate. In every nation-state in the world, choices like these turn national minorities into the wrong kind of people ... if [Rule] really wants to abolish national and cultural favoritism root and branch, he won't be able to accommodate any of the tribes."[51] But Walzer here presumes that every civic community conceives of itself as the political expression of membership in a tribe. This isn't clear to me. It is indeed true that even "civic" nations such as Canada and the United States privilege particular languages, holidays, cultural traditions, and so on. But does this prove that these political communities are just as tribal as states that define themselves in a more straightforwardly nationalist way? This surely cannot be the case with Canada at least, which at the moment is a binational state. But suppose Quebec does decide to leave in order to pursue its own "tribal" destiny. Will the residual Anglo-Canada be a political tribe like Israel? A Canadian state minus Quebec would overwhelmingly privilege English, and to some extent would reflect a residual Anglo-Canadian culture; but does that mean that Canada would then be a uni-national state in any meaningful sense? Would common ethnonational identity define citizenship for the Anglo-Canadians, Greek Canadians, Italian Canadians, Aboriginal peoples, West Indian Canadians, and so on, who would compose such a political community after the departure of Quebec?

If citizenship in Israel means citizenship in an expressly Jewish state, non-Jewish citizens are unavoidably second-class citizens in some sense, even if the state doesn't go out of its way to oppress them or to crush their minority culture. In a new state founded on the principle of *Québec pour les québécois*, anglophone Montrealers and Aboriginal peoples in northern Quebec will likewise be second-class citizens in some sense (at least until they assimilate to the francophone majority culture), even if the state of Quebec respects minority rights and affirms universal citizenship within its territorial boundaries. Non-nationalist conceptions of citizenship, by contrast, aspire to a trans-ethnic definition of political community (even if in practice they fall short of this ideal). There are immediate existential choices here (precisely the kinds of dilemmas that prompt one to embrace political philosophy as a quest for first principles): for Jews, citizenship in Israel versus citizenship in (say) a multicultural Canada; for Scots, citizenship in an independent Scotland versus citizenship in a trinational or quadranational Britain.[52] For thoroughgoing nationalists, there must be something suspect about the desire to house different ethnonational communities under the umbrella of a shared civic community (which is precisely what defines binational Canada or trinational Switzerland or quadranational Britain).

Liberal nationalism, it seems to me, seeks to blur the sharpness of these existential choices. Any *principled* nationalist would have to consider it foolhardy and perhaps incomprehensible for a Jew to live in Canada when emigration to Israel is an available option; and consider it demeaning and perhaps a self-betrayal for a Québécois to abide continued subordination within a federation populated by an anglophone majority when self-determination is so readily within reach by simply voting *oui* in a referendum. Of course, it is possible to opt for citizenship in a nationalist polity without embracing illiberalism, oppression of others, and violent conflict (contrary to what strident anti-nationalists sometimes suggest); in this respect the liberal-nationalist thesis is true. If I trade in my Canadian citizenship for citizenship in a nationalist Republic of Quebec, or for citizenship in a Zionist Israel, I will still be a citizen in a relatively liberal political community. Nonetheless, the possibility of liberal nationalism in this sense doesn't mean further normative scrutiny of the alternatives is unnecessary. There remains a normatively weighty choice of principle between, on the one hand, citizenship in a deliberately multinational or multicultural society, and on the other hand, citizenship expressly devoted to embodying "the passionate desire of men to be only with their own kind."[53] Political-philosophical debate ought to be able to illuminate our engagement with such alternatives.

To be sure, not every nationalist is a Milan Karadzic or Louis Farrakhan. There are more liberal and less liberal nationalists. There are, for instance, a great many liberal Zionists who not only have no sympathy for Jewish chauvinism but also considerable solicitude for the plight of Palestinians within a Jewish state (just as there are many liberal nationalists in Quebec who felt ashamed and sullied by the ethnocentric ranting of Jacques Parizeau on the night of 30 October 1995). On the other hand, I think there is some risk that liberal defenders of nationalism, in trying to take the illiberal sting out of nationalism, will remove from it some of the very things that make nationalism philosophically interesting. It is very important for the philosopher of nationalism to keep in mind that the national idea has been such a potent force in the modern world, and opens up a far-reaching philosophical alternative to liberal conceptions of the meaning of life (one that may or may not be vindicated at the conclusion of a fully developed philosophical interrogation of its claims), precisely because it involves profound ideas of national belonging, national destiny, rootedness in a community of experience, memories of a shared past, and so on. These are powerful notions, and I am not sure that one is able to do justice to them by seeking to split the difference between liberalism and nationalism.

The Ethnic/Civic Question

A good example of the liberal-nationalist defence of nationalism is an argument by Kai Nielsen which very vigorously opposes the depiction of Québécois nationalism as a form of ethnic nationalism.[54] My own view is that Nielsen is too quick to conclude that Quebec nationalism is entirely benign and innocent. Perhaps his account of cultural nationalism in Quebec would be more compelling if it were obvious that the French language and Québécois culture would be more secure in an independent Quebec than they are in binational Canada as it presently exists. But this is not obvious: maybe language and culture would be more secure; maybe not. There are plausible arguments on both sides of the question. At least the most militant Québécois nationalists seem driven by something else: namely, the ambition to turn a sovereign Quebec into a state of the (ethno-) Québécois, similar to what Israel, defined as the "Jewish state," is for Zionists, and what Croatia, defined as the "state of the Croats," is for Croatian nationalists.[55] No doubt it is unfair for Quebeckers who are not ethno-Québécois to assume that *all* Quebec nationalists are ethnic nationalists of the vicious sort: most are, as Nielsen argues, more liberal cultural-nationalists.[56] But those living in Quebec who are fearful of ethnic nationalism are not merely hallucinating, conjuring up ghastly phantoms that are, in reality, entirely absent from the scene. Thus Nielsen is being a bit too charitable in maintaining that the problem with Quebec nationalism is limited to a few "loose cannons."[57] (It surely says something about the less savoury side of Quebec nationalism when it turns out that one of these "loose cannons" happens to have been premier of Quebec, and hence titular leader of the nationalist movement – namely Jacques Parizeau: when Parizeau says *nous*, it is difficult to purge this of all ethnonational associations.) The issue here is *not* whether every nationalist movement will turn into a Rwanda-style bloodbath or a Yugoslav-style free-for-all of ethnocentric hatred. The issue is whether it is morally and politically attractive to give political priority (as nationalists do) to questions of national sovereignty and cultural self-affirmation. For instance, what are the broader consequences for the quality of political life in a multinational society of this politicization of cultural identity?

As Bernard Yack and Will Kymlicka rightly argue, the state can never be culturally and linguistically neutral, and therefore one should be careful not to oppose nationalist myths by positing the counter-myth of a liberal state that achieves a state of pure abstinence in relation to national concerns.[58] However, that said, it would be unwarranted to conclude that, explicitly or implicitly, all politics are nationalist politics. Being concerned with the preservation of a language and cultural identity does not suffice to make one a nationalist, for if it did, we would be required to call Pierre Trudeau a Québécois nationalist, which would be absurd. Trudeau was an antinationalist because, for all of his desire to preserve French culture in Quebec (and elsewhere in Canada!), he did not believe that the self-affirmation of the Québécois nation ought to trump all other political concerns nor to be definitive of one's ultimate political commitments.[59]

What defines nationalism is precisely the idea that concern over the national question trumps every other social-political concern. As Eric Hobsbawm rightly observes, the relationship between nationalism and, for instance, the choice between capitalism and socialism "is of no significance to nationalists, who do not care what this relationship is, so long as Ruritanians (or whoever) acquire sovereign statehood as a nation, or indeed what happens thereafter. Their utopia – by now at least as shopsoiled by practice as some others – consists precisely in the achievement of Ruritanian (and if possible Greater Ruritanian) independence and rule, if need be over the non-Ruritanians in their midst."[60] It goes without saying that, for instance in Quebec, there are all kinds of nationalists, more liberal and less liberal. But this fact doesn't lessen my inclination to say that for the "real" nationalists, nationalists in the strict sense, the issue is not adequate protection for the French language and culture, for which there is, arguably, already ample provision in the existing federation. Instead, the issue for them is Quebec's desire for a nation-state in the strict sense ("to be a normal country" is the standard nationalist formulation). This would not be too much of a problem, normatively speaking, if the citizens of Quebec were, like those of Norway or

Japan, more or less ethnically homogeneous.[61] But the minorities in Quebec justifiably perceive this ambition for a nation-state as an attempt to diminish their citizenship.

What motivates some critics of nationalism to distinguish "ethnic" and "civic" conceptions of nationhood is not the absurd notion that language and cultural identity are politically irrelevant.[62] Rather, what animates the "civic" conception is the vision of a shared citizenship and civic identity that would be in principle capable of transcending these cultural preoccupations, however legitimate they may be, in a political community where linguistic and cultural identities are in potential conflict. It doesn't require any blindness to the importance people place upon their linguistic and ethnic heritage to say that the Czechoslovak and Yugoslav federations embodied a noble impulse, and their collapse in the face of nationalist agitation in each case conveys a real tragedy, not just for the peoples concerned but for all human onlookers. If the Canadian federation succumbs as well, the same may be said of it. So I think that the ethnic nationalism/civic nationalism distinction, robustly criticized by some very acute theorists, or some version of that distinction, is still worthy of philosophical defence.[63]

The Existential Question

This, in many ways the most interesting of the questions surveyed here, is the one least addressed in the recent philosophical debates about the problem of nationalism. There is a reason for this neglect; the main explanation for it has to do with the dominance of liberalism within Anglo-American political philosophy and its strong preference for questions of the right (what is normatively *permissible*) over questions of the good (what are the most desirable ways to live a human life).[64] Let me illustrate this contrast in reference to Michael Walzer's argument concerning nationalism.[65] In "The New Tribalism," Walzer offers a persuasive case for accommodating nationalist aspirations. But even if we fully accept Walzer's argument, we might ask whether that argument exhausts the task of philosophical reflection on nationalism. Here one should distinguish between two quite different kinds of argument, namely:

1   The argument that if there is a clear desire on the part of a national community (Slovaks or Palestinians or Québécois) within an existing state to give political expression to its feelings of national belonging, the majority culture should allow it to separate or to be otherwise accommodated in its national aspirations.

2   The argument that it is existentially or politically desirable for the individuals composing this community to have these nationalist or separatist aspirations in the first place.

Accordingly, one can look at the problem from two different standpoints: that of a member of the majority confronted by the (already existing) national demands of a minority (should we concede to their nationalist demands? resist? compromise?); or, that of a member of that minority, confronted with the moral-political question of whether to embrace nationalist politics (should I be a nationalist? should we as a community commit ourselves to this set of political goals rather than some other vision of politics?). It seems entirely coherent to give pro-nationalist and anti-nationalist answers to these two different questions. For instance: to the question of whether to accommodate nationalist demands (say in the case of Czechoslovakia), we could see the reasonableness of answering: "Yes, of course they (namely, the Slovaks) should be *allowed* to have their divorce, if national divorce is what they want"; but to the question of whether life in a uni-national state is in principle preferable to a binational state (which is, so to speak, a "marriage" of nations residing under a shared political roof), we could still answer "no" (say, from the standpoint of a Slovak who must decide upon his or her own political commitment). Philosophical liberals will be reluctant to extend the reach of political philosophy beyond questions of the first kind for fear of presuming to second-guess how individuals choose to conceive their own ends of life. For me, on the other hand, it seems unreasonable to stipulate that the former question, but not the latter, falls within the competence of political-philosophic reflection. Both questions, it seems to me, are legitimate concerns of political philosophy. To express the point once again in the Rawlsian vocabulary of right and good: it doesn't suffice to answer the question of whether accommodations with nationalism comport with what is *right* (what is normatively permissible); one must also address the more ambitious question, is nationalism (as a way of shaping the conception of how one should live) *good?*

Political philosophy as an intellectual engagement, going back to Socrates, is at bottom an attempt to answer the question of how to live ("the good for human beings" is the classical formulation of this existential question). Philosophical reflection on nationalism must therefore seek somehow to offer an answer to the problem of how to orient oneself among the diversity of life's possibilities. Here, I think, Kedourie's critique of nationalism, notwithstanding the compelling criticisms of it made by Gellner and others, retains a considerable force. What Kedourie captures is the aspect of nationalism that entails not just sentiments of national belonging, as a matter of spontaneous feeling, but, so to speak, the *ideologization* of these sentiments (what one might call the "ismness" of nationalism: the politicizing of pre-political bonds of membership). According to a nationalist vision of the world, it doesn't suffice to feel a sense of attachment to one's national group; these feelings of attachment must be made a matter of ideological commitment, and enforced by political mobilization. From a consistently nationalist point of view, the noblest employment of political energies consists in striving to establish a one-to-one correspondence between ethnic-cultural identity and political identity. For *me*, being a nationalist would mean having to become a Zionist (therefore emigrating?), so as to align my (fairly attenuated and more or less assimilated) ethnic identity with a corresponding political identity. But in fact my political identity is completely different, defined by the idea of Canadian citizenship (which is itself imperilled by nationalist agitation). For a thoroughgoing nationalist, there must be something anomalous about this condition of non-coincident cultural and political identity (something "abnormal," in the terminology of Quebec nationalists), whereas for a non-nationalist like me, this disjunction between cultural identity and political identity seems entirely legitimate and proper.

To return to the Joycean dilemmas broached at the beginning of this essay: all nationalists offer some version of Miss Ivors's challenge to Gabriel Conroy (in "The Dead")[66] – namely, her insistence that he make national identity central to the understanding of his own life (why go for holidays on the Continent instead of "visiting your own land"? why learn French or German when you have "your own language to keep in touch with"?), and, concomitantly, her charge that failure to do so constitutes being a traitor to one's people. It may well be that philosophical defenders of nationalism are able to show that some forms of national aspiration are reconcilable with human rights, liberal principles, interethnic goodwill, and so on. It is much more doubtful that any political philosophers have offered, or ever can offer, a theoretical vindication of Miss Ivors's challenge in the fullness of its existential ambition.

Source

This chapter is a revised version of an essay that originally appeared as the Introduction to *Theorizing Nationalism*, ed. Ronald Beiner (Albany: State University of New York Press, 1999), 1-25.

Notes

1 James Joyce, *A Portrait of the Artist As a Young Man: Text, Criticism, and Notes*, ed. Chester G. Anderson (New York: The Viking Press, 1968), 203. Extract from *A Portrait of the Artist As a Young Man* reproduced with the premission of the Estate of James Joyce © Copyright, the Estate of James Joyce. For another brilliant Joycean dialogue on nationalism, see "The Dead," in James Joyce, *Dubliners* (New York: Penguin, 1968), 187-90. One easily gets the impression that the story was intended to express simple revulsion on Joyce's part toward the *völkisch* ideology conjured up in the figure of Miss Ivors, but this might be going too far. For a fine elaboration of the complexities in Joyce's position, see Conor Cruise O'Brien, *Ancestral Voices: Religion and Nationalism in Ireland* (Dublin: Poolbeg, 1994), 44-9. O'Brien emphasizes that Joyce was not thoroughly alienated from the claims of Irishness, but rather felt the inner tension between the impulse to yield to Irish nationalism and the (ultimately prevailing) impulse to resist it.
2 See Benedict Anderson, "Introduction," in *Mapping the Nation*, ed. Gopal Balakrishnan (London: Verso, 1996): "Given what seems today the vast role that nationalism has played over

two centuries of world-politics, why have so many seminal thinkers of modernity – Marx, Nietzsche, Weber, Durkheim, Benjamin, Freud, Lévi-Strauss, Keynes, Gramsci, Foucault – had so little to say about it?" (1). Cf. Ernest Gellner, *Nations and Nationalism* (Ithaca, NY: Cornell University Press, 1983), paraphrasing Eric Hobsbawm, "the disproportion between the importance of nationalism and the amount of thought given to it" (124, n. 1).

3 Benedict Anderson, *Imagined Communities*, rev. ed. (London: Verso, 1991), 5.

4 Bernard Yack, "Ethnos and Demos: A Political Theorist Looks at the Idea of the Nation," manuscript, 1-2. This is an earlier draft of chapter 5, entitled "The Myth of the Civic Nation," of *Theorizing Nationalism*, ed. Ronald Beiner (Albany: State University of New York Press, 1999) (hereinafter *TN*).

5 Cf. Anderson's reference to "the 'political' power of nationalisms vs. their philosophical poverty and even incoherence" (*Imagined Communities*, 5). Also Gellner, *Nations and Nationalism:* "Their precise doctrines are hardly worth analysing ... the prophets of nationalism were not anywhere near the First Division, when it came to the business of thinking" (123-4). Also Ernest Gellner, *Encounters with Nationalism* (Oxford: Blackwell, 1994): "Nationalism as an elaborated intellectual *theory* is neither widely endorsed, nor of high quality, nor of any historic importance" (65). It is a little misleading to call Gellner a "critic" of nationalism. To be sure, he is certainly no friend of the ideologies that propagate nationalism; but strictly speaking his view is that nationalism is a matter for sociological explanation rather than normative judgment, since it is pointless to bemoan something that is a sociologically determined requirement of the modern world.

6 Conor Cruise O'Brien, "Paradise Lost," *New York Review of Books*, 25 April 1991, 56-7. O'Brien argues that "nationalism-as-theory," to the extent that it exists at all, is always merely a façade for national feeling directed toward some particular national group.

7 F.M. Barnard, ed., *J.G. Herder on Social and Political Culture* (Cambridge: Cambridge University Press, 1969). The two most important heirs of Herder within contemporary political theory are Isaiah Berlin and Charles Taylor (no doubt influenced by Berlin's Herderianism). According to Taylor, Herder's idea of *Volk* implies the mutual recognition of all peoples "in their irreplaceable but complementary differences, because they form together the entire choir of humanity" (Taylor, "Les sources de l'identité moderne," in *Les frontières de l'identité: Modernité et postmodernisme au Québec*, ed. M. Elbaz, A. Fortin, and G. Laforest [Paris: L'Harmattan, 1996], 351, my translation). One finds a similar conception in Michael Walzer's idea of what he calls "reiterative universalism," which he illustrates with the case of Mazzini: "Like the man who wanted to dance at every wedding, Mazzini was eager to endorse every reiteration of Italy's national struggle." See Walzer, "Nation and Universe," in *The Tanner Lectures on Human Values XI: 1990*, ed. Grethe B. Peterson (Salt Lake City: University of Utah Press, 1990), 550. For a fine summary of Berlin's views, see Stuart Hampshire, "Nationalism," in *Isaiah Berlin: A Celebration*, ed. Edna and Avishai Margalit (London: Hogarth Press, 1991), 127-34.

8 Johann Gottlieb Fichte, *Addresses to the German Nation*, trans. R.F. Jones and G.H. Turnbull (New York: Harper and Row, 1968).

9 J.S. Mill, *Considerations on Representative Government*, chapter 16; Lord Acton, "Nationality," in *Essays on Freedom and Power*, ed. Gertrude Himmelfarb (Cleveland, OH: Meridian Books, 1955), 141-70. For an analysis of this debate, see chapter 12 below.

10 Ernest Renan, *Qu'est-ce qu'une nation?/What Is a Nation?* (Toronto: Tapir Press, 1996), a bilingual edition with a translation by Wanda Romer Taylor. It is worth noting, for instance, how Renan figures in the recent debate between Jürgen Habermas and Bernard Yack on whether some kind of civic nationalism can offer a viable alternative to cultural or ethnic nationalism (see pp. 110, 115-16, 203 in this book). Habermas is very critical of the idea of basing citizenship on national identity. In fact, his central purpose as a theorist of citizenship is to "de-couple" the idea of citizenship from the idea of ethnocultural identity. Yack, on the other hand, is much more comfortable with the idea that there is an inescapably cultural dimension to citizenship. Yet both cite Renan as supporting their case: see Habermas, "Citizenship and National Identity: Some Reflections on the Future of Europe," in *Theorizing Citizenship*, ed. Ronald Beiner (Albany: State University of New York Press, 1995), 258-9; and Yack, "The Myth of the Civic Nation," in *TN*, 116.

11 Julien Benda, *The Treason of the Intellectuals*, trans. R. Aldington (New York: Norton, 1969). For a contemporary work inspired by Benda, see Alain Finkielkraut, *The Defeat of the Mind*, trans. Judith Friedlander (New York: Columbia University Press, 1995); part 1 offers an excellent account of some crucial episodes in the history of nationalist thought. Of particular interest is Finkielkraut's reconstruction of a dialogue between Herder and Goethe that directly parallels the dialogue between Davin and Stephen cited at the beginning of this essay: again, the issue is whether the human spirit flies most freely when it has been liberated from its cultural roots to participate in a wider humanity, or whether this supposed liberation is in fact mere deracination, therefore spiritually deadening. For an eloquent restatement of the Herderian side of this debate, see Isaiah Berlin, "Two Concepts of Nationalism," *New York Review of Books*, 21 November 1992, 19-23 ("Like Herder, I regard cosmopolitanism as empty. People can't develop unless they belong to a culture," 22).

12 There have been interesting debates about whether to add Rousseau and Hegel to this list of essential theorists of nationalism. See, for instance, Anne M. Cohler, *Rousseau and Nationalism* (New York: Basic Books, 1970); John Plamenatz, "Two Types of Nationalism," in *Nationalism: The Nature and Evolution of an Idea*, ed. Eugene Kamenka (New York: St. Martin's Press, 1976), 24-5; Elie Kedourie, *Nationalism*, 4th ed. (Oxford: Blackwell, 1993), 28-9 n. 1; Gellner, *Nations and Nationalism*, 130; and Neil MacCormick, "Nation and Nationalism," in *TN*, 195. Certainly both Rousseau and Hegel believed that attachment to a national community would contribute in very important ways to attachment to the state. But for both of them the point is not to foster national feeling for its own sake (as would be the case for a nationalist); rather, the point is to draw upon it as a cultural resource in strengthening the *civic* community (the community of citizens holding membership in the state). In Hegel's case, I think we have decisive evidence of his non-nationalism. As Roger Scruton notes, it was Fichte's "experience of the helplessness of Germany before the Napoleonic armies that inspired" his nationalism. "In Defense of the Nation," in Scruton, *The Philosopher on Dover Beach* (Manchester: Carcanet, 1990), 325. This is certainly true, and it proves at the same time that Hegel, with his great enthusiasm for Napoleon, could not possibly have been a nationalist.

13 *TN*, 105. Yack's charge of Western-liberal self-congratulation against the civic/ethnic distinction ought to be taken seriously. Yet it is possible to defend the distinction without reference to politics in the West: for instance, there is all the difference in the world between the pan-Indian nationalism championed by Gandhi and Nehru and the Hindu nationalism that is presently gaining ground in India. Here, at least, is a case where it is a question not of celebrating "Western" nationalism relative to "Eastern" nationalism (Yack has in mind terms introduced by John Plamenatz), but of comparing two Asian nationalisms – one that is normatively attractive and another that is normatively repugnant (e.g., the Hindu militancy of the Bharatiya Janata Party). In fact, I am tempted to describe them as Nehru's pan-Indian "nationalism" versus the Hindu nationalism of the BJP, since it is not obvious to me or to other critics of nationalism that *nationalism* is the right term to describe a movement of trans-ethnic civic emancipation, whereas it *does* seem obvious that Hindu nationalist politics is an instance of nationalism in the purest and most odious sense.

14 According to Brian Barry ("Self-Government Revisited," in *TN*, 255-6, 258, 265, 275 n. 56), Acton's championing of multinationality is in the service of his more fundamental commitment to the cause of empire; this seems a rather deterministic and ungenerous interpretation. For another ungenerously reductionist interpretation of Lord Acton's argument against uni-national states, see David Miller, *On Nationality* (Oxford: Clarendon Press, 1995), 85 n. 5.

15 Elie Kedourie, *Nationalism*, 135. Cf. Ernest Gellner, "Nationalism," in *Thought and Change* (Chicago: University of Chicago Press, 1965): "Life is a difficult and serious business. The protection from starvation and insecurity is not easily achieved. In the achievement of it, effective government is an important factor. Could one think of a sillier, more *frivolous* consideration than the question concerning the native vernacular of the governors?" (153).

16 For a powerful account of the moral and political considerations that support this intuition, see Alan C. Cairns, "Empire, Globalization, and the Fall and Rise of Diversity," in *Citizenship, Diversity, and Pluralism: Canadian and Comparative Perspectives*, ed. Alan C. Cairns et al. (Montreal and Kingston: McGill-Queen's University Press, 1999), 23-57.

17 Isaiah Berlin, "The Bent Twig," in *The Crooked Timber of Humanity*, ed. Henry Hardy (New York: Vintage Books, 1992), 251.

18 As Walker Connor points out in *Ethnonationalism* (Princeton, NJ: Princeton University Press, 1994), however, calling this *national* self-determination is not unproblematic: "Although [the African and Asian independence movements] had been conducted in the name of self-determination of nations, they were, in fact, demands for political independence not in accord with ethnic distributions, but along the essentially happenstance borders that delimited either the sovereignty or the administrative zones of former colonial powers. This fact combined with the incredibly complex ethnic map of Africa and Asia to create, in the name of self-determination of nations, a host of multinational states" (5). Cf. E.J. Hobsbawm, *Nations and Nationalism since 1780*, 2nd ed. (Cambridge: Cambridge University Press, 1992), 169.

19 Cf. Eric Hobsbawm, "Some Reflections on 'The Break-up of Britain,'" *New Left Review* 105 (1977): "The virtual disappearance of formal empires ('colonialism') has snapped the main link between anti-imperialism and the slogan of national self-determination ... the struggle against [neocolonial dependence] simply cannot any longer be crystallized round the slogan of establishing independent political statehood, because most territories concerned already have it" (11).

20 See, for instance, Will Kymlicka, *Multicultural Citizenship* (Oxford, Clarendon Press, 1995), 1 and 196 n. 1; Hobsbawm, *Nations and Nationalism since 1780*, 66, 179, 186; Connor, *Ethnonationalism*, 77, 155, 166.

21 Ernest Gellner, "Do Nations Have Navels?" *Nations and Nationalism* 2, part 3 (1996): 369.

22 For Gellner's interesting reflections on potential nationalisms, see *Nations and Nationalism*, 44-5.

23 Cf. Sanford Levinson, "Is Liberal Nationalism an Oxymoron? An Essay for Judith Shklar" *Ethics* 105 (April 1995): 626-45: "There are far too many nations to make [a Wilsonian commitment to national self-determination] feasible, at least without bloodshed that would make Bosnia look almost mild. The phrase 'self-determination,' especially when it is interpreted as a call for political independence, is, as was said by Wilson's own secretary of state, 'simply loaded with dynamite. It will raise hopes which can never be realized. It will, I fear, cost thousands of lives.' Lansing's only error, of course, was the almost literally incredible underestimation of costs" (631).

24 Hobsbawm, "Some Reflections on 'The Break-up of Britain,'" 12-13.

25 Eric J. Hobsbawm, "Ethnicity and Nationalism in Europe Today," in *Mapping the Nation*, ed. Balakrishnan, 260.

26 For an excellent display of this kind of debate, see the recent exchange between Gellner and Anthony Smith: Anthony D. Smith and Ernest Gellner, "The Nation: Real or Imagined?" and Anthony D. Smith, "Memory and Modernity," in *Nations and Nationalism* 2, part 3 (1996): 358-70; 371-88.

27 Kenneth R. Minogue, "Olympianism and the Denigration of Nationality," in *The Worth of Nations*, ed. Claudio Véliz (Boston: Boston University Press, 1993), 74.

28 Roger Scruton, "The First Person Plural," in *TN*, 288. This may be a suitable place to correct what I now regard as a somewhat misleading previously offered characterization of Scruton's position. In chapter 1 above, I labelled Scruton a defender of "nationalism," whereas a more careful reading of his writings on this subject shows that he would certainly reject this as an appropriate category by which to describe his view. In his essay "In Defense of the Nation," 304, 311-13, and 318, Scruton distinguishes nationalism as an ideology used to "conscript" people to an artificial unity associated with the state, as opposed to the unconscripted bonds of national loyalty that are, presumably, by contrast quasi-natural; he even speaks of the "doctrine" of nationalism as something that "perverts" or "pollutes" the idea of the nation. It goes without saying that Scruton, in writing in celebration of national identity, must deny that it is any part of his purpose to conscript anyone to a redoubled devotion to waning national attachments.

29 For another interesting challenge to the modernist view, this time on behalf of Scottish nationalism, see Neil MacCormick's contribution to *TN*.

30 Anderson, *Imagined Communities*, 73 n. 17. Cf. Eric Hobsbawm, "Ethnicity and Nationalism in Europe Today," 259-60.

31 Cf. Gellner, *Nations and Nationalism*, 130.

32 Charles Taylor, "Nationalism and Modernity," in *TN*, 219-45.

33 Cf. Brian Barry, *TN*, 249, 260. A similar understanding of the strong linkage between nationalism and modern political principles is implicit in the following statement by Shlomo Avineri: "Nationalism is a two-headed animal. It is, on the one hand, a great emancipatory force, based as it is on ideas of liberty, self-determination and people defining their own culture and memory. But it also has the potential of turning xenophobic, intolerant of minorities, repressive of dissent" ("A Fate Worse than Communism?" *Jerusalem Post*, 8 September 1991). Cf. Jeff Spinner, *The Boundaries of Citizenship: Race, Ethnicity, and Nationality in the Liberal State* (Baltimore, MD: Johns Hopkins University Press, 1994): "Nationalism ... has been both a movement against oppression and a movement that itself oppresses" (141).

34 Cf. Taylor, "Les sources de l'identité moderne," 347-54.

35 It is striking that even as vehement a critic of nationalism as Elie Kedourie concedes that any decision concerning "whether nationalists should be conciliated or resisted ... is necessarily governed by the particular circumstances of each individual case" (*Nationalism*, xix). For some sensible suggestions concerning ways to accommodate and pacify nationalism in practice, see Elizabeth Kiss, "Five Theses on Nationalism," in *Political Order: NOMOS XXXVIII*, ed. Ian Shapiro and Russell Hardin (New York: New York University Press, 1996), 288-332.

36 Stephen Holmes, "Liberalism for a World of Ethnic Passions and Decaying States," *Social Research* 61, 3 (1994): 606.

37 For a clear statement of Habermas's challenge to nationalism, see "The European Nation-State – Its Achievements and Its Limits," in *Mapping the Nation*, ed. Balakrishnan, 281-94. Patchen Markell offers a helpful and insightful account of interesting tensions in Habermas's idea of constitutional patriotism, in "Making Affect Safe for Democracy? On 'Constitutional Patriotism,'" *Political Theory* 28, 1 (2000): 38-63. See also, for another good account of such tensions in Habermas, W. James Booth, "Communities of Memory," in *Canadian Political Philosophy: Contemporary Reflections*, ed. Ronald Beiner and Wayne Norman (Toronto: Oxford University Press, 2001), 263-81.

38 See, for instance, Perry Anderson, "Nation-States and National Identity," *London Review of Books*, 9 May 1991: what interests Habermas is "merely a generic parliamentary order as such ... such constitutional patriotism is vacuous ... we can be sure we have not heard the end of the quest for German identity" (7-8). Also relevant here is David Miller's challenge to Maurizio Viroli's idea of patriotism as an alternative to nationalism: "Nationalism helped to form an inclusive political community from people divided by attributes such as class and religion. Since that is still our predicament today, it may seem that a direct attempt to get back to republican patriotism is anachronistic: we need the cement of a common culture to underpin our democratic politics." Review of *For Love of Country* in *American Political Science Review* 90, 4 (1996): 886. For an acknowledgment by Habermas of such challenges, see "The European Nation-State – Its Achievements and Its Limits," 289-90.

39 Yael Tamir, *Liberal Nationalism* (Princeton, NJ: Princeton University Press, 1993).

40 For a similar response to Tamir, see Sanford Levinson, "Is Liberal Nationalism an Oxymoron?": "Tamir is considerably more liberal than she is nationalistic" (629); "It should be clear that zealous political nationalists will find relatively little attractive in *Liberal Nationalism*" (633).

41 Cf. Bernard Yack, "Reconciling Liberalism and Nationalism," *Political Theory* 23, 1 (1995): 172, referring to Tamir's "depoliticization" of national identity.

42 Tamir, *Liberal Nationalism*, 150.

43 Ibid., 145.

44 George Kateb, "Notes on Pluralism," *Social Research* 61, 3 (1994): 535.

45 As far as Israel's Law of Return is concerned, Tamir's position is that it "would only be justified if the largest minority in the state, namely, the Palestinians, would also have a national entity in which they could enact a similar law" (*Liberal Nationalism*, 160). This is

fine for Palestinians who become citizens of a Palestinian state, if and when such a state comes into existence; but it is hard to see how this stipulation elevates the civic status of Arab citizens within Israel.

46 Norman Spector, "Cultures Warring in the Bosom of a Single State," *Globe and Mail*, 7 September 1996, D3. Spector is a former Canadian ambassador to Israel.

47 Alex Weingrod, "Palestinian Israelis?" *Dissent* (Summer 1996): 110.

48 Avishai Margalit and Moshe Halbertal, "Liberalism and the Right to Culture," *Social Research* 61, 3 (1994): 495. Margalit and Halbertal tell the story of a Peace Now demonstration following the massacre in Hebron. Organizers decided that the demonstration should end with a minute of silence rather than the usual singing of "Hatikva" because it was felt "that a national anthem intended solely for Jews could not be sung at a joint demonstration of Jews and Arabs" (ibid., 494-5).

49 James B. Rule, "Tribalism and the State" (with a reply by Walzer), *Dissent* (Fall 1992): 519-24; "Letters," *Dissent* (Winter 1993): 127-8; "Letters," *Dissent* (Spring 1993): 268-70. The debate between Rule and Walzer was occasioned by the original publication of Michael Walzer, "The New Tribalism: Notes on a Difficult Problem" (reprinted as chapter 11 of *TN*). Cf. Amos Elon, "Israel and the End of Zionism," *New York Review of Books*, 19 December 1996, 22-30. Elon argues for a "post-Zionist" conception of Israel, that is, the adoption of "a more Western, more pluralistic, less 'ideological' form of patriotism and of citizenship" (26-7).

50 Walzer's response to Rule, "Tribalism," 524.

51 Ibid.

52 It seems to me uncontroversial that Britain is a political union of (at least) the English, the Scottish, and the Welsh. It is obviously more complicated how the citizens of Ulster (with their divided identities) figure in this union, but even if one leaves them to one side, one can perhaps count the Cornish as a fourth (quasi-)nation.

53 George Steiner, "Israel: A View from Without," in *Imagination and Precision in the Social Sciences*, ed. T.J. Nossiter, A.H. Hanson, and Stein Rokkan (London: Faber and Faber, 1972), 339. Cf. Berlin, "Two Concepts of Nationalism": "To be human meant [for Herder] to be able to feel at home somewhere, with your own kind" (19).

54 *TN*, chapter 6.

55 For a very powerful vindication of the idea of the multiethnic state as a "political community of all of its citizens," and, correspondingly, a powerful indictment of the ethnic state (for instance, the kind of ethno-Croat state created by Franjo Tudjman), see Bogdan Denitch, *Ethnic Nationalism: The Tragic Death of Yugoslavia*, rev. ed. (Minneapolis: University of Minnesota Press, 1996). In Israel, the Basic Law forces all political parties to acknowledge "the state of Israel as the state of the Jewish people" rather than as the state of all its citizens: see Brian Barry, *Culture and Equality: An Egalitarian Critique of Multiculturalism* (Cambridge: Polity Press, 2001), 346 n. 73.

56 On the other hand, it is interesting how tricky it can be, even for a resolute federalist such as Charles Taylor, to avoid getting drawn into an ethnic definition of Quebec's nationhood. For instance, in Taylor's brief to the Bélanger-Campeau Commission (19 December 1990), he took as his starting point the following two facts: "1 Quebec is a distinct society, the political expression of a nation, and the great majority of this nation lives within its borders. 2 Quebec is the principal home of this nation, but branches of it have settled elsewhere in Canada and North America." *Reconciling the Solitudes*, ed. Guy Laforest (Montreal and Kingston: McGill-Queen's University Press, 1993), 141. In other words, those individuals who live within the territorial boundaries of "Quebec" (= civic) yet who do not belong to the relevant (francophone) nation cannot be counted as full citizens of "Quebec" (= ethnic) defined as "the political expression of a nation." Taylor would surely resist the idea that Quebec should be defined as an ethnic state, yet that is precisely what his own statement asserts. As Walker Connor emphasizes throughout his book *Ethnonationalism*, even if nationalists *want* to purge their nationalism of "ethnonationalist" connotations (or at least want it to be seen that they want this), one shouldn't be surprised to find implicit appeals to *ethnos* lurking somewhere in the background. Cf. Yael Tamir, "The Enigma of Nationalism," *World Politics* 47, 3 (1995): "The more we learn about the emergence of nations and

about the origins and the development of nationalism, the less credible is the nationalist image of nations as homogeneous, natural, and continuous communities of common fate and descent. Yet, it is precisely this image that nurtures the unique power of nationalism" (420).

57   Kai Nielsen, "Cultural Nationalism, Neither Ethnic nor Civic," in *TN*, 127.

58   See *TN*, chapters 5 and 7.

59   This should not be interpreted as an endorsement of Trudeau's politics with respect to the national question in Quebec. On the contrary, my view is that Trudeau's interventions in the Meech Lake and Charlottetown debates in the late 1980s and early '90s helped decisively to defeat possible political compromises between federalists and nationalists, and therefore contributed to the present polarization in the debate concerning Quebec. I have discussed these issues in chapter 10 below.

60   Hobsbawm, "Some Reflections," 11-12.

61   Let me hasten to add that normative questions are not absent even in the case of the homogeneous nation, since, for instance, in the Japanese example, the national homogeneity is acquired by keeping out immigrants. There is also, of course, the issue of ethnocentric attitudes in Japan toward the (numerically very small) ethnic Korean minority.

62   Again, Kymlicka replies very effectively to those who would postulate the linguistic and cultural "neutrality" of the civic-national state: "National minorities are no different from the members of majority nations [in regard to attachment to their own language and culture]. Anglophones in Ontario (or Illinois) are as deeply attached to their language and culture as Francophones in Quebec or the Flemish in Belgium. If the demographics were reversed, and Anglophones in the United States were outnumbered by Francophones or Hispanics, then they, too, would mobilize to gain official recognition and support for their language and culture. The only difference is that Anglophones in North America can take their national identity for granted. As Seton-Watson put it, national identity is 'passively treasured by nearly all citizens of modern societies, even if they do not know it,' since they take it for granted. But were their identity to be threatened, national majorities would mobilize in just the same way as minorities. [note:] Or as George Bernard Shaw put it, 'A healthy nation is as unconscious of its nationality as a healthy man of his bones. But if you break a nation's nationality, it will think of nothing else but getting it set again.'" Will Kymlicka, "The Sources of Nationalism," in *The Morality of Nationalism*, ed. Robert McKim and Jeff McMahan (New York: Oxford University Press, 1997), 62, 65 n. 11.

63   A big part of the problem in pursuing this project is that different people use the term *civic nationalism* for radically different purposes (nationalists use it to fend off accusations that their nationalism is exclusionary and ethnocentric, whereas critics of nationalism use it to cast a moral cloud over "real" nationalism, i.e., ethnic nationalism). Wayne Norman rightly points out that when someone like Michael Ignatieff describes himself as committed to civic nationalism, it suggests, misleadingly, that this is a particular species of nationalism, whereas Ignatieff himself, of course, intends it as a reproach to all forms of nationalism strictly speaking. "Les paradoxes du nationalisme civique," in *Charles Taylor et l'interprétation de l'identité moderne*, ed. Guy Laforest and Philippe de Lara (Quebec: Les Presses de l'Université Laval, 1998), 162, 168. Therefore it might clarify the debate somewhat simply to drop the term *civic nationalism* and replace it with references to citizenship (or Habermas's constitutional patriotism).

64   John Rawls's *A Theory of Justice* (Oxford: Oxford University Press, 1971) did more than any other work to establish and define this constricted philosophical agenda within liberal political philosophy.

65   *TN*, chapter 11.

66   See n. 1 above.

7
Reflections of a Diaspora Jew in Israel

> Exile is the nursery of nationality, as oppression is the school of liberalism.
>
> Lord Acton

I am a Diaspora Jew. I am in Israel for four months. It is my first visit to Israel. (Luckily, for any Zionist credentials I might want to possess, I arrived before the missiles stopped dropping.)

Life in Israel is scary and perplexing for an outsider in ways that it is perhaps not (or less so) for an Israeli. For instance, one of the things that makes living in Israel a bit hard to navigate for a Diaspora Jew is that it is not always easy, apart from Jews who wear a kippa, to tell who is a Jew and who is an Arab. (At the same time, as a Jew out on the street you can't help feeling a bit guilty that you are *not* wearing a kippa, since you must be less of a target than the Jews who do wear one.) "Is that guy walking behind me, who *may* have a knife, a Jew or an Arab?" (You would not have quite the same *kind* of anxiety if, say, you were walking anxiously on a street in the slums of Washington, DC.) Of course, as the newspapers inform us, the Arabs (the ones who do the stabbings) have exactly the same problem – so maybe it is not *just* an outsider's problem after all. "Is that guy walking ahead of me, whose back is an inviting target, an Arab or a Jew?" So the Arab, intending to stick his knife into the back of a Jew, not uncommonly sticks it into the back of a fellow Arab by mistake. This offers a kind of unhappy commentary on the contingency and evident arbitrariness of the division of the human race into nations.

Strangely enough, we can find a twisted recognition of this truth about the moral arbitrariness of nations in the opposing ideologies of two arch-nationalists: the pan-Arabism of Saddam Hussein (the distinction between the Iraqi and the Kuwaiti nation is artificial), and the pan-Arabism of Ariel

Sharon (the distinction between the Jordanian and the Palestinian nation is artificial). If even diehard nationalists such as these are able to realize, however perversely, the dependence upon paltry accidents of history of the boundaries between seemingly established nations, then perhaps there is some ground for hope that more moderate nationalists will come to entertain similar insights that might be subversive of nationalism in general.

Is it possible, as a Jew, to have a real desire to experience life in Israel without the slightest twinge of Zionist longing? I think you can quite easily. But I think perhaps many Israelis find this a little hard to imagine, and therefore find the Diaspora Jew a bit incomprehensible. It is, I would say, one of the lesser ironies of life in this society that Israeli Jews, hugely dependent on the Diaspora for moral and financial support, find these Jews on whom they so depend, at bottom, somewhat incomprehensible (perhaps *essentially* incomprehensible).

Life in contemporary Israel makes a nonsense of the UN's outrageous "Zionism is racism" resolution. Indeed, with the current massive immigration of Jews from Kiev to Addis Ababa, contemporary Israel is one of the world's great experiments in trying to create a *multi*racial society. After all, what other non-African country in the world is so eager to welcome in poor African refugees? Perhaps only the United States in the heyday of its immigration offers a comparable case of such an experiment in multiracialism. Nevertheless, I don't think life in Israel entirely alleviates one's worries about Zionism as a nationalist ideology. Even if Israel is an unqualified good, my philosophical conscience tells me that nationalism tends to be something bad. (This will be admitted by any nationalist who stops to reflect on *another* people's nationalism.) Yet of course Israel is founded on a nationalist ideology, and would not exist were it not so. How can one affirm the product of an ideology and not affirm the ideology that produced it? (Willing the end implies willing the means, Kant said.) Perhaps the only way a Diaspora Jew can squirm out of this paradox is to express enormous relief that some people were (and continue to be) strongly enough motivated by nationalism to have founded this state, even though he or she cannot possibly share in this nationalistic motivation. While it is wonderful for Israel that it is attracting Soviet Jews in such large numbers, we should also remember that these Soviet immigrants are coming here in order to escape a land being torn apart by nationalisms.

The meaning of the paradox may be spelled out a little further as follows. In principle, a non-national or trans-national state would certainly be best, in conformity with Lord Acton's dictum: "The co-existence of several nations under the same State is a test ... of its freedom." (This is of course what the PLO *claims* to want, although this claim is a little hard to credit in the case of a movement whose primary sources include militant Arab nationalism.) No less certainly, however, peoples that find themselves as beleaguered minorities in every land they inhabit have no choice but to embrace a defensive nationalism in order not to be prey to the aggressive nationalisms of other peoples. Such was the case of the Jews prior to the establishment of Israel, and as we all now know, such is the case of the Kurds today. In the case of Israel, though, what is distressing to the outside observer (and to many insiders as well) is the way in which a legitimate defensive nationalism evolves into modes of aggressive nationalism, while simultaneously the aggressive nationalism threatening it from outside its borders is constrained to become a defensive nationalism within its borders. Naturally there are complexities on both sides here – that is, elements of defensive nationalism and aggressive nationalism on *both* sides of the *intifada* – but the point is that this moral ambiguity is inescapable as long as the conflict between peoples takes the form, on both sides, of a struggle between nationalisms.

My experience of life in Israel, brief as it is, has brought home to me that what defines Zionism is the idea that immigration to Israel is the core of a proper human existence. It is not hard to get the sense, living here, that in the eyes of many Israelis, Diaspora Jews, just because they have no inclination to share the risks and burdens of life in the homeland, show themselves to be cowards, hypocrites, and generally lacking in moral substance. I think that American Jews who support Israel with great sums of money would be more than a little shocked if they realized how little the deep care and affection they feel for their Israeli brethren is reciprocated by Israeli affection for their brethren in the United States and elsewhere (unless they are potential immigrants). And for those in whom one detects this lack of requited affection, the money sent from abroad does not increase the affection.

As these words attest, spending time in Israel has not really put to rest my unease concerning Zionism (although it has certainly made me much more appreciative of the territorial insecurities of Israelis). If Zionism means that the world is an immeasurably better place because Israel exists, then I am a Zionist. But I suspect that Zionism means something more than this for those who live here; it means that I should want to live here. Nationalism, as Elie Kedourie conveys very well in his little book on the subject, is the "ideologization" of nationality. Nationality is more or less a given. (Being a Jew is more or less a fact of birth, something you are born into.) National*ism* makes it an ideological duty to affirm with all your heart this given. This is, I think, borne out by Zionism as you experience it here. And Diaspora Jews, of course, fail the test miserably. Zionism makes it exceedingly simple to measure how committed you are to being a Jew – immigration to "Eretz Yisrael." "Aliya" is the magic word of this society. So, according to Zionism's definition of Jewishness, to be a Diaspora Jew is *by definition* to be a bad Jew.

I read editorials and letters to the editor that say outsiders who express alarm about the expansion of settlement activity in the occupied territories do so because they want to oblige Arabs who find Jews so odious that they want land that they might later regain by negotiation to be *Judenrein*. And I wonder to myself, can Israelis think that Jews in the Diaspora are so alienated from what it is to be a Jew that they would really oppose settlement activity for *that* reason?

Does a Diaspora Jew have a right to pass judgment on Israel? Yes and no, I would say. Naturally, it is an impertinence for an outsider, someone who doesn't serve in the army and whose children will not serve in the army, to pass judgment. I can imagine that there are even some Peace Now activists who might think to themselves, "I have the right to say that. He doesn't." But critical judgment is *always*, to a greater or lesser extent, an impertinence. And there is no guarantee that the greater the impertinence, the less valid the judgment. Yet the outsider who makes the judgment should at the very least *remember* that it is an impertinence, should at least have the sense to find it intelligible that insiders would see it that way. I don't think that I, as a Jew, have more of a right to pass judgment than a Gentile, and, in the same measure, I don't think that I, as a Diaspora Jew, have less of a right to pass judgment than an Israeli Jew. (Do only Iraqis have the right to pass judgment on Saddam?) On the other hand, I don't believe I have the right to be listened to with the same attention and patience that an Israeli might accord to a fellow Israeli who shares the same risks and bears the anxiety of seeing his or her children share the same risks. To be aware of this impertinence, as an outsider, is not to withhold judgment but to hesitate, and so I hesitate in offering these reflections of a Diaspora Jew.

Source
This chapter is a time-bound piece. It was written in the spring of 1991, in the aftermath of the Gulf War. I have not attempted to update it or alter its time-bound character. An abbreviated version of the essay was first published in the *Jerusalem Report*, 6 June 1991.

8
Hannah Arendt As a Critic of Nationalism

There really is such a thing as freedom here [in the United States] ... The republic is not a vapid illusion, and the fact that there is no national state and no truly national tradition creates an atmosphere of freedom.

Letter to Karl Jaspers, 29 January 1946

"Love of the Jews" would appear to me, since I am myself Jewish, as something rather suspect. I cannot love myself or anything which I know is part and parcel of my own person.

Letter to Gershom Scholem, 24 July 1963

Hannah Arendt is sometimes regarded as an important source of, or inspiration behind, contemporary communitarian political thought.[1] There is some measure of truth to this view, but to think of her political theory as distinctively communitarian is more than a little misleading. For what characterizes communitarianism as a philosophical challenge to liberalism is a highlighting of how the self is constituted by collective or group identity, and an argument that insufficient concern with thick shared identities marks a central deficiency of liberal-individualist conceptions of political community. If, however, a properly communitarian argument emphasizes the collective constitution of selfhood, and the political salience of the shared identity so constituted, one would expect communitarians to exhibit significant sympathy for the politics of nationalism – a form of politics that places shared identity and thick communal attachments at the very core of its understanding of political life.[2] Yet, as we shall see, Arendt's thought shows itself to be, in this respect, pronouncedly anti-communitarian. Thus an examination of Arendt's stance toward nationalism should help to clarify those aspects of her thought that are located at the furthest remove from specifically communitarian concerns. Though the Arendtian and communitarian critiques of liberalism do overlap in important ways, there is a fundamental respect in which Arendt's criticisms of liberalism are motivated by a very different set of theoretical concerns than those characteristic of the communitarian critique.[3]

The easiest entry point into the Arendtian view of nationalism is to look at her stance toward contemporary Zionism.[4] Zionism is a classic species of nationalist politics because it makes a shared experience of Jewish national belonging the foundation of a claim to statehood, and it makes shared nationality the pivot of an entire political universe. Arendt's political writings of the mid- to late 1940s on the problem of Jewish politics sound a consistent theme. In these writings, notably in four important articles analyzing developments in the Zionist movement in the crucial lead-up to the formation of the State of Israel, Arendt presents Zionist politics as having opted for an obsolete conception of political community, and thereby having betrayed both the genuine aspirations of an oppressed people and its own better impulses.[5] Arendt seems to suggest that in the epoch in which it first arose, namely the nineteenth century, nationalism offered a coherent and quite attractive political doctrine: after referring to nationalism as "this once great and revolutionary principle of the national organization of peoples," she claims that it becomes a force of evil once political circumstances change such that the nationalist principle "could no longer either guarantee true sovereignty of the people within or establish a just relationship among different peoples beyond the national borders."[6] Therefore the first thing to understand about Zionism is its ideological character, where for her ideology is more or less synonymous with the distortion of political reality. The Zionism of those "who may be truly called political Zionists," as distinct from the basically nonpolitical idealists who comprised the *kibbutz* movement, belongs, she writes, "to those nineteenth-century political movements that carried ideologies, *Weltanschauungen,* keys to history, in their portmanteaus ... it shares with [socialism or nationalism] the sad fate of having outlived their political conditions only to stalk together like living ghosts amid the ruins of our times."[7]

Arendt's essential view of Zionism is that it is a "sectarian ideology," employing the "categories and methods of the nineteenth century," and that it needs urgently to reconsider "its whole obsolete set of doctrines."[8] Theodor Herzl, she suggests, was a political thinker shaped by the political realities of the nineteenth century, and therefore his political vision "could hardly express itself in any other form than that of the nation-state. In his period, indeed, the claim for national self-determination of peoples was almost self-evident justice as far as the oppressed peoples of Europe were concerned, and so there was nothing wrong or absurd in a demand made by Jews for the same kind of emancipation and freedom."[9] This being so, Herzl could not be blamed for having failed to foresee "that the whole structure of sovereign national states, great and small, would crumble within another fifty years."[10] The main problem with the Zionist movement was the unfortunate fact of bad timing: Zionism "did not ask for a state at a time when it might have been granted by everybody, but did ask for one only when the whole concept of national sovereignty had become a mockery."[11] Again, Arendt insists that nationalism is "outdated" because what has been witnessed in our time is "the catastrophic decline of the national-state system": Europe has come to the unavoidable realization "that the national state is neither capable of protecting the existence of the nation nor able to guarantee the sovereignty of the people."[12] These passages were written before Zionism achieved its objective of securing its own nation-state, and more than four decades before the end of the Cold War gave dramatically new impetus to the nation-state principle. Arendt claims that the way in which Herzl formulated his demand for a Jewish state, namely by an appeal to national self-determination, shows just how time-bound his political thinking was.[13] In retrospect, it's hard not to conclude that Arendt was much more time-bound in her dismissal of the nation-state principle than Herzl was in his embrace of it.

Central to her analysis is the conception of a kind of Zionism that had been seized on by intellectual elites that involved kowtowing to Great Powers and selling out to imperialist potentates in the hopes of securing a quick and easy shortcut to a European-style nation-state in Palestine.[14] She thinks that twentieth-century Zionists fell for "the delusion of nationhood," in the sense of a political ideal that was no longer meaningful, and that Zionist leaders put themselves at the service of imperialist interests in order to reassure themselves that the delusion was still an attainable goal.[15] To Zionism thus characterized she opposes what she thinks could have been a more authentically revolutionary movement of Jewish political emancipation (although she is vague about the content of this more revolutionary Zionist politics).[16] She writes that "all those national-revolutionary movements of small European peoples whose situation was equally one of social as of national oppression" embodied a healthy amalgam of socialism and nationalism; but in the case of Zionism, there was from the outset an unfortunate split "between the social-revolutionary forces which had sprung from the east European masses" and the Herzlian ambition for strictly *national* emancipation.[17] The historically dominant Zionism was an elite contrivance that passed over "the genuine national revolutionary movement which sprang from the Jewish masses."[18] "The alternative to the road that Herzl marked out, and [Chaim] Weizmann followed through to the bitter end, would have been to organize the Jewish people in order to negotiate on the basis of a great revolutionary movement. This would have meant an alliance with all progressive forces in Europe"; what was actually unfolded in the Zionist movement of the first half of the twentieth century was the dismaying "spectacle of a national movement that, starting out with such an idealistic élan, sold out at the very first moment to the powers-that-be – that felt no solidarity with other oppressed peoples whose cause, though historically otherwise conditioned, was essentially the same – that endeavored even in the morning-dream of freedom and justice to compromise with the most evil forces of our time by taking advantage of imperialistic interests."[19] In short, "the true revolutionary possibilities of Zionism for Jewish life" came to be sacrificed by the machinations of the Zionist leadership.[20] All of this appears to suggest that, in Arendt's view, there was the possibility of a kind of Jewish nationalist politics that would be genuinely emancipatory, focused on a broader social-revolutionary agenda, but that these possibilities were sabotaged by the sell-out mentality of Zionist leaders: contingent political choices were made that channelled the movement into a course of political action defined by a more narrowly nationalist ideology. In a sense, and one not without paradox, it more or less follows from Arendt's argument that nationalism was the undoing of Zionism.[21]

Another constant theme of her Jewish political writings is the disastrousness of the ambition for a uni-national state, and not just the desirability of, but the imperative need for, Jewish-Arab federalism. This line of criticism clearly cuts more deeply at the very heart of a nationalist politics. The essential thrust of Arendt's critique of Zionism in these writings is that instead of preoccupying themselves with how their political project stood in relation to the Great Powers of the time, Zionists ought to have paid more attention to the problem of building relations of trust with their Arab neighbours. Indeed, the "good" Zionists (supported politically by Arendt) did just that. The problem is that the good Zionists (notably, the Ihud group led by Judah L. Magnes) were marginal to the main Zionist movement, and became steadily more marginal. As Palestinian Jewry moved closer to statehood, Arendt's unhappiness with the Zionist project increased rather than diminished. In the wake of the UN's 1947 endorsement of the partition of Palestine and formation of a Jewish state, she remained opposed to partition and opposed to creation of a Jewish state.[22] She deeply regretted the evaporation of a non-Zionist opposition within Jewish politics that would formulate alternative political visions.[23] "With the support of a Jewish state by the great powers, the non-Zionists believed themselves refuted by reality itself."[24]

Obviously, with the unfolding of events, there came a time when Arendt had to recognize that her own non-Zionism was refuted by reality, but in 1948 she was still a non-Zionist.[25] Part of the story here, of course, was simply fear about wagering all on a Jewish-Arab war that the Jews after all might have lost, with incalculable consequences for the identity and even continued existence of the Jewish people; the stakes were simply too high to risk another (post-Holocaust) catastrophe.[26] And even if the Jews were to win the war, the creation of a garrison state surrounded by a sea of Arab hostility would consume all Jewish energies, and therefore undo what was already most impressive in the accomplishments of the Jewish community in Palestine, such as the *kibbutz* movement.[27] It is in this sense that she writes: "at this moment and under present circumstances a Jewish state can only be erected at the price of the Jewish homeland."[28] However, it seems fair to categorize these as prudential considerations: weighing up risks, balancing gains against losses; one might say that alongside (or perhaps underlying) these judgments, Arendt has a more principled basis for resisting the idea of a Jewish nation-state. She is profoundly committed to Jewish-Arab federalism, and even as Jewish-Arab warfare escalated in Palestine, she refused to give up on the notion that a kind of political community could be constituted in Palestine founded on concrete experiences of Jewish-Arab friendship and cooperation. Arendt concludes her article "To Save the Jewish Homeland" with a statement of principles that lays out clearly enough her alternative (non-Zionist) vision of Palestine: "The real goal of the Jews in Palestine is the building up of a Jewish homeland. This goal must never be sacrificed to the pseudo-sovereignty of a Jewish state"; "the independence of Palestine can be achieved only on a solid basis of Jewish-Arab cooperation."[29] The ultimate goal is a "federated structure [resting on] Jewish-Arab community councils": "local self-government and mixed Jewish-Arab municipal and rural councils, on a small scale and as numerous as possible."[30] Again, part of the argument is a prudential one: Palestine is so small a territory that partition would leave two political communities, neither of which would be really viable and capable of meaningful independence.[31] "National sovereignty which so long had been the very symbol of free national development has become the greatest danger to national survival for small nations."[32] However, the deeper argument is straightforwardly normative: the world needs to be shown that two very different peoples are capable of cooperating within the compass of a binational political community.[33]

As seems entirely fitting for works of political journalism, Arendt's arguments appear highly historicized and contextual. If uni-national statehood is a disaster for small nations contesting a crowded territory, does nationalism continue to be a legitimate principle for large nations commanding a more expansive territory? If nationalist leaders were less interested in cutting deals with the big powers of the day and were more concerned with democratic mobilization, would that redeem their nationalism? If nationalism shows itself to be a species of ideological delusion because it no longer fits the political realities of twentieth-century political life, does that mean that the argument against nationalism is a historically specific one rather than one at the level of universal principles? The core of Arendt's challenge to the nation-state concerns its alleged obsolescence.[34] But as a political thinker who herself put abundant theoretical energies into championing arguably obsolete forms of political community, it is far from clear why this historicist standard should be normatively decisive.[35]

It seems clear that Arendt wanted Jewish politics but not Jewish nationalism, wanted a Jewish homeland but not a Jewish nation-state. To what extent are these the theoretical judgments of a political philosopher as opposed to the "merely" political judgments of a political onlooker and somewhat engaged political actor? To be sure, Arendt felt only a weak identity as a political philosopher, and the badge of the political philosopher was one she was reluctant to wear.[36] Be that as it may, if we seek a more general theoretical ground for her anti-nationalism, we ought to turn to her analyses of national movements and the nation-state in the middle volume of her towering historical-theoretical work, *The Origins of Totalitarianism*. The work as a whole is directed at showing how modern ideologies disfigure political life, and Arendt is in no doubt that nationalism counts as a full-fledged ideology in her culpable sense.

Arendt's main discussion of nationalism occurs in the context of a narrative explaining how the late-nineteenth-century to early twentieth-century pan-movements (Pan-German and Pan-Slav) contributed to the horrors of the totalitarian movements. Her basic idea is that there is an intrinsic and deep tension (if not a contradiction) between "nation" and "state" in the synthetic idea of a nation-state, and when confronted with the evil dynamism of the pan-movements and then full-blown totalitarianism, this tension was intensified to the point where the nation-state itself as it were exploded.[37] According to Arendt, the pan-movements used claims to national rights to self-determination as "a comfortable smoke screen" for national-imperial expansionism.[38] While these movements borrowed their means of self-legitimation from nationalist ideology by claiming "to unite all people of similar folk origin, independent of history and no matter where they happened to live," they in fact embodied a "contempt for the narrowness of the nation-state."[39] Once the existing state system proved itself unable to contain this imperialistic nationalism, the way was clear for totalitarian movements to finish off the job of demolishing the very idea of a nation-state that claims to offer protection for its national citizens and respects the right of other nation-states to do likewise. The nation-state (with its defining idea of nation-based citizenship) both contributed to, and was ultimately the helpless victim of, much more dangerous and predatory ideologies that simply trampled over the mere state. The simplest way in which to encapsulate Arendt's analysis is to say that the pairing of the state with the nation sets in motion a dialectic whose eventual outcome is the destruction of the state as a moral-juridical shelter for its citizens. Nationalism is a pathology of citizenship that, having subordinated the state to the idea of the nation, generates a further pathology in a more expansionary notion of nationhood that surpasses the boundaries (and therefore the moral limits) of the state: with this double pathology, the nation-state itself gets utterly subverted. Therefore, following through this evil dialectic requires us to rethink the whole idea of the nation-state (and ideally, to conceive other non-national forms of political association as a basis for citizenship).

Having offered a quick overview, let us now look more closely at how Arendt understands this tension between state and nation at the heart of the nation-state idea. Arendt begins with a contrast between what she calls "Western nationalism" and what she calls "tribal nationalism" – corresponding more or less to what is now standardly referred to as the distinction between civic and ethnic nationalism:[40]

> The nation-state, with its claim to popular representation and national sovereignty, as it had developed since the French revolution through the nineteenth century, was the result of a combination of two factors that were still separate in the eighteenth century and remained separate in Russia and Austria-Hungary: nationality and state. Nations entered the scene of history and were emancipated when peoples had acquired a consciousness of themselves as cultural and historical entities, and of their territory as a permanent home, where history had left its visible traces, whose cultivation was the product of the common labor of their ancestors and whose future would depend upon the course of a common civilization.[41]

The fact that the process of fusing state and nationality commences with the French Revolution's assertion of popular sovereignty explains why Arendt consistently refers to France as the "nation par excellence" (that is, the paradigm of Western nationalism, not tribal nationalism).[42] "Sociologically the nation-state was the body politic of the European emancipated peasant classes ... Western nationalism ... was the product of firmly rooted and emancipated peasant classes."[43] Conversely, "in the Eastern and Southern European regions the establishment of nation-states failed because they could not fall back upon firmly rooted peasant classes."[44] In these regions of Europe, the "peasant classes had not struck deep roots in the country and were not on the verge of emancipation ... consequently, their national quality appeared to be much more a portable private matter, inherent in their very personality, than a matter of public concern and civilization ... they had no country, no state, no historic achievement to show but could only point to themselves, and that meant, at best, to their language ... at worst, to their Slavic, or Germanic, or God-knows-what soul."[45] With the constant changing of frontiers and continuous migration of populations, "no conditions existed for the realization of the Western national trinity of people-territory-state."[46] Tribal nationalism, she concludes, "grew out of this atmosphere of rootlessness."[47] (And it was this sort of nationalism, in turn, that provided a breeding-ground for totalitarianism.)

Leaving aside this pathological variant of nationalism, Arendt sees still grave problems in the nation-state idea even in its best (that is, Western) version:

> The state inherited as its supreme function the protection of all inhabitants in its territory no matter what their nationality, and was supposed to act as a supreme legal institution. The tragedy of the nation-state was that the people's rising national consciousness interfered with these functions. In the name of the will of the people the state was forced to recognize only "nationals" as citizens, to grant full civil and political rights only to those who belonged to the national community by right of origin and fact of birth. This meant that the state was partly transformed from an instrument of law into an instrument of the nation.[48]

In short, the state was conquered by the nation – that is, the nation, in appropriating the state for national purposes, diverted the state from functions that are proper to it *qua* state. Arendt relates this development politically to the downfall of absolute monarchy and sociologically to the rise of classes: "The only remaining bond between the citizens of a nation-state without a monarch to symbolize their essential community, seemed to be national, that is, common origin ... [and] in a century when every class and section in the population was dominated by class or group interest, the interest of the nation as a whole was supposedly guaranteed in a common origin, which sentimentally expressed itself in nationalism."[49] She also relates it to liberal individualism, and to a simultaneous centralization of state administration: "It seemed to be the will of the nation that the state protect it from the consequences of its social atomization ... only a strongly centralized administration ... could counterbalance the centrifugal forces constantly produced in a class-ridden society. Nationalism, then, became the precious cement for binding together a centralized state and an atomized society."[50]

What ensues is what Arendt characterizes as a "secret conflict between state and nation" that was coeval with "the very birth of the modern nation-state, when the French Revolution combined the declaration of the Rights of Man with the demand for national sovereignty":

> The same essential rights were at once claimed as the inalienable heritage of all human beings *and* as the specific heritage of specific nations, the same nation was at once declared to be subject to laws, which supposedly would flow from the Rights of Man, *and* sovereign, that is, bound by no universal

law and acknowledging nothing superior to itself. The practical outcome of this contradiction was that from then on human rights were protected and enforced only as national rights and that the very institution of a state, whose supreme task was to protect and guarantee man his rights as man, as citizen and as national, lost its legal, rational appearance and could be interpreted by the romantics as the nebulous representative of a "national soul" which through the very fact of its existence was supposed to be beyond or above the law. National sovereignty, accordingly, lost its original connotation of freedom of the people and was being surrounded by a pseudomystical aura of lawless arbitrariness.[51]

Nationalism, Arendt concludes, "is essentially the expression of this perversion of the state into an instrument of the nation and the identification of the citizen with the member of the nation."[52]

Crucial to this whole analysis is the idea of "the conquest of the state by the nation."[53] Arendt draws the notion from J.-T. Delos, and in a highly sympathetic review of Delos's two-volume work *La Nation,* Arendt provides additional formulations of the state-nation tension.[54] She writes: "The fundamental political reality of our time is determined by two facts: on the one hand, it is based upon 'nations' and, on the other, it is permanently disturbed and thoroughly menaced by 'nationalism'"; therefore we need "to find a political principle which would prevent nations from developing nationalism and would thereby lay the fundamentals of an international community, capable of presenting and protecting the civilization of the modern world."[55] Nation and state represent opposing principles:

A people becomes a nation when [it arrives at a historical consciousness of itself]; as such it is attached to the soil which is the product of past labor and where history has left its traces. It represents the "milieu" into which man is born, a closed society to which one belongs by right of birth. The state on the other hand is an open society, ruling over a territory where its power protects and makes the law. As a legal institution, the state knows only citizens no matter of what nationality; its legal order is open to all who happen to live on its territory.[56]

Here, contrary to how Arendt elsewhere depicts the relation between the state and the nation, she suggests that it is the "open" power-seeking of the state that encourages expansionary ambitions on the part of the nation, whereas the nation, as a "closed" community, is wedded to its own territory. Hence, "the old dream of the innate pacifism of the nations whose very liberation would guarantee an era of peace and welfare was not all humbug."[57] However, reversing direction, Arendt immediately goes on to present the nation as the more sinister partner in this unhappy alliance:

> The conquest of the state through the nation started with the declaration of the sovereignty of the nation. This was the first step transforming the state into an instrument of the nation which finally has ended in those totalitarian forms of nationalism in which all laws and the legal institutions of the state as such are interpreted as a means for the welfare of the nation. It is therefore quite erroneous to see the evil of our times in a deification of the state. It is the nation which has usurped the traditional place of God and religion.[58]

So there seems to be a genuine vacillation here on the question of whether the state corrupts the nation or the nation corrupts the state. In any case, the fusion of state and nation is a fatal one, with the imperialistic ambitions of the state henceforth claimed (and with greater potential for evil) on behalf of the nation.

"There is little doubt that civilization will be lost if after destroying the first forms of totalitarianism we do not succeed in solving the basic problems of our political structures."[59] Arendt's reference to "first" forms of totalitarianism clearly implies that the process whereby nationalism turned into fascism, the nation-state turned into the totalitarian state, can be replicated unless the nationalist bacillus can be neutralized. How can this be done? The key here is once again to drive a wedge between state and nation. "The state, far from being identical with the nation, is the supreme protector of a law which guarantees man his rights as man, his rights as citizen and his rights as a national ... Of these rights, only the rights of man and citizen are primary rights whereas the rights of nationals are derived and implied in them," Arendt writes.[60] "While these distinctions between the citizen and the national, between the political order and the national one, would take the wind out of the sails of nationalism, by putting man as a national in his right place in public life, the larger political needs of our civilization ... would be met with the idea of federation. Within federated structures, nationality would become a personal status rather than a territorial one."[61]

In her 1967 preface to part 2 of *The Origins of Totalitarianism*, Arendt states that the volume on *Imperialism* "tells the story of the disintegration of the nation state."[62] What does it mean to assert that the nation-state as such has disintegrated? Arendt attempts to answer this question in an important chapter entitled "The Decline of the Nation-State and the End of the Rights of Man."[63] The most obvious problem with a system of nation-states in Europe following the First World War was that with all the minorities who could not possibly be accommodated by the nation-state principle, there was a vast number of "nationally frustrated peoples."[64] And since the nation-state model furnished by the French Revolution had promulgated the notion of the inseparability of human rights and national sovereignty, the tens of millions of nationless people in Europe were also in principle rightless, because the nation-state principle had left them without an effective political guarantor of their rights. An equally (or in fact much more) grave problem was the situation of those suffering wholesale population transfers, peoples who were "repatriated" without a national home where they could be properly patriated.[65] If national minorities were "half stateless," the masses of deported refugees and de-naturalized aliens were completely stateless with respect to the protection of fundamental rights.[66] The idea of human rights that was born with the French Revolution was intended to be universal. But the states that embraced these doctrines of human rights were decidedly not universal, and the evolution of the state into the nation-state gave a correspondingly national definition to the scope of the community whose human rights were to be enforced. Those who found themselves lacking their own nation-states (again, a considerable proportion of the population of Europe) also discovered that "universal" human rights had a very insecure application to them, to put it mildly. The Rights of Man signified an assertion of ultimate human sovereignty, but

> man had hardly appeared as a completely emancipated, completely isolated being who carried his dignity within himself without reference to some larger encompassing order, when he disappeared again into a member of a people. From the beginning the paradox involved in the declaration of inalienable human rights was that it reckoned with an "abstract" human being who seemed to exist nowhere ... The whole question of human rights, therefore, was quickly and inextricably blended with the question of national emancipation; only the emancipated sovereignty of the people, of one's own people, seemed to be able to insure them. As mankind, since the French Revolution, was conceived in the image of a family of nations, it gradually became self-evident that the people, and not the individual, was the image of man ... The Rights of Man, after all, had been defined as "inalienable" because they were supposed to be independent of all governments; but it turned out that the moment human beings lacked their own government ... no authority was left to protect them and no institution was willing to guarantee them.[67]

This "identification of the rights of man with the rights of peoples" didn't escape the attention of those whom it left undefended, namely the minorities and the stateless.[68] They themselves became convinced "that loss of national rights was identical with loss of human rights, that the former inevitably entailed the latter. The more they were excluded from right in any form, the more they tended to look for a reintegration into a national, into their own national community."[69] The widespread condition of degraded rights for minorities and rightlessness for the stateless in the twentieth century (continuing right up to our own day) establishes beyond a possibility of dispute the legitimacy of those anxieties. Thus the lesson of the ghastly politics of our century seems to be that supposedly universal human rights are meaningless unless rooted in a national community that is committed to enforcing these rights for its co-nationals; the fundamental "right to have rights" presupposes some particular state agency that will guarantee human rights only for those it considers to be properly its own members.[70] "Loss of national rights in all instances" entailed, for Arendt, "the loss of human rights."[71]

Here there seems a real paradox in Arendt's argument. She argues that the principal human right is the right to have rights, which means the right to have a (national) state that will assume responsibility for guarding and enforcing one's rights. Thus (despite the fact that Arendt presents herself as a strong critic of a nationality-based conception of the state, and is committed to the notion of its obsolescence), the logic of her argument would seem to dictate a return to the nation-state rather than its supersession.[72] To the extent that Arendt has an answer to this paradox, her answer seems to be that given our experience in the twentieth century, with its spectacle of the "disintegration" of the nation-state in the face of proto-totalitarian and totalitarian challenges, the only way the state can be made a safe repository of human rights for its citizens is by taking the nation out of the nation-state.[73] (Arendt clearly believed that the United States as a political community had achieved this condition of nationless statehood.)[74] The way to do this is by meshing the state in a web of federal relations, both below and beyond the state, therefore getting away from the state as a site of *sovereignty*. Insofar as nationalism as an ideology is bound to the claim to national sovereignty, this reconfiguration of the state depends upon liberating ourselves from the nationalist legacy.[75]

It seems that fundamentally what Arendt meant by the decline and "disintegration" of the nation-state is that states organized on a principle of national belonging had, by their treatment of national minorities and stateless refugees, so thoroughly discredited themselves in the twentieth century that human beings would be obliged to conjure up some quite different way of conceiving citizenship. But we can't derive a conclusion concerning the historical prospects of this kind of state from a moral critique of the conduct of various nation-states: a catalogue of the sins committed by the twentieth-century nation-state doesn't by itself guarantee the historical supersession of this idea of the state, nor cancel out the widespread desire of people, rightly or wrongly, to define their citizenship in terms of shared nationhood.[76]

To conclude, let me offer two reflections on Hannah Arendt's theoretical legacy in the light of that watershed year, 1989. On the one hand, 1989 redeemed Arendt's prescient claim in *On Revolution* that revolution "will stay with us into the foreseeable future ... this century ... most certainly will remain a century of revolutions."[77] On the other hand, the increased salience of nation-state politics after 1989 (each defeat of communism became a triumph for nationalism) underscores the inadequacy of her theoretical response to nationalist politics. Like generations of liberals and Marxists before her, Hannah Arendt was too quick to assume that the nation-state had already been tossed on the dust-heap of history.[78] Given her general immunity to historicist arguments, it seems surprising that we need to make the following point with respect to her thinking concerning nationalism: if nationalism strikes one as offering a deficient basis for modern politics, one must respond to its theoretical and political challenge with a normative counter-argument rather than with a historicist trust that the sun has finally set on the nation-state.

Source

This chapter was originally published in *The Cambridge Companion to Hannah Arendt,* ed. Dana Villa (Cambridge: Cambridge University Press, 2000), 44-62.

Notes

1   For instance, see Bernard Yack, *The Problems of a Political Animal* (Berkeley: University of California Press, 1993), 13, where Arendt's misleading account of Aristotle is connected to contemporary communitarian concerns. See also Stephen Holmes, *The Anatomy of Anti-liberalism* (Cambridge, MA: Harvard University Press, 1993), xi-xii; and Thomas L. Pangle, *The Spirit of Modern Republicanism* (Chicago: University of Chicago Press, 1988), 48-9.

2   Charles Taylor and Michael Walzer both offer arguments intended to encourage greater sympathy for nationalist politics: see, for instance, their chapters in *Theorizing Nationalism* (ed. R. Beiner [Albany: State University of New York Press, 1999], 219-45 and 205-17 respectively), as well as Walzer, "Nation and Universe," *The Tanner Lectures on Human Values XI: 1990,* ed. Grethe B. Peterson (Salt Lake City: University of Utah Press, 1990), 509-56. While Michael Sandel rarely discusses contemporary nationalism (see *Democracy's Discontent* [Cambridge, MA: Belknap Press, 1996], 338-50, for a highly abbreviated discussion), there is good reason to think that his view of nationalism would be similar to those of Taylor and Walzer. Alasdair MacIntyre, too, is reticent on the question of nationalism, but his view seems to be that national sentiment is good whereas the modern state, and therefore the nation-state, is bad. It goes without saying that it is hard to approve of nationalism if one disapproves of the nation-state. Hence MacIntyre's anti-statism cancels out any sympathy for nationalism he might otherwise display. (For MacIntyre's most recent statement of his position on this question, see Alasdair MacIntyre, *Dependent Rational Animals: Why Human Beings Need the Virtues* [Chicago: Open Court, 1999], 132-3.)

3   Bonnie Honig, in a round-table exchange with George Kateb published in *Hannah Arendt and Leo Strauss,* ed. P.G. Kielmansegg, H. Mewes, and E. Glaser-Schmidt (Cambridge: Cambridge University Press, 1995), 186, rightly draws attention to Arendt's anxieties about identity-based politics and her hostility toward a politics geared to group identities. Cf. Margaret Canovan, *Hannah Arendt: A Reinterpretation of Her Political Thought* (Cambridge: Cambridge University Press, 1992), 243-9, where Canovan argues (again rightly) that what Arendt desired was an understanding of citizenship that was *not* communitarian. See also Albrecht Wellmer, "Hannah Arendt on Revolution," in *Hannah Arendt in Jerusalem,* ed. Steven E. Aschheim (Berkeley: University of California Press, 2001), 38. Jeremy Waldron writes, "Arendt is ambivalent about the politics of national identity." Waldron, "Arendt's Constitutional Politics," in *The Cambridge Companion to Hannah Arendt,* ed. Dana Villa (Cambridge: Cambridge University Press, 2000), 205. This formulation understates Arendt's hostility to nationalism. Waldron reaches the conclusion about her ambivalence by giving special attention to a text in which she is untypically open to nationalist categories:

Arendt, *Eichmann in Jerusalem: A Report on the Banality of Evil,* rev. and enlarged ed. (New York: Viking Press, 1965), 262-3.

4 For a very clear and helpful summary of Arendt's critical responses to Zionism, see Richard J. Bernstein, *Hannah Arendt and the Jewish Question* (Cambridge, MA: MIT Press, 1996), chapter 5. For a quite harsh assessment of Arendt's views concerning Zionism, see Walter Laqueur, "The Arendt Cult: Hannah Arendt As Political Commentator," in *Hannah Arendt in Jerusalem,* ed. Aschheim, 52-5. For much more sympathetic responses to her critique of Zionism, see the chapters by Amnon Raz-Krakotzkin, Moshe Zimmerman, and Richard J. Bernstein in the same volume.

5 These four articles are: "Zionism Reconsidered" (1945); "The Jewish State: Fifty Years After" (1946); "To Save the Jewish Homeland" (1948); and "Peace or Armistice in the Near East?" (written in 1948 but published in 1950). They are republished in Hannah Arendt, *The Jew As Pariah: Jewish Identity and Politics in the Modern Age,* ed. Ron H. Feldman (New York: Grove Press, 1978).

6 Ibid., 141.

7 Ibid., 140. Cf. Hannah Arendt, *On Revolution* (New York: Viking Press, 1965): "The nineteenth-century ideologies – such as nationalism and internationalism, capitalism and imperialism, socialism and communism ... though still invoked by many as justifying causes, have lost contact with the major realities of our world" (1).

8 Arendt, *The Jew As Pariah,* 163.

9 Ibid., 173.

10 Ibid.

11 Ibid.

12 Arendt, *The Jew As Pariah,* 161.

13 Ibid., 173. In a letter to Karl Jaspers dated 22 August 1960, Arendt seems to reject the principle of national self-determination: "Self-determination as a right of nations applies to constitutional form and domestic political arrangements and by no means needs to include the so-called right to national self-determination"; the context is a discussion of German reunification. *Hannah Arendt – Karl Jaspers: Correspondence 1926-1969,* ed. L. Kohler and H. Saner, trans. R. Kimber and R. Kimber (New York: Harcourt Brace Jovanovich, 1992), 398.

14 Arendt, *The Jew As Pariah:* "Nationalism is bad enough when it trusts in nothing but the rude force of the nation. A nationalism that necessarily and admittedly depends upon the force of a foreign nation is certainly worse. This is the threatened fate of Jewish nationalism" (132-3).

15 Ibid., 162. Cf. ibid., 182-3.

16 Cf. Bernstein, *Hannah Arendt and the Jewish Question,* 112; Laqueur, "The Arendt Cult," 53-4. As an alternative to Herzlian Zionism, Arendt counterposes the Jewish nationalism of Bernard Lazare: see "Herzl and Lazare" (1942), in *The Jew As Pariah,* 125-30. Also, ibid., 171, and ibid., 153, where she characterizes Lazare as a kind of Zionist who "trusted the Jewish people for the necessary political strength of will to achieve freedom instead of being transported to freedom" and who "dared to side with the revolutionary forces in Europe."

17 Arendt, *The Jew As Pariah,* 136-7.

18 Ibid., 142.

19 Ibid., 152-3. She immediately adds that one "should in fairness consider how exceptionally difficult the conditions were for the Jews who, in contrast to other peoples, did not even possess the territory from which to start their fight for freedom." This concession considerably blunts what would otherwise seem an extremely harsh assessment of the Zionist movement.

20 Ibid., 149.

21 In "Peace or Armistice in the Near East?" Arendt suggests that there have been nationalist and non-nationalist versions of Zionism. The Herzlian tradition, which ultimately prevailed, offered classic nineteenth-century nationalist ideology, and would settle for nothing less than "a full-fledged sovereign Jewish state." A counter-tradition, which Arendt associates with Ahad Ha'am and which, she argues, had its finest fruition in the *kibbutzim* and the founding of the Hebrew University, was more interested in Palestine as a Jewish cultural

centre; the latter tradition resisted "the crude slogans of a Balkanized nationalism," and rejected a vision of Palestine based on "ethnic homogeneity and national sovereignty" (ibid., 213).

22 Subsequent to the UN's partition vote, the United States backtracked and instead supported trusteeship for Palestine. Arendt agreed with the (revised) US policy: "Trusteeship over the whole of Palestine would postpone and possibly prevent partition of the country" (ibid., 190). Trusteeship would also "have the advantage of preventing the establishment of sovereignty whose only sovereign right would be to commit suicide" (ibid.).

23 Arendt, *The Jew As Pariah,* 184-5.

24 Ibid., 184.

25 Even *after* the creation of the State of Israel, Arendt continues to follow Magnes and the Ihud group in arguing for a binational Palestinian Confederation (ibid., 218).

26 Ibid., 185.

27 Ibid., 187-8. Arendt writes that "loss of the kibbutzim [in the event of Jewish defeat] ... would be one of the severest of blows to the hopes of all those, Jewish and non-Jewish, who have not and never will make their peace with present-day society and its standards. For this Jewish experiment in Palestine holds out hope of solutions that will be acceptable and applicable, not only in individual cases, but also for the large mass of men everywhere whose dignity and very humanity are in our time so seriously threatened by the pressures of modern life and its unsolved problems" (ibid., 186). Cf. ibid., 214.

28 Ibid., 188.

29 Ibid., 192.

30 Ibid., 191, 192.

31 Ibid., 190-1. According to Arendt, what prevented both sides from recognizing the advantages for each of interdependence was *ideology*: on the Jewish side, "a Central European ideology of nationalism and tribal thinking"; on the Arab side, an anti-Western ideology that romanticized underdevelopment (ibid., 208-9).

32 Ibid., 222.

33 Ibid., 186. Cf. the statement Arendt quotes from Judah Magnes: "What a boon to mankind it would be if the Jews and Arabs of Palestine were to strive together in friendship and partnership to make this Holy Land into a thriving peaceful Switzerland ... A bi-national Palestine could become a beacon of peace in the world" (ibid., 212). In "Peace or Armistice in the Near East?" Arendt, following Magnes, goes on to argue that federal or confederal arrangements in Palestine should be the stepping stone to a larger regional federation: "Nationalist insistence on absolute sovereignty in such small countries as Palestine, Syria, Lebanon, Iraq, Transjordan, Saudi Arabia and Egypt can lead only to the Balkanization of the whole region and its transformation into a battlefield for the conflicting interests of the great powers to the detriment of all authentic national interests. In the long run, the only alternative to Balkanization is a regional federation" (ibid., 217).

34 Cf. K.R. Minogue, *Nationalism* (London: Methuen, 1969), 21. Minogue quotes Hans J. Morgenthau – "That the traditional nation-state is obsolescent in view of the technological and military conditions of the contemporary world is obvious" – and then asks, "But is it obvious that the nation-state is obsolescent?"

35 In other contexts, Arendt is rightly suspicious of the appeal to historical trends as a basis for political principles. The problem is acutely highlighted when Arendt celebrates Russia's "entirely new and successful approach to nationality conflicts, its new form of organizing different peoples on the basis of national equality," and urges that this be looked up to as a model for "every political and national movement in our times" (Arendt, *The Jew As Pariah,* 149). We may indeed sympathize with the Soviet ideal of forging a multinational federation, but the idea that we can bank on history turning its back on the nation-state turns out to be hopeless – the nation-state has a habit of bouncing back!

36 See Hannah Arendt, *Essays in Understanding 1930-1954,* ed. Jerome Kohn (New York: Harcourt Brace, 1994), 2.

37 See Hannah Arendt, *Imperialism,* part 2 of *The Origins of Totalitarianism* (New York: Harcourt, Brace and World, 1968), bottom of 110, where she refers to the state-nation relationship as a contradiction.

38 Ibid., 106.
39 Ibid., 103-4.
40 This distinction, as the basis for a normative rather than sociological argument, has recently come under a lot of fire from political philosophers: see, for instance, the chapters by Bernard Yack, Kai Nielsen, and Will Kymlicka in *Theorizing Nationalism*, ed. Beiner, 103-18, 119-30, 131-40 respectively. For criticism directed at Arendt's version of the distinction, see Joan Cocks, "On Nationalism: Frantz Fanon, 1925-1961; Rosa Luxemburg, 1871-1919; and Hannah Arendt, 1906-1975," in *Feminist Interpretations of Hannah Arendt*, ed. Bonnie Honig (University Park: Pennsylvania State University Press, 1995), 237.
41 Arendt, *Imperialism*, 109.
42 See, for instance, ibid., 156; Hannah Arendt, *Antisemitism*, part 1 of *The Origins of Totalitarianism* (New York: Harcourt, Brace and World, 1968), 50, 79.
43 Arendt, *Imperialism*, 109-10.
44 Ibid., 109.
45 Ibid., 111-12.
46 Ibid., 112.
47 Ibid. She goes on: "Rootlessness was the true source of that 'enlarged tribal consciousness' which actually meant that members of these peoples had no definite home but felt at home wherever other members of their 'tribe' happened to live." Hence the pan-movements, and their successors, the totalitarian movements, had no inclination to respect existing state boundaries. The more Arendt thinks about the nation-state in juxtaposition to these tribal nationalisms, the more sympathetic she becomes to the bounded (Western) nation-state: see ibid., contrasting the pan-movements with "national emancipation" within the "bounds of a national community," "the true national liberation movements of small peoples." Nationalism as such is a perversion of the state, but the authentic nation-state, "even in its perverted form, [by comparison with the tribal nationalism of the pan-movements] remained a legal institution, [so that] nationalism was controlled by some law, and ... was limited by definite boundaries" (Arendt, *Imperialism*, 111).
48 Ibid., 110.
49 Ibid.
50 Arendt, *Imperialism*, 111.
51 Ibid., 110-11; cf. 152, 155, 170-2. See Istvan Hont, "The Permanent Crisis of a Divided Mankind: 'Contemporary Crisis of the Nation State' in Historical Perspective," *Political Studies* 42 (1994): 206-17. Apropos Arendt's critique of nationalism, Hont suggests that Arendt is really driven by a cosmopolitan longing "to see the world as a brotherhood or family of republics" (216); therefore the ultimate target of her critique is an idea of sovereignty that is inherent to the concept of the modern state (with or without the nation as the seat of sovereignty). Accordingly, despite the misleading way in which she appears to put the chief blame on the nation, "her objection to *national* sovereignty is really a complaint about the notion of modern sovereignty *tout court*" (209). It is significant in this connection that in *On Revolution* (see, for instance, 152), Arendt becomes very critical of sovereignty as such – and correspondingly, becomes much more critical of Jacobin republicanism, with its own claims to sovereignty (cf. Canovan, *Hannah Arendt*, 32 n. 70). In "Zionism Reconsidered," Arendt had referred to "the grand French idea of the sovereignty of the people," and complained that, owing to Zionism's "uncritical acceptance of German-inspired nationalism," this grand idea was "perverted into the nationalist claims to autarchical existence" (*The Jew As Pariah*, 156). Clearly, by the time she writes *On Revolution*, Arendt is no longer so enamoured of the French Revolution's idea of popular sovereignty, which she comes to associate with the nationalist idea of an integral national will (see *On Revolution*, 154-5). With respect to the latter claim, William E. Scheuerman argues that Arendt carries her repudiation of French revolutionary thought much too far: see "Revolutions and Constitutions: Hannah Arendt's Challenge to Carl Schmitt," in *Law As Politics: Carl Schmitt's Critique of Liberalism*, ed. David Dyzenhaus (Durham, NC: Duke University Press, 1998), 252-80. A pivotal text, both for Arendt and for her critics, in interpreting the kind of nationalism inscribed in the French Revolution is Emmanuel Joseph Sieyès, *What Is the Third Estate?* ed. S.E. Finer, trans. M. Blondel (London: Pall Mall Press, 1963).

52 Arendt, *Imperialism,* 111.
53 Ibid., 110.
54 Hannah Arendt, "The Nation," *Review of Politics* 8, 1 (1946): 138-41. In fact, Arendt draws heavily on her Delos review in the theoretical account of the nation-state summarized above (*Imperialism,* 109-11).
55 Arendt, "The Nation," 138.
56 Ibid., 139.
57 Ibid.
58 Ibid.
59 Arendt, "The Nation," 140.
60 Ibid., 140-1.
61 Ibid., 141. In *Imperialism,* 111-12 n. 32, Arendt associates this proposal to personalize or de-politicize nationality with Karl Renner and Otto Bauer, two Austro-Marxists who had addressed the nationality question. See *Austro-Marxism,* ed. and trans. Tom Bottomore and Patrick Goode (Oxford: Clarendon Press, 1978), 102-25.
62 Arendt, *Imperialism,* ix. Significantly, Habermas continues to use the same language: "The classic form of the nation-state is at present disintegrating." Jürgen Habermas, "Citizenship and National Identity," in *Theorizing Citizenship,* ed. R. Beiner (Albany: State University of New York Press, 1995), 256-7.
63 For a very helpful summary of Arendt's account, see Canovan, *Hannah Arendt,* 31-6.
64 Arendt, *Imperialism,* 151-2; see 152 n. 8 for some suggestion of the numbers involved.
65 Ibid., 156-70.
66 Ibid., 156. Arendt notes the grim irony, which is obviously of some relevance to her critical judgments concerning the Zionist project, that those who were Europe's worst victims of minority status, de-naturalization, and statelessness proceeded to establish their own nation-state, thereby casting hundreds of thousands of Arabs who fled Palestine into precisely the condition of statelessness and rightlessness that the Jews had finally escaped (ibid., 170).
67 Ibid., 171-2.
68 Ibid., 171.
69 Ibid., 172.
70 Ibid., 176.
71 Ibid., 179.
72 Arendt seems to concede as much when she makes the following important acknowledgment with respect to the recovery of human rights by the Jews through the establishment of a Jewish nation-state: "the restoration of human rights, as the recent example of the State of Israel proves, has been achieved so far only through the restoration or the establishment of national rights" (ibid.). This supports Cocks's judgment that Arendt sees the national question "as a riddle with no solution" ("On Nationalism," 238).
73 Cf. Arendt, *Imperialism:* "The danger of this development [semi-citizenship and stateless-ness] had been inherent in the structure of the nation-state since the beginning" (155). Also, Arendt, "The Nation": "Almost all modern brands of nationalism are racist to some degree" (138-9).
74 See Arendt, *The Jew As Pariah:* "The United States ... is not a national state in the European sense of the word" (158). For a contrary view, see Roger Scruton, "The First Person Plural," in *Theorizing Nationalism,* ed. Beiner, 289-90.
75 Contrary to this argument, the fact is that nationalists today are less and less inclined to assert national sovereignty: witness the enthusiasm of Scottish nationalists for European federalism, or the keenness of Québécois nationalists to be included in sovereignty-undermining arrangements such as NAFTA. Arendt is right that "modern power conditions ... make national sovereignty a mockery except for giant states" (*Imperialism,* 149), and that national sovereignty "has become the greatest danger to national survival for small nations" (*The Jew As Pariah,* 222); but contemporary nationalists seem to have taken this point.
76 Cf. Canovan, *Hannah Arendt,* 246: Arendt was determined to believe that "the future lay with non-national political forms" (federations or empires), and, Canovan notes, persisted in this view even while "nationalism revived in Europe and spread around the world." Also

see ibid., 36 n. 80. Cf. Judith N. Shklar, *Political Thought and Political Thinkers*, ed. Stanley Hoffman (Chicago: University of Chicago Press, 1998), 367.
77 Arendt, *On Revolution*, 8.
78 Hannah Arendt's husband, Heinrich Blücher, who, as we know from his published letters in the Arendt-Jaspers correspondence, was an even harsher critic of nationalism than Arendt was, shared the same view: "As Hölderlin once said, the time of kings is past; and now the time of nations is past." *Correspondence 1926-1969*, ed. Kohler and Saner, 278.

9

National Self-Determination: Some Cautionary Remarks on the Rhetoric of Rights

My purpose in this essay is not to specify a set of theoretical criteria to help decide when national groups within a state seeking to renegotiate their citizenship are advancing just or unjust – or more just or less just – moral claims. Rather, my intention is to focus attention on the kind of moral language in which these moral claims are advanced and debated, and on how the character of different moral vocabularies makes a difference to the conduct of nationalist and anti-nationalist politics. In pursuing this argument, I'll be drawing upon one strand of the so-called liberal-communitarian debate. It will be recalled that a notable feature of the so-called communitarian challenge to liberalism was the articulation of an anxiety about the hegemony of rights discourse within liberal society, along with a hostility toward, or at least skepticism about, the place occupied by "rights" as the pre-eminent moral category within liberal theory. I want to make an analogous argument against the language of rights as applied to political-philosophical debates about nationality: whether one wants to opt for an expansive or restricted approach to the moral claims of politicized nationalities, affirming a general *right* to national self-determination, so I will be suggesting, is not a helpful way to deal with the complex predicaments that these nationalist claims invariably generate.

What's Wrong with Rights Talk?

In the first section of chapter 6, we summarized a set of considerations that give us good reason to be wary of embracing the idea of national self-determination: acknowledging this idea as a universal moral entitlement would be both difficult and hazardous to honour in practice. The purpose of the present chapter is to lay out a further set of arguments according to which expression of these moral claims in the language of rights makes matters considerably worse, especially when we consider that nationalist political actors can be expected to make a sometimes cynical and opportunistic use of whatever legitimizing slogans we place at their disposal.

In order to pursue this argument, I'll need to rehearse certain themes from what in the 1980s came to be called the communitarian critique of liberalism.[1] The appeal to rights as the central moral-political category is so familiar to us in contemporary liberal democracies, we are so thoroughly habituated to it, that we tend to take this moral language for granted, failing to see its distinctive features as one moral language among others and overlooking the ways it often expresses the social and political pathologies of contemporary liberal society. Therefore, critics of rights language (some more militant, some less militant) such as Alasdair MacIntyre, Charles Taylor, Michael Sandel, William Galston, and Mary Ann Glendon have performed an immense service in helping us to be more attentive to the deficiencies of this pervasive moral vocabulary. Common to all these critics is the idea that the more we find ourselves relying on rights discourse to articulate all of our social-political commitments, the more we know ourselves to be inhabiting a moral universe characterized by brittle relationships between individuals and groups; diminished social trust; a propensity to assert absolutist claims; stridency; a propensity to reduce complex social issues to simple slogans; and a constant proliferation of new supposed rights that demand satisfaction at whatever cost to society.[2] As Glendon summarizes this challenge to "rights talk": "A tendency to frame nearly every social controversy in terms of a clash of rights ... impedes compromise, mutual understanding, and the discovery of common ground."[3]

As theorists such as Taylor and Sandel articulated very effectively, we have reason to feel deep anxiety about the quality of the moral bonds between citizens of modern liberal societies to the extent that our political relationships are founded exclusively on a procedural-juridical conception that finds its natural expression in the language of rights.[4] Although Sandel, in his first book, didn't present himself explicitly as a critic of the morality of rights, it's implicit in his general critique of the Rawlsian notion that justice is the first virtue of social institutions.[5] To quote an important Sandelian formulation of this critique, in the light of the Humean account of justice as a response to a condition of conflicting interests and aims, "justice appears as a remedial virtue, whose moral advantage consists in the repair it works on fallen conditions ... the virtue of justice [and the question of its primacy or non-primacy] is measured by the morally diminished conditions that are its prerequisite."[6] However, if Rawlsian justice is not the first virtue of social institutions but merely the response to our "fallen conditions," this critical perspective applies with much greater force to a moral world in which the appeal to rights is the only currency to which citizens of a liberal society can resort in conducting their public discourse, and in which political community is defined by a compulsive insistence that our rights be protected. In line with Sandel's account of justice as a remedial virtue, rights are intended as a remedy to the deformations of a social condition that is assumed to be less than ideal.[7] The language of rights is never a language of shared projects or collective co-involvement (the language of friends or fellow citizens engaged in joint deliberation concerning a common good); instead, rights are always a means of enforcing inviolable boundaries against those (strangers, anonymous officials of the state, or estranged spouses) we have some reason to distrust – a protection against encroachment. As Glendon rightly points out, "the assertion of rights is usually a sign of breakdown in a relationship."[8] Or as another famous critic of rights discourse has put the point, "Since in modern society the accommodation of one set of wills to the purpose of another continually requires the frustration of one group's purposes by those of another, it is unsurprising that the concept of rights, understood as claims against the inroads of marauding others in situations where shared allegiances to goods that are goods of the whole community have been attenuated or abandoned, should become a socially central concept."[9]

For many theorists, the real problem is the *individualism* of rights language, with the presumption that discourse about rights necessarily privileges the claims of individuals over against other individuals. I think this is a serious misconception. If critics of rights talk are right about the infirmities of this moral language, the same critique of individual rights applies with equal force to group rights.[10] The simple fact of calling one's moral claim (whether on behalf of oneself *or* on behalf of one's group) a *right* automatically renders one less inclined to compromise this claim or submit it to a process of mutual accommodation. To illustrate, I'll borrow an example I've used elsewhere: "consider an argument between two individuals of differing political persuasions concerning whether it would be good for the society as a whole if the state were to make available a certain social service (say, universal state-funded daycare). Now imagine how the tone of the debate would be altered if it suddenly turned into a contest between the *right* of one of the parties to receive the service in question and the *right* of the other party not to be burdened by the higher taxes necessary to supply the service."[11] What the example illustrates is that the very fact that each side phrases its claims in the language of rights indicates that the barricades have already been erected by the two rival positions. Exactly the same point applies to group rights: it makes a difference, socially and politically, when one translates a set of claims about political good into the language of rights, which presupposes a social universe where individuals or groups are subject to the unjust depredations of other individuals and groups, and require binding protections or absolute guarantees against these violations of their rights, hence an implication of the non-negotiability of these protections or guarantees.

The Impact on Nationalism

To summarize the argument thus far: contrary to what may be suggested by some of those who criticize the centrality of rights discourse within contemporary politics, the fundamental problem with rights discourse is not its individualism. Rather, the deeper problem with this discourse is its absolutism: that is, the notion that a right, if genuine, cannot be trumped or compromised. If so, the critique of rights discourse can be applied to collective rights, not just individual rights. This in turn suggests that the critique of rights language presents an important challenge to nationalism, with its foundational appeal to a universal *right* to self-determination. The purpose of our inquiry is to consider the possibility that a political philosophy that feels driven to articulate its social vision in the language of rights is for that very reason theoretically unattractive, and if we are right, this thesis has direct application to the philosophical problem of nationalism.

What's required here is a contrast between alternative forms of public rhetoric, and to make this as concrete as possible, imagine two different ways of conducting the argument for the secession of Quebec:

1   We (Québécois) no longer feel allegiance to Canada. We appreciate the past benefits of the union, of how we have grown and matured as a nation during this period of national cohabitation, but we feel we have *out*grown this marriage of nations – we can flourish better on our own, without the constant constitutional squabbling, without the quarrelling over jurisdictions, without the feeling on the part of the other provinces that we are the spoiled brat of confederation. We go without rancour, even with some nostalgia for an interesting 130 years of this binational experiment. But we are ready for a new experiment.
2   Give us our rights! We are a nation. We can determine our own fate. We have an inviolable *right* as a historical people to rule ourselves. You, as a separate nation, a separate people, have no right to involve yourselves in our national destiny.

It seems obvious that it makes a world of difference, practically speaking, whether one makes one's claim for nationhood in the first rhetoric or in the second. The second we might call nationhood with a clenched fist. I think there is an intimation of this second rhetoric in the appeal to national *rights* as such. I also think it's fairly clear that the second rhetoric is the preferred rhetoric of Quebec nationalism as it presently exists (nor is it an accident – if the critique of rights talk is on the mark – that this is the dominant rhetoric).[12] However, nothing in principle precludes Quebec nationalists from switching to the first kind of rhetoric; and in fact Quebec nationalists in the past have sometimes used the first rhetoric with considerable effectiveness.[13] If nothing else, the choice of presecession rhetoric will make some difference to the quality of postsecession relations between the two divorced nations; just as in a literal marriage between two spouses, you can be sure that you're in for a pretty nasty divorce as soon as both partners start demanding their rights.

"Rights talk" is a form of political discourse that is intended as the verbal equivalent of shaking your fist in the direction of those with whom you are in a state of political disagreement. (That, at least, is its function in liberal societies; I allow that rights discourse serves a different function in nonliberal societies subject to regimes that persecute, torture, and otherwise oppress their citizens.) I don't want to suggest that nationalists are the only offenders here. In fact, it would be equally easy to illustrate the same point by looking at the other side of the barricades in Quebec. Consider the current (and never-ending) language debate. It is possible to make all sorts of plausible arguments about why it's reasonable and desirable to show respect for the anglophone minority by allowing a certain measure of English presence in the public face of Quebec. But anglophones at present insist on using the language of rights: they have a *right* to advertise in English – their fundamental human rights are being violated by Quebec language laws. Once again, this rights rhetoric is a form of fist-waving. It raises the political temperature, and inflames both sides, while doing little to advance the debate by tempering differences and locating means of mutual accommodation.

To formulate one's grievances in the language of rights (what one might call "the juridification of political claims") is a politically familiar way of saying: "To hell with you! Give me what I want or I'll sue you. I'll take you to the Supreme Court or the International Tribunal in The Hague if I have to." The basic point here is that we *can* discuss these matters without waving the banner of rights and therefore making the agents of nationalist secessions (and perhaps their adversaries as well) more truculent and morally self-righteous. In place of the question "Do the Québécois have a *right* to exercise their national will by seceding from Canada?" one could substitute these questions: "How far is it prudent to go in seeking to accommodate the national aspirations of the Québécois?" (Stating the question in this form doesn't rule out secession as an appropriate answer.) "How is it good for Canada as a political community to constrain Quebeckers to remain a part of the federation if a majority of them declare in a clear way their determination to withdraw allegiance?" "What are the substantive gains and losses for *both* sides in the dispute?" In principle, it seems that one could address all the relevant moral-political issues while entirely avoiding reference to national rights; it must not be assumed that one *has to* formulate these issues in the language of rights. Above all, we want an accommodation of conflicting political purposes, and it seems unlikely that the idiom of national or group rights, any more than the idiom of individual rights, will be helpful in the attainment of a reasonable outcome.

Rights Talk in Common Currency

What concerns me in this discussion is not the "logic" of rights language in any rigorous sense, but rather what we might call the "grammar" of rights talk in something like a Wittgensteinian sense – that is, a mode of moral-political self-articulation rooted in particular forms of life, and expressive of social and political practices that naturally lend themselves to conceptualization in rights categories. I certainly don't rule out that sophisticated rights theorists in the academy can define rights in a way that avoids the pathologies I discuss (and philosophers who defend a "right to secede" or "right to self-determination" are generally very careful to define these rights in a way that is far from unbounded or unqualified). On the other hand, I suspect that it is these very pathologies that contribute to the attractiveness of the appeal to rights within societies where rights are such a popular coin of public rhetoric (and my suspicion is shared by all those critics of rights talk referred to earlier).

To pursue this discussion, I want to identify what I'll call various rhetorical functions of the language of rights. I'll focus on three in particular: the "trumping function"; the "levelling function"; and the "short-circuiting function." Again, what's being addressed here is not the idea of a right as we encounter it in the most refined versions of professional philosophers, but rather, what we might call the "pragmatics" of rights rhetoric as it actually operates in real political life.

A "right," according to its most modest definition, is simply a shorthand for a morally warranted political claim. But there is a price to be paid (rarely acknowledged by rights theorists) for the use of this shorthand. Ronald Dworkin made clearer the nature of this price with his famous image of "rights as trumps."[14] Just as in the realm of individual rights, one has a right to freedom of expression if the claims of free expression "trump" whatever other social goods might be in conflict with the exercise of this right, so in the realm of collective rights, a group has a "right" to national self-determination if the claim to self-determination "trumps" other social goods that may be in conflict with the exercise of this right. The problem, from our point of view, is that this trumping function will become considerably more mischievous when we move from political philosophy to political practice. Someone who is the holder of a presumed right will say: "Look, we're not just talking about any old moral claim here, we're talking about a *right* – the token of an essential moral guarantee, the boundary-marker of an inviolable moral space. It's non-negotiable." Obviously, calling the moral claim a "right" is intended to add extra force to the urgency of attending to the moral claim. Once everyone becomes habituated to talking in this way, we can easily find ourselves in a situation of political deadlock, where moral and political deliberation is stymied on all sides.

The choice of a moral vocabulary doesn't just condition substantive outcomes; more broadly, it structures possible lines of theoretical debate and moral deliberation. To take an absurd example: if, in response to my compulsive consumption of a hundred Twinkies a day, someone puts the challenge, "Don't you realize what you are doing to yourself by eating so many Twinkies?" I can reply: "It's my *right* as a free individual to eat as many Twinkies as I desire." In other words, I short-circuit the discussion of welfare or what's good for me by invoking my individual rights (as I suppose them to be). I'm certainly not trying to suggest that all appeals to rights are as frivolous as this. For the sake of balance, let's call to mind someone who invokes his or her right not to be deprived of regular physical exercise while incarcerated. The latter, unquestionably, embodies a legitimate moral claim. However, I also want to suggest that the absolutism of rights claims, as they operate within the common discourse of a rights-conscious society, tends to have a "levelling" effect: that is, my right to consume Twinkies free of moral scrutiny is asserted as if it were on the same moral level as any other right (such as the more morally weighty demand not to be incarcerated in a way detrimental to my basic welfare); or as if the questioning of the first "right" would offend my humanity as grievously as the denial of the second. This levelling effect, I want to suggest, is central to how a rhetoric of rights operates in a society sensitive to that rhetoric.

Let's now transpose the discussion to the problem of putative rights to national self-determination. It is not hard to see how a similar set of considerations apply; how, here too, a sort of levelling effect is at work once one frames one's moral claims in a rhetoric of rights. Consider, first, the case of a national group such as the East Timorese, who have been trampled on by their Indonesian captors, and have had to endure conditions that approach, or that actually constitute, systematic genocide (the plight of Kurds in Northern Iraq would be an equally apt example).[15] One would have to be morally obtuse to an extreme degree not to see the justice of the demand by the East Timorese for self-determination, since they have little or no reason to expect from the Indonesian state any respect for their cultural integrity or even their physical survival. The only way they can be assured of their cultural and physical security is by reassuming control over their own fate. This example clearly corresponds to the case, in the domain of individual rights, of the prisoner who demands not to receive abusive treatment from his or her jailers. In both cases, we have a set of claims that possess a profound moral seriousness. But if we grant a universal moral right to self-determination, then groups with a much more frivolous basis for their national claims will borrow the moral authority rightly granted to national groups that are genuinely oppressed. Hence the levelling of moral entitlements: nations that suffer merely symbolic slights from the majority culture; that aspire to what Wayne Norman has referred to as "vanity seces-sions";[16] that succumb to the demagogic promptings of nationalist entre-preneurs – all of these will presume that they have a moral entitlement no less sacred or inviolable than that of the most oppressed national minority. Here we have a group-rights equivalent to our Twinkie glutton to whom the language of rights has yielded the moral high ground.

Part of the problem here is the essential universalism of rights claims. The whole point of asserting a rights claim is to identify an aspect of human existence that is so fundamental that its violation, anywhere, at any time, constitutes an affront to human dignity as such. For instance, if we have a right not to be tortured, *any* instance of torture, anywhere, at any time, is morally intolerable. Applying this logic to the problem of the moral status of nationalities raises a problem, for it puts a moralistic language at the disposal of nationalists everywhere, who, as such, are in the business of playing the ethnic grievances game. This isn't, of course, to suggest that there aren't, in various situations, ethnic grievances that are morally serious; in some cases, they are of the utmost moral seriousness. As I suggested above, no reasonable person, I think, could deny the moral claims of the East Timorese or the Iraqi Kurds. But phrasing these moral claims in the universalistic language of rights at the same time equips entrepreneurs of nationality politics whose moral claims are much more dubious – extending even to the absurd "Padanian" project of opportunists in Northern Italy, as discussed in chapter 6.

I want to say a little more about what I've called the short-circuiting func-tion of rights discourse. What does an argument about nationalism look like when it's conducted in the language of good rather than the language of rights? It seems fairly obvious that judgments about the attractive or unattractive character of the nation-state project are shaped by competing conceptions of political good. For instance, with respect to my own political commitments, I support Canadian federalism, rather than Canada's partition into two states, each of which would be closer to the classic nation-state paradigm, because I am convinced that there are goods associated with binational partnership that override those to be found in the more simpli-fied bonds of membership in the nation-state (in the narrower sense). It may be that political community founded on binational or multinational partnership is unobtainable in a particular case; it may be that the binational state that already exists in Canada turns out to be impossible to sustain; but what is in question here is not an issue of practicality but what is desirable as a matter of principle. Now it might be said that in the Canadian case, my judgments are hardly impartial; as a member of (not exactly the majority culture in Canada, but certainly) the majority linguistic community, I have some kind of vested interest in Quebec's continued subscription in the larger political community. I suppose this is true. But here I would like to think that if (a counterfactual, to be sure) I were a francophone Quebecker, I would have the same preference for binational political partnership that I do as an anglophone Canadian.[17] And if (here the counterfactual involves less of an existential leap, and so my thought experiment has more credibility) I were once again an anglophone Quebecker in a Quebec that *did* decide to be an independent state, I would certainly oppose the "partitionist" efforts of anglophone communities in Quebec, and *for exactly the same reason:* namely, allegiance to the idea that binational or multinational coexistence is a more noble political adventure than uni-national solidarity. But here the nationalist as such sees group belonging or national togetherness as the overriding good, and correspondingly, is unmoved by what strikes me as the more attractive political ideal of binational partnership. The nationalist regards each nation as flourishing best on its own, and sees the strains of mutual accommodation within a political marriage of nations not as a noble (though sometimes unsustainable) cause, but rather, as a futile undertaking that's bound to cause more trouble than it's worth.[18]

Now it seems clear that one could have an interesting moral debate between these two opposing conceptions of political good. But once again, the appeal to rights has the effect of short-circuiting moral deliberation conducted within the discourse of good.[19] Instead of debating the alternative goods of political life shared with a co-national partner versus those of a smaller and more exclusive national community that forgoes the challenge of federal or consociational partnership, as soon as one invokes the *right* to go one's own way as a nation with its own state, further deliberation about goods is beside the point. (Think again of the rights-claiming Twinkie eater. There's no point asking if it's *good* for my health or sanity to consume so many Twinkies; it's my sovereign *right* as an autonomous individual to eat as many of them as I please.)

It's important to emphasize once again that if we eschew the language of rights, we don't necessarily wind up with different substantive moral outcomes. We may well conclude that the claims to secession on the part of oppressed East Timorese are morally warranted *whether or not* we see fit to express this moral claim in the language of universal rights. But the point is not simply whether we get this moral outcome or that moral outcome; the point is to appreciate the significance of the moral vocabulary by which we arrive at these outcomes.

Conclusion

I noted earlier that those political philosophers who treat the politics of nationalism within the horizon of the morality of rights tend to be careful not to define the rights in question in an absolutist or unqualified fashion, and are by and large quite sensitive to the risks of encouraging recklessness or of opening the floodgates to secessionist claims that would be likely to have destructive consequences. It might be helpful to conclude this discussion by considering how these rights theorists seek to qualify or hedge the moral rights they defend, and whether these theories succeed in staunching the anxieties about the rhetoric of rights that I have tried to identify.

To start with, let me survey various theoretical possibilities, so we have a better sense of the range of options.

1   Needless to say, anyone who is hostile to nationalism will be correspondingly hostile to the idea of national self-determination. As we saw in chapter 6, this is Kedourie's position, and it is a consistent view. No one can coherently think that nationalism is one of the plagues of the modern world while nonetheless believing that national self-determination stated as a universal moral principle is politically benign and philosophically defensible.

2   One can be relatively sympathetic to (at least some kinds of) nationalism, but nonetheless think that national self-determination as a general principle is a misguided notion. Consider the following argument advanced by Bernard Yack: "History has left us sufficient barriers to establishing broader political identities without multiplying them by using the concept of rights to erect and maintain new ones. Where past conflicts and injustices have erected such barriers, it may be wise, as a matter of political prudence, to offer special national rights ... But introducing such cultural rights as a general principle would unnecessarily harden perceptions of cultural opposition and thereby promote greater mutual suspicion and contention within political communities. Translating nationalism into the liberal language of rights leads [one] to ignore the social and historical context of political problems."[20] I take Yack to be suggesting here that it is one thing to try to cope with national conflicts as they arise; but declaring a universal *right* has the effect of egging people on to fight for the attainment of that right in situations where they might not otherwise have felt oppressed by the majority culture. Another political philosopher who has a large measure of sympathy for liberal versions of nationalism but who is nervous about applying the language of rights to these issues is David Miller.[21] Miller, too, recognizes that the notion of an across-the-board "right" is a very blunt instrument in weighing up the complex and historically mediated considerations presented for moral judgment in any instance of national conflict, and therefore his preferred way of talking about these matters is not to say that a secessionist nation is the bearer of a right but merely to say "prima facie the group has a good case."[22]

3   One can support a just right to secede, provided that it is consistent with standard liberal principles, but be skeptical about, if not downright hostile toward, nationalist accounts of what renders secession justifiable. This is more or less Allen Buchanan's position. In Buchanan's book *Secession*,

the nationalist account of self-determination is only the eighth of twelve pro-secession arguments that he considers (which in itself says quite a lot), and when he does finally get around to considering it, Buchanan finds it one of the weakest arguments for secession.[23] He concludes: "the normative nationalist principle is a recipe for limitless political fragmentation."[24]

4   One can embrace a so-called right of national self-determination, but try to interpret it in a way that steers nationalism away from claims to statehood. This is a plausible description of Yael Tamir's project.[25]

5   One can, of course, be a full-blown nationalist, and endorse a right to self-determination on standardly nationalist grounds.[26] Among the various liberal defenders of nationalism, Avishai Margalit and Joseph Raz come closest to defining self-determination on a characteristically nationalist basis.[27]

6   Finally (although this hardly exhausts the possibilities), one can opt for a relatively ambitious right of self-determination, but see bonds of national identity as irrelevant to the issue: if a group of individuals wishes to opt out, national solidarity on the part of the seceders is not a necessary condition for the justice of their secessionist claims. This position deserves to be listed after the properly nationalist view, since it subsumes, and therefore is of wider scope than, a strictly nationalist justification of secession. A good example of this kind of theory is that of Harry Beran, who embraces a *more* expansive right of secession than would be entailed by a universal right of national self-determination.[28]

What emerges from this brief sketch of various theoretical positions is that there are three different indices at play here: (1) one's attitude toward nationalism in general; (2) one's acceptance or rejection of some notion of a right to national self-determination; and (3) one's acceptance or rejection of a just right to secede. There is no reason to assume that there will be a simple correspondence between one's positions along these three indices, or that each index will, as it were, "line up" with the other two. To illustrate this lack of alignment, consider, for instance, my own position with respect to these three dimensions of the question: in general, I'm not warmly disposed toward nationalism; I am a skeptic about rights claims in general and nationalist rights in particular; but I am nonetheless reasonably open to liberal-nationalist secessions (certainly more so than would be dictated by Buchanan's principles of rightful secession).[29] I'm led to an acceptance (grudging, not enthusiastic) of secessionism not because I have any great sympathy for nationalism, and certainly not because I think every ethnic group and self-proclaimed "people" has a right to its own state, but for a different reason altogether: because one is unlikely to have a happy and flourishing political community where a substantial and territorially concentrated minority has a minimal or less than minimal allegiance to the political community to which it happens to belong, and where the alienation is permanent, that is, where there is no prospect at all of wooing back allegiance.[30] This way of thinking about the problem is deliberately phrased in the language of good (of what is choiceworthy) rather than the language of rights (of what is permissible).[31] Of course it would be vastly preferable to work out special constitutional arrangements, including federal institutions with sufficient authority to secure greater allegiance on the part of subcommunities with a distinctive identity. However, as Canadians already know and as Britons may come to find out as they move in a more federalist direction under the new Blair government, there is no guarantee that a highly decentralized federation with robust powers exercised by regional parliaments will solve the problem. It is always possible that giving nationalists their own parliament will simply furnish them with stronger instruments by which to pursue their more ambitious objectives. So in the end one might have little choice but to let them go their own way in the world (as the Czechs let their federal partners go), even if they are mistaken in thinking this will advance their own interests and mistaken in thinking that a uni-national political community is in principle normatively superior to a binational or multinational federation.

None of the theorists considered in our survey endorses rights without qualification; all of them want hedged rights – whether we're talking about rights to secede or rights of nations to determine their own political fate.[32] It would be perfectly easy for these defenders of the morality of rights to argue that my dire depiction of the language of rights at its worse has no application whatever to their own efforts as rights theorists. Buchanan, for instance, in a response to the communitarian critique of rights talk, made the point that it is unfair for communitarians to saddle liberals "with the implausible view that individual civil and political rights are absolute, that is, that they never may be justifiably infringed or restricted," and he would no doubt make the same complaint against the present challenge to rights discourse.[33] However, I don't think that this rejoinder gets liberal-nationalist rights theorists entirely off the hook, and I'll try to explain why.

First, though, let me review once again a few of the theories that are on offer, some of which are rather complex. Buchanan, as we've already seen, forthrightly rejects any right of national self-determination, but he still uses the language of rights to characterize those claims to secede that he does accept. In fact, he's a strong defender of rights theory, although, interestingly enough, he intimates that he's only weakly committed to pursuing his theory of secession in the idiom of rights. In one noteworthy passage, he states that, although in his own view the advantages of rights talk outweigh the drawbacks, he recognizes that other theorists may be more averse to the language of rights, and he lets it be known that he "would not protest too loudly if those who abhor the notion of a right wish to translate" his talk about rights into some other moral vocabulary.[34] As we've already seen, other theorists (such as Miller and Yack) are more sympathetic to nationalist claims than Buchanan is, but less inclined to formulate these claims in the language of rights.

Buchanan has a very restrictive view of the conditions of just secession (he says that his aim is to "domesticate" the right to secede, which surely implies making the conditions for permissible secession sufficiently stringent that the encouragement given to secessionists by moral philosophers will be minimized).[35] But it is striking how hedged and full of qualifications are the theories of even those philosophers who embrace a much more expansive account of the scope of just secessions. For instance, Margalit and Raz, who *seem* to affirm a quite ambitious right of self-determination, say that "the wish for a state must be shared *by an overwhelming majority,* reflecting deep-seated beliefs and feelings *of an enduring nature,* and not mere temporary popularity."[36] (What will the institutional embodiment of this right look like? Will Quebec sovereigntists have to win three referenda in a row, with 80 percent or more in each referendum?) Daniel Philpott, another defender of a moral right to self-determination, endorses "high procedural hurdles" and he says that while his theory is in principle more expansive than Buchanan's, "I doubt that there are many cases to which my own theory would give a green light, but to which Buchanan's would grant a red or yellow light."[37] This suggests that he would deny self-determination to the Québécois, since it's fairly clear that Québécois secessionism falls well short of satisfying Buchanan's principles. And Margaret Moore, who also appears to embrace an expansive right of self-determination, sees a compelling case for self-determination when "the vast majority" of a national group expresses its will in a plebiscite.[38] Secessionists (sovereigntists in Quebec, for instance) could be expected to respond to these "friends" of self-determination by saying, "Who needs this? What's the point of granting us a right to self-determination if the conditions for the permissible exercise of the right are so narrow that our national rights are in effect voided? What you give us with the right hand, you take away with the left!"

If philosophical theories of national rights are so heavily qualified, why would one be left with any cause for concern that the philosophical defence of a right to self-determination would contribute to secessionist recklessness? There are several reasons to be anxious still:

First, most of the self-determination theorists state a strong preference for federalist accommodation of national distinctiveness over secession.[39] But, for reasons laid out by Margalit and Raz, it is not clear how the statement of this preference is consistent with self-determination in a strict sense. Margalit and Raz write that "A group's right to self-determination is its right to determine that a territory be self-governing ... the right to self-determination

answers the question 'who is to decide?' not 'what is the best decision?' ...
if it has the right to decide, its decision is binding even if it is wrong."[40] If
I have understood them correctly, Margalit and Raz are saying that what a
right to self-determination serves to do is not to assert the wisdom or advisa-
bility of governing oneself in this way or that way but simply to specify the
morally relevant community that gets to decide this question. If we grant
self-determination to the Québécois, *they* alone are authorized to decide their
preferred form of self-governance. If so, then it is illegitimate to define self-
determination in a way that privileges autonomy without secession over full
secession: if granted self-determination, the group that aspires to secede gets
to choose between autonomy and secession, otherwise self-determination
isn't really self-determination. Philpott can speak of "a presumption against
secession," but if Margalit and Raz are right, self-determination means that
the group gets to decide *for itself* what's appropriate, rather than have this
dictated by some set of universal moral-political principles.

Most self-determination theorists proceed by granting a general right but
then qualifying it by requiring the secessionists to make various guarantees in advance, such as a pledge to institute a liberal regime of individual
rights and the promise of protections for national minorities within the
new state. As critics of self-determination theory have pointed out, there is
a problem here, which yields the second reason for anxiety. David Miller,
for instance, makes the important point that "once the new state is formed
and recognized, powerful norms of international non-interference come
into play," so third-party states may have the power to grant recognition
to seceding states but little power to regulate the consequences of having
legitimized the secession (he cites the Yugoslavian mess).[41] Of course, *no*
political movement with nationalist-secessionist aspirations is going to *say*
that it intends to oppress its own national minorities after independence:
if there are qualifications attached to the right to self-determination, the
secessionists will have nothing to gain by admitting their intention to violate
the qualifications and everything to gain by pledging their absolute fidelity to these qualifications. But surely the secession isn't revocable if all hell
breaks loose after their claims to self-determination have been granted. It
would make sense for the secessionists to agree to whatever conditions are
laid down by the international community, and then, with recognition in
their back pocket, conduct themselves pretty much as they please, as most
existing states now do. As Miller says, "We cannot [simply] take whatever
reassurances the secessionists may give at face value."[42] So the principle
of national self-determination awards moral credentials to the nationalist
group without being able to guarantee that the nationalists won't yield to
the temptation to pocket the right while paying little attention to the "fine
print" (the hedges attached to the right).

All the liberal defenders of self-determination want self-determination hedged by prudence, but once one lets the rhetoric of self-determination loose upon the world prudence may be seriously handicapped, which generates a further reason for concern. It is not hard to think of examples of how acknowledgment of a right of national self-determination would handcuff political prudence in coping with the challenges posed by nationalists. Even if one thought that the Yugoslav federation was doomed, the rhetoric of self-determination would encourage one to grant a more hasty recognition of the secessionist states than might be necessary, with severe injuries to the cause of prudence. It can be plausibly argued that the over-hasty recognition of Croatia and Slovenia by the EC (under German pressure) in fact contributed to the subsequent disaster in ex-Yugoslavia.[43] Or, to pick an example that is still playing itself out: speaking about self-determination in the idiom of rights helps nationalists in Quebec to convince themselves and other Quebeckers that the rest of Canada has no business meddling in Quebec's control over its own destiny (for instance, by becoming involved in the choice of a suitable referendum question); if, on the other hand, one rejects this rhetoric, one leaves more room for compromise and negotiation.[44]

Finally, we can ask why, if philosophers such as Margalit and Raz, Philpott, and Moore are as anxious about the right of self-determination getting out of hand as they say they are, they think it's reasonable or prudent to continue speaking of a "right" of self-determination. If Philpott, for instance, thinks his principle of self-determination has very limited application (see the discussion above concerning red lights and green lights), why does he see fit to continue using the language of a "right" of self-determination – with its universalistic-sounding associations – rather than a commitment to *ad hoc* consideration of the pros and cons of greater communal autonomy in this or that case?[45] Why start off with the presumption of legitimacy, which is what the "right" announces, and *then* worry about how to limit and qualify exercise of the right (clawing back the right, so to speak), rather than, as seems more prudent, put the onus on nationalists and secessionists to make their case for the reasonableness, in their own situation, of sovereignty or self-determination? Donald Horowitz refers to the debate within international law "over whether self-determination is still merely a principle or is now a right."[46] This nicely captures the point that it *does* make a real difference whether we formulate a given moral claim in the language of rights.[47] If we hand this particular ball to partisans of nationalist politics, we can be sure they'll run with it, and the philosophers who hand them the ball may wind up being surprised at just how far they run. The politics of self-determination is full of perils, and the bolstering of this politics with the rhetoric of rights is likely to make these perils even more fearsome.

Source

This chapter is a revised version of an essay originally published in *National Self-Determination and Secession,* ed. Margaret Moore (Oxford: Oxford University Press, 1998), 158-80.

Notes

1 In various places, I've tried to explain why I find the communitarian label more confusing than helpful: see, for instance, Ronald Beiner, *What's the Matter with Liberalism?* (Berkeley: University of California Press, 1992), chapter 2; and Beiner, *Philosophy in a Time of Lost Spirit: Essays on Contemporary Theory* (Toronto: University of Toronto Press, 1997), chapter 1.

2 Cf. Mary Ann Glendon, *Rights Talk: The Impoverishment of Political Discourse* (New York: Free Press, 1991), x-xi, 14, 16.

3 Ibid., xi.

4 See, for instance, Charles Taylor, "Alternative Futures," in *Reconciling the Solitudes: Essays on Canadian Federalism and Nationalism,* ed. Guy Laforest (Montreal and Kingston: McGill-Queen's University Press, 1993), 87-119. For my own version of this argument, see Beiner, *What's the Matter with Liberalism?* chapter 4.

5 Sandel's criticisms of the culture of rights become more explicit in his later work on the "procedural republic."

6 Michael J. Sandel, *Liberalism and the Limits of Justice* (Cambridge: Cambridge University Press, 1982), 31-2. Cf. Allen E. Buchanan's characterization of the communitarian critique of justice: "Assessing the Communitarian Critique of Liberalism," *Ethics* 99 (July 1989): 853.

7 Cf. Edward Andrew, *Shylock's Rights: A Grammar of Lockian Claims* (Toronto: University of Toronto Press, 1988): "[It's not the case that] the more rights, the better the society. [On the contrary,] rights are to be understood as necessary evils, as claims against others that are necessary to societies based on conflict and competition ... to be conceived more as claims *against* others rather than as joint entitlements constituting a moral community. We have rights *against* others as we have duties *towards* one another" (17-20).

8 Glendon, *Rights Talk,* 175.

9 Alasdair MacIntyre, "Rights, Practices and Marxism," *Analyse and Kritik* 7 (1985): 239.

10 Glendon implicitly accepts this point when she mentions that the rhetoric of rights serves to legitimate "individual *and* group egoism." *Rights Talk,* 171, my italics.

11 Beiner, *What's the Matter with Liberalism?* 42.

12 For a small but typical example, see Susan Delacourt, "Spectre of Split Spawned Plan B Strategy," *Globe and Mail,* 30 October 1996, referring to the "angry Quebec commentary about [Ottawa's] alleged interference in the province's right to self-determination" (A10). If there were indeed a national *right* to self-determination in a stringent sense, it would be quite true that it would be illegitimate for the rest of the country to "interfere" in Quebec's exercise of that right (including deciding for itself the conditions of its exercise). But it is worth mentioning that the political initiative that aroused this heated reaction, namely the federal government's attempt to clarify the conditions of a lawful secession, which as such presupposed an acknowledgment of the possibility of secession, would be considered as *exceeding* the requirements of justice by many of the philosophers who defend a right to secede!

13 For instance, there are certainly strong elements of the first rhetoric in René Lévesque, *An Option for Quebec* (Toronto: McClelland and Stewart, 1968). In typical speeches of Lucien Bouchard, on the other hand, despite the fact that he is hardly the most immoderate among Quebec nationalists, the second rhetoric clearly tends to be predominant.

14 See Ronald Dworkin, "Rights As Trumps," in *Theories of Rights,* ed. Jeremy Waldron (Oxford: Oxford University Press, 1984), 153-67.

15 See Allen Buchanan, "Theories of Secession," *Philosophy and Public Affairs* 26, 1 (1997): 36, 37; more generally, see Allen Buchanan, *Secession: The Morality of Political Divorce from Fort Sumter to Lithuania and Quebec* (Boulder, CO: Westview Press, 1991), 64-7.

16 Wayne Norman, "The Ethics of Secession As the Regulation of Secessionist Politics," in *National Self-Determination and Secession,* ed. Margaret Moore (Oxford: Oxford University Press, 1998), 52-5.

17 When I speak of partnership, I mean shared citizenship in a full federation. Of course, Quebec sovereigntists also say they desire some kind of postindependence partnership with English-speaking Canada, but it remains very questionable whether anything would come of this promised partnership.

18 I don't mean to suggest that Quebec nationalists *welcome* partition along ethnic lines. Clearly, nothing infuriates them more than the claims made upon Quebec territory by non-francophone partitionists. On the other hand, whether these nationalists are willing to acknowledge it or not, the "right" of non-francophone communities to secede from an independent Quebec corresponds to the logic of the nationalists' own project to partition the existing federation.

19 Cf. William A. Galston, "Political Economy and the Politics of Virtue: U.S. Public Philosophy at Century's End," in *Debating Democracy's Discontent: Essays on American Politics, Law, and Public Philosophy*, ed. Anita L. Allen and Milton C. Regan Jr. (New York: Oxford University Press, 1998): "There is a temptation to regard the language of rights, standing alone, as an adequate moral vocabulary. But of course it is not. The assertion 'I have the right to do X,' even if accurate, does not warrant the conclusion that 'X is the right thing to do.' The gap between rights and rightness can only be filled with a moral discourse that goes well beyond rights-talk" (76).

20 Bernard Yack, "Reconciling Liberalism and Nationalism," *Political Theory* 23, 1 (1995): 174; the context is a criticism of Yael Tamir's theory of nationalism.

21 David Miller, "Secession and the Principle of Nationality," in *National Self-Determination and Secession*, ed. Moore: "I say 'a claim' rather than 'a right' in order to signal that the claim in question is not necessarily an overriding one, but may be defeated by other considerations" (65). The point here is that the implication of "overridingness" is a familiar feature of the language of rights.

22 Ibid., 69. Cf. David Miller, *On Nationality* (Oxford: Clarendon Press, 1995): "It devalues the currency of rights to announce rights which in their nature are sometimes incapable of fulfilment ... this applies to the alleged right of national self-determination. I have therefore couched the proposition that I wish to defend in terms of a 'good claim' to political self-determination, recognizing that there will be cases where the claim cannot be met" (81).

23 Buchanan, *Secession*, 48-52. Although Buchanan presents his book as a defence of *group* rights, it is somewhat astonishing to what extent he subordinates issues of nationality, ethnicity, and cultural identity to issues of distributive justice.

24 Ibid., 49. Also: "An unlimited right to secede for any and every ethnic group or 'people' would be a dangerous thing indeed" (20); and "this principle [the right of self-determination as a normative nationalist principle], and hence its use as a justification for secession, must be resolutely rejected" (102). Cf. Buchanan's criticisms of "the Nationalist Principle" (or what he calls the "Ascriptive-Group variant of Primary Right Theory") in "Theories of Secession," 44-61.

25 Yael Tamir, *Liberal Nationalism* (Princeton, NJ: Princeton University Press, 1993): "The right to national self-determination ... stakes a cultural rather than a political claim, namely, it is the right to preserve the existence of a nation as a distinct cultural entity ... national claims are not synonymous with demands for political sovereignty" (57). According to Tamir's self-description of the project, what she offers is "a cultural interpretation of the right to national self-determination" (58). Yack ("Reconciling Liberalism and Nationalism," 172) refers to Tamir's "depoliticization" of national identity, which seems a fair characterization of Tamir's nationalism.

26 Philosophers will assume that the way to be a nationalist is to affirm a *universal* right to self-determination, but those with a more historical bent may be inclined to be rather skeptical about how reliably universalistic most nationalists in fact are. See, for instance, Eric Hobsbawm, "Identity Politics and the Left," *New Left Review* 217 (1996): "Zionist Jewish nationalism, whether we sympathize with it or not, is exclusively about Jews, and hang – or rather bomb – the rest. All nationalisms are. The nationalist claim that they are for *everyone's* right to self-determination is bogus" (43). A good test of Hobsbawm's thesis is to see how Quebec nationalists react to the claims to national self-determination on the part of Aboriginal groups in Quebec: see Ramsay Cook, *Canada, Québec, and the Uses of Nationalism*,

2nd ed. (Toronto: McClelland and Stewart, 1995), 81, 245, 264 n. 23, and 286 n. 20. Michael Walzer is sympathetic to neo-nationalism, yet he acknowledges "the consistent failure of new nation-states to meet the moral test of the nation that comes next, to recognize in others the rights vindicated by their own independence." "The New Tribalism," in *Theorizing Nationalism,* ed. Ronald Beiner (Albany: State University of New York Press, 1999), 214. See also Walzer, "Nation and Universe," in *The Tanner Lectures on Human Values XI: 1990,* ed. Grethe B. Peterson (Salt Lake City: University of Utah Press, 1990), 549-52.

27 Avishai Margalit and Joseph Raz, "National Self-Determination," *Journal of Philosophy 87,* 9 (1990): 439-61. See also Kai Nielsen, "Secession: The Case of Quebec," *Journal of Applied Philosophy* 10, 1 (1993): 29-43.

28 Harry Beran, "A Liberal Theory of Secession," *Political Studies* 32, 1 (1984): 21-31. See Buchanan's helpful typology of theories in "Theories of Secession"; Buchanan labels Beran's theory an "Associative-Group variant of Primary Right Theory."

29 It should be noted, however, that it is not Buchanan's purpose to *prohibit* secessions where these are agreed to by the parties involved. Presumably, he would not object to Quebec secession if it was accepted by the Canadian political community as a whole, but he would say that Quebeckers could not *insist* on their secession on grounds of justice if the rest of Canada said no (and I assume the same goes for the Czech-Slovak divorce). As Buchanan puts it, "Remedial Right Only Theories are not as restrictive as they might first appear" ("Theories of Secession," 36).

30 I certainly don't mean to present this argument as the basis for a general right, for reasons offered in Yack's critique of Tamir, cited above. In agreement with Yack, it seems to me self-evident folly to make judgments of what is advisable or inadvisable in advance of knowing a great deal about the historical context shaping particular nationality conflicts.

31 Cf. Andrew, *Shylock's Rights*: "Rights ... function to secure choice rather than direct us to what is choiceworthy" (20).

32 See for instance Margalit and Raz, "National Self-Determination": "the right to self-determination is neither absolute nor unconditional" (461); Daniel Philpott, "Self-Determination in Practice," in *National Self-Determination and Secession,* ed. Moore, 80-1.

33 Buchanan, "Assessing the Communitarian Critique of Liberalism," 855.

34 Buchanan, *Secession,* 152.

35 Ibid., 20, 103-4.

36 Margalit and Raz, "National Self-Determination," 458, my italics.

37 Philpott, "Self-Determination in Practice," 96-7, 90.

38 Margaret Moore, "The Territorial Dimension of Self-Determination," in *National Self-Determination and Secession,* ed. Moore, 150.

39 Philpott, for instance, speaks of "a presumption against secession" ("Self-Determination in Practice," 83); he also refers to secession as "a last resort" (ibid., 86, 87, 90). This seems to be Moore's position as well ("The Territorial Dimension of Self-Determination," 154).

40 Margalit and Raz, "National Self-Determination," 454.

41 Miller, "Secession and the Principle of Nationality," 71. Philpott, too, concedes that there is a legitimate worry that having won recognition of its independent statehood, the new state will be able to evade "follow up" on the part of the states granting recognition (which *ought to* provide long-term oversight and enforcement of the new state's commitments but may fail to do so) ("Self-Determination in Practice," 86). As Philpott puts it in the original draft of this essay: "We face ... the prospect of enforcing the principle, but not the qualifications."

42 Miller, "Secession and the Principle of Nationality," 71. Cf. Donald L. Horowitz, "Self-Determination: Politics, Philosophy, Law," in *National Self-Determination and Secession,* ed. Moore: "The inability to forecast the emergence of an illiberal regime with any degree of reliability renders [qualifications such as the insistence on minority rights] illusory" (198).

43 See Bogdan Denitch, *Ethnic Nationalism: The Tragic Death of Yugoslavia,* rev. ed. (Minneapolis: University of Minnesota Press, 1996), 12-13, 51-3. See also Horowitz, "Self-Determination: Politics, Philosophy, Law," 189; and Philpott, "Self-Determination in Practice," 88.

44 Cf. Anthony D. Smith, *Theories of Nationalism* (London: Duckworth, 1971): "Nationalism confuses principles with interests. It makes conflicts that much less amenable to a negotiated peace, because men will not compromise over principles" (10). Naturally, the main culprit here is precisely the principle of national self-determination.

45 Cf. Eric Hobsbawm, "Some Reflections on 'The Break-up of Britain,'" *New Left Review* 105 (1977): "Any finite number of [sovereign] states must exclude some potential candidates from statehood ... the argument for the formation of any independent nation-state must always be an *ad hoc* argument, which undermines the case for *universal* self-determination by separatism. The irony of nationalism is that the argument for the separation of Scotland from England is exactly analogous to the argument for the separation of the Shetlands from Scotland; and so are the arguments against both separations" (13).

46 Horowitz, "Self-Determination: Politics, Philosophy, Law," 200.

47 As cited earlier (see n. 21 above), David Miller makes the same point when he explains his reluctance to apply the term *rights* to this question.

10
Citizenship and Nationalism: Is Canada a "Real Country"?

My concern with the problem of citizenship first arose out of an interest in Hannah Arendt. Arendt, of course, tried to formulate, in books such as *The Human Condition* and *On Revolution,* an argument for a more robust, more muscular conception of political agency than liberal societies typically make available, and she argued, in *On Revolution* in particular, that the history of liberal America had betrayed its own original civic-republican revolutionary impulse. It goes without saying that implicit in all this is a radical challenge to everything we normally associate with liberal conceptions of civic membership. But in thinking more about this whole problem, I gradually came around to the conclusion that, despite appearances, Arendt is only to a very limited degree a bona fide theorist of citizenship. For what distinguishes thought about citizenship is the effort to answer the question: why commit one's political allegiance to *this* political community rather than *that* political community? What are the *bounds* of political community, and on what basis do citizens commit themselves emotionally and existentially (as actually defining their own identity) to some specific, identifiable community of fellow citizens? In other words, in theorizing citizenship, we must take up questions of *membership, national identity, civic allegiance,* and all the commonalities of sentiment and obligation that give effect to the legal and ethical bonds constitutive of a given political community. These questions one will never find addressed in Hannah Arendt. In that sense, she is a theorist of *political agency* rather than a theorist of *citizenship* properly speaking: she treats the bounds of the political community as if it were a given, whereas much of the drama of contemporary political life, as we see all around us today, consists in efforts to define and redefine boundaries of political community that are anything but given. Hence the irony of attempts by various people influenced by the communitarian theories of the 1980s to appropriate Arendt as a good communitarian. In fact, there is *nothing* "communitarian" about Arendt's theorizing: she displays no interest in questions about communal attachments, shared culture, or national or subnational identity as bases for political agency. If anything, she tends to be *hostile* to the idea of grounding civic participation in communal attachments of any kind. Part of the story here, of course, is her intense antipathy to nationalism, and here, I must confess, I fully share her anxieties. But this leaves us with the problem of supplying *some* account of why citizens commit themselves to the particular locus of political agency that they do, and Hannah Arendt, I'm afraid, offers no answer to this sort of question.

Rival Conceptions of Citizenship

I do not want to pretend that I have fully developed theoretical answers to these puzzles. But if political philosophy is to be helpful to us in providing a source of theoretical alternatives, it should at least be possible, as a necessary preliminary, to survey the range of possibilities among theories of citizenship. The following is hardly an exhaustive treatment of the topic, but it can at least serve as a sketch of some alternative conceptions of citizenship, along with some very brief suggestions as to why each of them falls short of a satisfactory solution to the conundrum we face.

1 *The liberal conception of citizenship*   Citizenship = allegiance to the state as something that enforces the rule of law and acts as a protector of universal human rights. But it is not clear why one should be especially committed to state X rather than state Y if state Y is *also* a protector of human rights. Moreover, liberalism seems philosophically to entail a cultural cosmopolitanism that dissolves civic boundaries and ultimately subverts citizenship as membership in a bounded community.[1] In any case, it is not clear that liberalism provides a sufficiently robust experience of civic identity, that is, a sufficiently robust basis for civic membership, especially in the face of the challenge of twentieth-century nationalism.[2]

2 *The pluralist conception of citizenship*   Citizenship = provision by the state of an open framework for the flowering of group identity or group purposes, either in civil society, or in multicultural subgroups. This conception is available in both liberal and leftish versions. In chapter 1 of this volume, I offer some criticisms of such conceptions under the heading of "groupism" or groupist ideologies.[3] The basic argument is that if the state exists to serve a set of more partial group identities, allegiance to these constitutive group identities ultimately "trumps" allegiance to the larger civic community. Naturally, defenders of this groupist politics frame their justification in terms of "inclusivity," and would be reluctant to concede that any of this poses a threat to the idea of citizenship. Nonetheless, I think an argument can be made that the logic of their view points in a direction that may ultimately be subversive of the notion of a *shared* civic membership.[4]

3 *The welfarist conception of citizenship*   Citizenship = allegiance to the state defined by receipt of benefits and social services dispensed by the welfare state. The problem, as we saw very dramatically in the 1980s, is that when

[handwritten margin notes: THIS IS WHY E.U. CANNOT INCLUDE SOC. C'R. RIGHTS IN ITS CITIZ'P AND WHY IT MUST HAVE A CITIZ'P; CAUSE NATION STATE CITIZ'P THAT INVOLVES ONE WAY TO THE COLLAPSE]

the welfare state undergoes a "fiscal crisis," with shrinking revenues and mounting social responsibilities, this form of citizenship threatens to collapse. The welfarist conception is associated with what T.H. Marshall called "social rights"; the kinds of crisis experienced by this definition of citizenship are nicely summed up in Michael Ignatieff's writings on citizenship.[5] The crisis highlighted by Ignatieff is by no means limited to the 1980s – it continues today. In any case, there is a more general problem here, which matches the one we identified in the case of liberal citizenship: namely, to the extent that two states offer identical social benefits, upheld by a social morality that the two societies more or less share (e.g., Norway and Sweden), there must be some further dimension to civic consciousness that explains why we have two welfare states here rather than one.[6]

4 *Nationalism* Citizenship = the vehicle for the furthering of national identity (where "national" isn't taken to be merely a synonym for "civic," but refers to some more specific ethnolinguistic, cultural, or religious community). This alternative does at least provide a definite answer to the question of the bounds of civic membership. But it exacts a heavy price: what we might call a contraction of our *human* identity.[7] Proponents of so-called liberal nationalism want to believe that we can have our cake and eat it, that is, have a robust attachment to national identity without lessening our commitment to universal humanity, but everything that we have experienced in world politics since the epochal year of 1989 encourages skepticism about the prospects of an easy reconciliation between nationalism and liberalism.

5 *"Arendtian" citizenship* Citizenship = the means for giving effect to our noblest human capacities: our power to realize ourselves as political animals. This is what Richard Flathman labels: "high citizenship."[8] This conception is attractive insofar as it highlights the deficiencies of liberalism without falling into the trap of nationalism. But as I discussed above, it offers very little in answer to the question of why political agency should be enacted within one political community rather than another.

The Problem of Citizenship:
Why It Matters to (for Instance) Canadians

As suggested already, the problem of citizenship as a challenge for political philosophy (to say nothing of the challenge it poses for political practice) is a problem of locating a principled basis for delineating the boundaries of political membership. Perhaps there is more of an excuse for neglecting or abstracting from these questions of the bounds of political community if you are writing about citizenship in the contemporary United States, where the boundaries of political community are more or less a given. (Or at least they are so *today* – they certainly weren't so at the time of the Civil War. In fact, even today they aren't entirely a given, if, say, you belong to the

Nation of Islam, or to an Aboriginal community asserting sovereignty or quasi-sovereignty.) In any case, these questions are absolutely inescapable if you are trying to think about citizenship in contemporary Canada (to say nothing, for the moment, of the Balkans, the former Soviet Union, Lebanon, Northern Ireland, South Africa, Israel, etcetera, etcetera). It is no secret that Canada has been struggling with these dilemmas of political self-definition for several decades, and the constitutional wrangling that culminated in the Charlottetown Accord referendum in the autumn of 1992 was animated by the desire to arrive at a nationally agreed definition of civic community, and as such, ended in a failure of colossal proportions.

Perhaps we can all come to an agreement on a resolve not to talk about our constitutional quandaries – at least for a certain period of time. But what we *cannot* do is to sustain a political community indefinitely as if those quandaries never existed, or as if they had actually been resolved – just as two spouses who fundamentally lack a shared understanding of what their marriage is about may be so wearied by their arguments that they agree, for a time, to act as if there were no underlying problem, but what they cannot do is sustain a conjugal relationship permanently in default of a basic shared understanding of what defines it. (As if to prove my point, the Chrétien government came into power in October 1993 with a promise to say nothing more about the festering constitutional mess; today, the constitutional problem is back at the centre of the government's preoccupations.) I recall reading a couple of years ago an article by Kenneth Whyte, who used to write a weekly column in the *Globe and Mail* defining the perspective of "The West" (i.e., Western Canada), in which he cited a study by an academic in Alberta who had calculated exactly what each province contributes to the national government in tax revenues and exactly what each province receives back in payments and services.[9] It struck me when I read this that you cannot sustain a country, as an integral political community, where these sorts of things are calculated and quantified. Again, one can't help thinking of domestic analogies: a family where what each family member contributes and what they receive back in "subsidies" from other family members is quantified and compared is no longer really a family at all.

In all of these respects Canada offers an excellent model of what it is to engage in theoretical reflection on the nature of citizenship, and the perplexities and challenges of trying to sustain a civic community in the late twentieth century. Let no one be deluded about the magnitude of the stakes involved: once citizenship is up for grabs, there is no telling where the process of contestation and dissolution will end. This is, alas, no longer a merely theoretical problem, for since the 30 October 1995 referendum there has arisen an extremely vocal "partitionist" movement among Quebec anglophones, arguing that if Canada is divisible, so too would an independent Quebec be divisible, and that if Quebec secedes it ought to be partitioned along basically ethnic lines. These partitionist notions have been given some encouragement by new Minister of Intergovernment Affairs Stéphane Dion, Prime Minister Jean Chrétien, and especially Minister of Indian Affairs Ron Irwin. So Quebec nationalism, as all nationalisms do, seems to have aroused a kind of counter-nationalism, even within the island of Montreal. Naturally, the more moderate elements of the Montreal anglophone community have realized that these are Bosnian or Belfast-like scenarios, and are to be avoided at all costs. But the Crees in Northern Quebec have an especially forceful case (their claims to national self-determination are undeniable once one accepts the legitimacy of nationalist discourse, and they, unlike the Québécois, have backed up their claim with a 96.3 percent endorsement of the Cree "general will" in a vote held on 24 October 1995). If there is a flashpoint in any possible conflagration in Quebec, this is it. In any case, the theoretical challenge here seems inescapable: how can one affirm national self-determination for the Québécois in relation to Canada and yet deny national self-determination to the Crees in relation to an independent Quebec? Or, to take a non-Canadian example that is exactly parallel: how can one affirm national self-determination for Ukraine in relation to the former Soviet Union, and yet deny national self-determination to the Russians in Crimea in relation to Ukraine? Yet nationalists *do* typically claim national self-determination for themselves and reject it for the next subcommunity demanding nationhood as the civic community slides perilously down the slippery slope.[10] Nationalists in Quebec have scarcely begun to think through the ultimate meaning of these theoretical predicaments, nor have they given sufficient thought to where this might lead politically should the process of civic re-definition begin to spin out of control. I recall a former colleague of mine in Israel once expressing surprise that it never occurred to Canadians, in their charming innocence, simply to send in the troops to put down Quebec's challenge to Canadian sovereignty. Naturally, I was quite shocked by this suggestion, and I guess that he might have been shocked that I was shocked. But what is *really* shocking is that, these days, many Canadians are themselves beginning to think the unthinkable (for instance, using the power of the federal armed forces to defend the territory of the Quebec Crees against the involuntary imposition of Québécois sovereignty). It may be an unhappy thought, but the fact is that no one can guarantee that armed confrontation is an impossibility in *any* society where the boundaries of civic community are subject to renegotiation. Of course, Canada is not Yugoslavia, and I don't think anyone imagines that English- and French-speaking Canadians are about to start fighting each other with the ferocity of Serbs and Croats. On the other hand, it suffices to think of the level of political tension during the Oka crisis in Quebec in the summer of 1990 to realize that even in a society as peace-loving as Canada, one simply cannot rule out the arising of circumstances that might provoke a resort to violent conflict. All of these rather sobering reflections serve merely to highlight the importance of coming to a better theoretical understanding of the basis upon which a people, or several peoples together, can secure a durable ground for shared civic identity.

The Nationalist Challenge to Canadian Citizenship

In an earlier section I sketched five rival conceptions of citizenship. Of these, the one that is of most interest to me for present purposes is the one that identifies citizenship and national belonging (where, again, "national" connotes some more robust pre-political allegiance than mere civic membership). My own actual citizenship – that is, membership in "Canada" as a political community – gives me some especially urgent reasons for giving privileged attention to the relation between citizenship and nationalism; for as readers may or may not know, the meaningfulness of Canadian citizenship has recently been challenged and impugned by Lucien Bouchard, the leader of the sovereigntist movement in Quebec, and the newly acclaimed premier of Quebec (acclaimed, of course, not by the electorate of Quebec, but by the membership of the ruling party of Quebec, the Parti Québécois). The new federal minister of intergovernmental affairs, Stéphane Dion, soon after his appointment made the observation that if Canada's boundaries are not sacred and immutable, it was unclear why Quebec should assume that *its* boundaries *are* sacred and immutable. To this (politically provocative but theoretically incontestable) suggestion, Bouchard gave the following reply: "We are a people, we are a nation; and as a nation we have a fundamental right to keep and maintain our territory. Canada is divisible because Canada is not a real country. There are two peoples, two nations and two territories. And this one is ours."[11] Lucien Bouchard is not only a leading political figure in my country (in fact, the one who may have the greatest sway over its future destiny); he was also, until very recently, the leader of Her Majesty's Loyal Opposition in the *federal* Parliament, was at earlier stages of his career both *Canada's* representative as ambassador to France and a *federal* cabinet minister, and he remains today, like me, a citizen of Canada. Yet notwithstanding these facts, he declares that Canadian citizenship denotes membership in a phantom country, and that those citizens of Canada who believe themselves to hold civic membership in a real country are deluded.

A Snapshot of the Quebec Scene

This artillery burst was immediately followed by a war of words, conducted in the Montreal newspapers, between Bouchard and former prime minister Pierre Trudeau, each of whom accused the other of being a traitor to democracy and a traitor to Quebec. Before pursuing a few theoretical implications of this battle between nationalists and anti-nationalists in Quebec, it might be helpful to non-Canadian readers to present a thumbnail sketch of the political situation in Quebec. Quebec has a population of roughly seven million. Of these, about 82 percent are francophone, 9 percent are anglophone, and 9 percent are what in Quebec one calls "allophone," that is, immigrants whose language of origin is neither French nor English. In addition, and of enormous significance for Quebec politics, there are approximately 80,000 members of various Aboriginal groups (Cree, Mohawk, Inuit, Montagnais, etcetera).

The referendum of 30 October 1995 was profoundly traumatizing for English Canada – there is no question about it. Technically, the federalist side won the referendum, so why the trauma? The non-francophone populations in Quebec, anglophone and allophone, are solidly against the sovereigntist project, so that means that the pro-sovereignty vote is almost entirely francophone. The vote in the 1980 referendum was 60 percent *non* and 40 percent *oui,* which means that francophone support for the *oui* side was just under 50 percent. The 1995 vote was dramatically different: 50.5 percent *non* and 49.5 percent *oui* (and this, in a referendum that the federalist side assumed, until virtually the last week, that it would win fairly easily and by a healthy margin), which means that a *majority* of francophones, thought to be in the vicinity of 63 percent, voted *oui.* Having to confront the fact that 60 to 65 percent of francophone Quebeckers could vote in favour of sovereignty is like learning that the country has just had a death sentence passed upon it (or it could easily be perceived as such).

Perhaps there is a minority of francophone Quebeckers who are what one might call "hardline federalists," that is, Trudeauite anti-nationalists, but despite Trudeau's own popularity and the popularity of his party in Quebec during the Trudeau years (1968-84), this minority, if it exists, is more or less politically insignificant. The majority of francophones today are either so-called soft nationalists or else they are less-soft nationalists.[12] As regards the latter, it can be assumed that they number somewhere between 40 and 50 percent of the total population of Quebec, or between 50 and 65 percent of the francophone population. The sovereigntist vote in the last federal and provincial elections gives us a rough guide here: in the Quebec provincial election of 12 September 1994, the PQ's percentage of the total vote was 44.7 percent (approximately 53 percent of the francophone population); in the federal election of 25 October 1993, the Bloc Québécois vote in Quebec was just under 50 percent – virtually the same as the *oui* vote in the 1995 referendum.[13]

Occasionally, leaders of the sovereigntist movement such as Jacques Parizeau slip up and make self-incriminating references to *québécois de souche* (old-stock Quebeckers) or *québécois pur laine* (true Quebeckers). However, the mainstream nationalist movement in contemporary Quebec is desperately anxious to present itself as a *non-ethnic* nationalist movement advancing the political aspirations of Quebec interpreted as a *territorial* community of (francophone, anglophone, allophone, and Aboriginal) citizens. Admittedly, it is not easy to make this argument, given that only a tiny minority within the non-francophone communities have any sympathy for the sovereigntist project; the vast majority regard this project with nothing but dread and loathing, and many of these non-francophones emigrate from the province every time it appears that the nationalists have taken another step closer to attaining their goal. Most damaging of all to the nationalist insistence on the trans-ethnic character of their project is the fact that the Aboriginal communities are vehemently opposed to it: in the week prior to the 30 October referendum, several of the Aboriginal communities held their own referenda, and in each case rejected the project of Quebec secession by near-unanimous margins (ranging from 95 to 99 percent). At the present conjuncture, one would have to say that the people for whom there is the most likelihood of blood being shed in the name of Canadian citizenship are the Crees in Northern Quebec. It is hard to believe that they would go to this extremity out of a profound affection for Canada or a deep attachment to Canadian political community (they have their own nationalism, and therefore their own claims to quasi-sovereignty). Rather, their motivation would surely be their resolute *aversion* to a Québécois definition of citizenship that the Crees obviously regard as more threatening to their own identity and way of life than the Canadian status quo. However weak may be their attachment to Canadian political membership, they infinitely prefer it to the prospect of a battle between two warring nationalisms.

I began this section by mentioning the latest Trudeau-Bouchard duel, so let me come back to these two titanic figures, who "metaphysically," one might say, dwarf all the other contemporary players. Pierre Trudeau has devoted his entire political career, in fact pretty much his entire adult life, to the battle against nationalism in Quebec. He remains even today the most formidable voice of anti-nationalism in Canada, just as Lucien Bouchard is today the most formidable voice of Quebec nationalism. For Quebec nationalists, Trudeau is certainly the one who remains the "Great Satan" of Canadian federalism. Pierre Trudeau has been out of office for twelve years and since leaving public office has only very rarely made public statements or public interventions, yet he has been extraordinarily important in the continuing debates. It is perhaps hard for non-Canadians to comprehend how an ex-politician holding no elected office can be so central to constitutional politics in Canada; however, it is a plain fact that even to this day, he can stand up to the nationalists with a political authority that no other federalist politician can command (certainly the present prime minister of Canada doesn't come remotely close!). With but a few forceful and carefully chosen forays from his life as a private citizen, Trudeau managed to help turn the tide against the two major constitutional initiatives of the Mulroney Conservatives, the Meech Lake Accord and the Charlottetown Accord. The Trudeau argument is that the genuine political aspirations of francophone Canadians focused on two concrete objectives: more power for French-speaking Canadians in the federal government in Ottawa; and nationally enforced individual rights to (judicial and bureaucratic) services in French.[14] Trudeau argues that his regime fully satisfied both demands (and secured constitutional protection for the latter with the 1982 Charter of Rights and Freedoms). Trudeau further argues that any other demands emanating from the nationalist movement are not intended as determinate objectives for negotiation, but merely movable tokens in a game of endless grievance-mongering.

My own view is that most of what Pierre Trudeau says about Quebec nationalism is true. But it can be a bad and destructive politics to try to hold a political community to standards of theoretical truth. Thus I find myself here somewhat mired in the ironies of theory and practice: *as a theorist,* I'm basically on Trudeau's side in his polemics against nationalism; *as a citizen,* however, I'm against him, and regard him as having done serious damage to the prospects of Canadian unity. In his recent exchanges with Premier Bouchard, Trudeau deployed a rhetoric of fearless truth-telling. But one may question whether a stance of uncompromising truth-telling is the best way to sustain a political community; it occurs to me that in his days as a student of political theory, Trudeau might have spent more of his time imbibing the wisdom of Burke.

Here again, the analogy with domestic life sheds helpful light on the matter. In order to sustain a marriage, one may need to accommodate oneself to much that one's spouse believes, simply because that is what he or she believes and not because one thinks those beliefs are true or are capable of ultimate theoretical vindication. To treat one's conjugal partner as an interlocutor in a philosophy seminar is to do unavoidable violence to the marriage one hopes to sustain. The same thing applies to the relation between national partners within a political community. Now, to be sure, things may eventually reach the point in a strained marriage where the weight of falsehood or mythification that one is required to accommodate for the sake of the marriage becomes so large that the marriage itself loses its attraction, and so it collapses. It is possible that Canada as a political community is approaching a collapse of this kind. But for those, like myself, who continue to feel an undying attachment to the idea of Canada as a political community, this is a harsh pill to swallow. In any case, this is the judgment that Trudeau and his followers have evidently embraced: namely, that it would be preferable for Canada as a political community to cease to exist than for it to continue abiding the falsehoods and mythification of nationalists in Quebec. Better to have no country at all than to have it on terms that require concessions to the nationalist vision of the world![15]

The political reality is that Trudeau's hardline anti-nationalism has very little support among francophone Québécois today (notwithstanding the fact that they voted for the Trudeau Liberals in federal elections from the late 1960s to early '80s); instead, Trudeau's following in Quebec at the moment is for the most part limited to the more extreme, less compromising segment of anglophone opinion. (In the other nine provinces, the Trudeau vision of Canada continues to have a substantial following, although here things are complicated by the fact that many who share Trudeau's hostility to Quebec nationalism, e.g., Reform Party supporters in the West, never accepted Trudeau's policies of official bilingualism and enhanced francophone presence in Ottawa.) As I noted above, Quebec francophones are divided into "soft nationalists" and "hard nationalists," and neither group has much sympathy for Trudeau's view of federalism (though admittedly the latter express their disdain for Trudeau with much more vehemence – and vice versa). According to the current nationalist narrative, Trudeau was the chief culprit in the two slaps in the face administered to Quebec by English-speaking Canada during the last decade and a half: in the early 1980s, the patriation of the Canadian Constitution over Quebec's objections; and in the late '80s, the collapse of the Meech Lake Accord. Needless to say, Trudeau made no apology for his words and deeds in these major constitutional events, and he responded to his accusers by making the countercharge that these ways of telling the story were mere inventions of nationalist mythology.

Let me elaborate what I meant in saying that while much of Trudeau's critique of nationalism is true, its practical consequences cannot be anything other than very damaging. What are the truths that Trudeau is resolved to tell in the face of nationalist mythmaking? They are, basically, these: that Quebec nationalism is backward-looking, resentful, that its exaggerated displays of wounded pride are the expression of an underlying inferiority complex and that it sustains an inflated sense of victimization by giving too much weight to past grievances and not enough weight to the fact that the Québécois are no longer an oppressed people and have ample instruments at both the federal level and provincial level for protection of their culture.[16] Trudeau is right that Canada is already a highly decentralized federation, even without taking into account the announced readiness of the present federal government to negotiate further decentralization.[17] Trudeau is certainly right that no amount of decentralization short of outright sovereignty will satisfy the nationalists. I believe a strong case can be made for the truth of most of these claims, yet Trudeau's forceful articulation of the case against nationalism has had and continues to have practical consequences that are anything but helpful. Canada cannot be Canada without Quebec, and therefore the avoidance of secession is a practical imperative of the first order. The political reality, however, is – once again – that the majority of francophones in Quebec will not buy the Trudeau line on the adequacy of status-quo federalism, and so if secession is to be avoided, a set of political responses must be designed that accommodates nationalist sentiment: the latter is what Trudeau's aggressive rhetoric of anti-nationalism entirely rules out.[18]

That, at a very quick glance, is the landscape of Quebec-Canada nationalist and anti-nationalist politics.

Restatement of the Theoretical Problem, and Its Practical Urgency

Let's come back to Premier Bouchard and his slander against Canadian citizenship.[19] Various theorists of nationalism have noted the fascinating discrepancy between "the 'political' power of nationalisms [and] their philosophical poverty and even incoherence."[20] This observation applies in principle to all nationalisms: we shouldn't be surprised, then, that we can find ample illustration of it in nationalist discourse in Quebec. During the October 1995 referendum, one of the notable slogans of the *oui* campaign led by Parizeau and Bouchard was that the object of Quebec's aspirations was to be a "normal country." The clear implication was that Canada, as it now exists, is a freak, an aberration, one of nature's misbegotten. But there is surely something odd about this idea of "normality." Ernest Gellner points out that, taking language alone as one's index for the presence of a national culture, the potential candidates for political nationhood must be in excess of eight thousand, whereas the number of states in the world is presently around two hundred, many of which fail to count as bona fide nation-states.[21] If one were really serious about the assertion that the norm consists in a one-to-one correspondence between nation and state, there ought to be well over eight thousand nation-states (matching up language/culture and statehood) rather than two hundred or so states, some of which conform more or less to the nation-state model and some of which more or less depart from it.[22] Again, one must have a rather strange notion of "normality" in order to arrive at the nation-state as the *norm*, in relation to which a multination-state such as Canada counts as an abnormal monstrosity. In fact, as Will Kymlicka points out at the beginning of *Multicultural Citizenship*, it would be much more plausible to regard the multination-state as the contemporary norm: "In very few countries can the citizens be said to share the same language, or belong to the same ethnonational group." (South Korea, North Korea, and Iceland constitute rare exceptions to this rule.)[23] When Lucien Bouchard declares that "Canada is not a real country," this naturally invites the challenge: if Quebec were to secede, would *it* be a real country? For it too would be a multination-state, embracing different ethnicities, different cultures, and even subcommunities such as Aboriginal groups with no less a sense than the Québécois of their own nationhood. If the nation-state in a very exacting sense is the norm, one suspects that the independent Republic of Quebec would *also* be abnormal, aberrational.

These points may have some theoretical force, but it is mere realism to acknowledge that arguments of this kind do little to blunt the political efficacy of the nationalist challenge. In order to face up to the challenge, theoretically and politically, it has to be recognized that in the struggle between Canadian citizenship and Québécois nationalism, there is an important sense in which the latter has the upper hand. For whether one finds the nationalist idea attractive or unattractive, the fact remains that it does offer a pretty robust conception of what defines citizenship: namely the promotion or advancement of national identity, national belonging. As we explored earlier in this chapter, the alternative conceptions of citizenship are all in various ways problematical or deficient. The uncomfortable truth, then, is that when Bouchard impugns Canada's reality as a political community, there is no ready answer in the form of a coherent and equally robust rival conception of citizenship on the basis of which the nationalist challenge can be rebuffed. This highlights very emphatically the urgency of theorizing anew the meaning of citizenship.

Source

This chapter is a particularly time-bound piece: it was written more or less in the aftermath of the 1995 Quebec secession referendum. I have not attempted to update it or alter its time-bound character. It was first published in *Citizenship after Liberalism*, ed. Karen Slawner and Mark E. Denham (New York: Peter Lang, 1998), 185-204. I wish to thank Nelson Wiseman and Simone Chambers for helpful criticisms of an earlier version of this essay, and Karen Slawner, whose editorial suggestions prompted this revised version.

Notes

1 See Joseph Carens, "Aliens and Citizens: The Case for Open Borders," in *Theorizing Citizenship*, ed. Ronald Beiner (Albany: State University of New York Press, 1995), 229-53; and see chapter 1 above, pp. 21-2, 33.

2 Jürgen Habermas has proposed what he calls "constitutional patriotism" as an alternative to nationalist definitions of citizenship – namely, shared attachment to liberal-democratic norms as a foundation for civic allegiance and civic identity: see Habermas, "Citizenship and National Identity: Some Reflections on the Future of Europe," in *Theorizing Citizenship*, ed. Beiner, 255-81. This seems like a promising possibility, however it is not entirely clear whether this Habermasian conception takes us any further than the legalistic idea of citizenship already supplied by liberalism. Perhaps it's just a fancier name for liberal citizenship: see, for instance, Perry Anderson, "Nation-States and National Identity," *London Review of Books*, 9 May 1991, 8.

3 See chapter 1 above, esp. pp. 23-9.

4 As the title of Iris Marion Young's contribution to *Theorizing Citizenship* (175-207) makes explicit, the target of her theoretical criticism is "the ideal of universal citizenship." In *Multicultural Citizenship* (Oxford: Clarendon Press, 1995), Will Kymlicka embraces Young's idea of "differentiated citizenship," but I think that there is a greater emphasis in Kymlicka's argument than there is in Young's argument that the purpose here is not sheer affirmation of difference, but rather *integration* into what ought to be a fully inclusive civic community. For an argument that is explicitly "integrationist" without being assimilationist, see Jeff Spinner, *The Boundaries of Citizenship: Race, Ethnicity, and Nationality in the Liberal State* (Baltimore, MD: Johns Hopkins University Press, 1994), 62; cf. 135.

5 See Michael Ignatieff, "The Myth of Citizenship," in *Theorizing Citizenship*, ed. Beiner, 53-77; and Ignatieff, "Citizenship and Moral Narcissism," in *Citizenship*, ed. Geoff Andrews (London: Lawrence and Wishart, 1991), 26-37.

6 Cf. Wayne Norman, "The Ideology of Shared Values," in *Is Quebec Nationalism Just?* ed. Joseph H. Carens (Montreal and Kingston: McGill-Queen's University Press, 1995),

137-59, esp. 141-2. When it is a question of holding together a state threatened by secession, Norman makes a persuasive argument that appeal to so-called shared values won't do the trick.

7   Cf. chapter 1 above, esp. pp. 28-34.

8   See Richard E. Flathman, "Citizenship and Authority: A Chastened View of Citizenship," in *Theorizing Citizenship*, ed. Beiner, 105-51.

9   Kenneth Whyte, "So the Prime Minister Feels Toronto's Pain, Does He? Whadda Card!" *Globe and Mail*, 5 February 1994, D2.

10 For a classic statement of the slippery slope argument (namely, the argument that once the boundaries of civic community are thrown into question, there is in principle no limit to the propagation of smaller and smaller micro-states), see Pierre Elliott Trudeau, *Federalism and the French Canadians* (Toronto: Macmillan, 1968), 158, 192. For a recent attempt to respond to the slippery slope argument, see Michael Walzer, *Thick and Thin: Moral Argument at Home and Abroad* (Notre Dame, IN: University of Notre Dame Press, 1994), chapter 4.

11 Rhéal Séguin, "Cabinet Edgy As Bouchard Takes Over," *Globe and Mail*, 29 January 1996, A4.

12 As Lucien Bouchard put it in one speech: "[even] Quebec federalists are Quebec nationalists, first and foremost." This seems to be true. *Canadian Speeches: Issues of the Day* 9, 8 (speech in the House of Commons, 29 November 1995): 13.

13 It goes without saying that one should be extremely cautious in interpreting exactly what ultimate political preferences are expressed in these votes. While English Canadians have good reason to be traumatized by the size of the *oui* vote on 30 October 1995, it would be foolish to assume that every vote for the PQ, for the BQ, and for the *oui* side in a sovereignty referendum is intended as a vote for the outright secession of Quebec. On the contrary, it is generally assumed that the politics of Quebec nationalism involves a considerable measure of "strategic voting," that is, voting sovereigntist in order to promote a "better deal" for Quebec, or to give Quebec greater leverage in renegotiating Canadian federalism. According to a poll taken after the 1995 referendum, 60 percent of Quebeckers wanted Premier Bouchard to seek a renegotiated federalism rather than to pursue his declared goal of full sovereignty. "Quebeckers Prefer Canada 2-1, Poll Says," *Globe and Mail*, 26 March 1996, A6. This surely indicates that at least some of the Quebeckers who voted *oui* on 30 October (and who may well do likewise in the next referendum) desired something other than independent statehood for Quebec. Quebec offers an excellent illustration of the following observation by E.J. Hobsbawm, *Nations and Nationalism since 1780*, 2nd ed. (Cambridge: Cambridge University Press, 1992): "We know what national parties and movements read into the support of such members of the nation as give them their backing, but not what these customers are after as they purchase the collection of very miscellaneous goods presented to them as a package by the salesmen of national politics" (78-9).

14 Pierre Elliott Trudeau, "Lucien Bouchard, Illusionist," *Montreal Gazette*, 3 February 1996, B3; for the subsequent exchanges in the Trudeau-Bouchard debate, see Lucien Bouchard, "Bouchard: Trudeau's 'I Accuse' Smacks of Déjà Vu," *Globe and Mail*, 12 February 1996, A19, and Pierre Elliott Trudeau, "Bouchard Had No Answer," *Montreal Gazette*, 17 February 1996, B5.

15 This seems to be the clear implication of Trudeau's famous statement that "if [Canada] is going to go, let it go with a bang rather than a whimper"; see Pierre Trudeau, "We, the People of Canada," in *Pierre Trudeau Speaks out on Meech Lake*, ed. Donald Johnston (Toronto: General Paperbacks, 1990), 105.

16 With only very short interruptions since 1968, the prime ministers of Canada have been Quebeckers. Quebeckers, with a quarter of Canada's population, have a guaranteed claim to three out of nine seats on the increasingly important Supreme Court. Whatever may be Pierre Trudeau's sins in the eyes of Quebec nationalists, it is nonetheless a fact that the status of the French language in Canadian life and Canadian political institutions made very considerable advances during his regime. Add to all of this the very substantial powers of the Quebec government referred to in the next note. Those who feel that their ultimate civic allegiance is to Quebec are entitled to seek to carry this to its ultimate political conclusion, namely statehood for Quebec, but it has become decreasingly plausible that this is required as the only possible release from English domination.

17 Cf. Stéphane Dion, "Explaining Quebec Nationalism," in *The Collapse of Canada?* ed. R. Kent Weaver (Washington, DC: Brookings Institution, 1992): "The province of Quebec is the most powerful subnational government in all of the OECD countries in terms of its share of resources and its scope of intervention" (78); "Today the Quebec government and institutions form a quasi state with exclusive or joint responsibility over education, health, welfare, natural resources, municipal affairs, housing, culture, energy, immigration, industry, and language" (102).

18 Note that even as vehement a critic of nationalism as Elie Kedourie concedes that any decision concerning "whether nationalists should be conciliated or resisted ... is necessarily governed by the particular circumstances of each individual case." *Nationalism,* 4th ed. (Oxford: Blackwell, 1993), xix.

19 After I wrote this paper, Lucien Bouchard offered a quasi-retraction of the infamous statement referred to in my subtitle: see "Bouchard Extends Hand to Anglos," *Montreal Gazette,* 12 March 1996, A8. I say a "quasi" retraction because what he actually said was not that Canada *is* a real country but, "I am well aware that Canada is a very real country for the people in this room" (he was addressing an audience of Montreal anglophones). At the same time, he stated that his preferred formulation was that "there are two real countries here," namely, Quebec and English-speaking Canada, which implies that Canada as it currently exists, that is, the status quo of a binational state, is still not a real country.

20 Benedict Anderson, *Imagined Communities,* rev. ed. (London: Verso, 1991), 5.

21 Ernest Gellner, *Nations and Nationalism* (Ithaca, NY: Cornell University Press, 1983), 44-5. Cf. Gellner, "Do Nations Have Navels?" *Nations and Nationalism* 2, part 3 (1996): we live in a world that "has only space for something of the order of 200 or 300 national states" (369). See also Hobsbawm, *Nations and Nationalism since 1780*: "The number of national movements, with or without states, is patently much smaller than the number of human groups capable of forming such movements by current criteria of potential nationhood" (77); "the apparent universal ideological domination of nationalism today is a sort of optical illusion. A world of nations cannot exist, only a world where some potentially national groups, in claiming this status, exclude others from making similar claims, which, as it happens, not many of them do" (78); "it should never be forgotten that [the cases where multi-ethnic and multi-communal states have fractured, or are close to breaking] are special cases in a world where multi-ethnic and multi-communal states are the norm" (179); "probably not much more than a dozen states out of some 180 can plausibly claim that their citizens coincide in any real sense with a single ethnic or linguistic group" (186).

22 It should be mentioned that for Gellner himself, the nation-state *is* the modern norm (though not for nationalist reasons), because in the industrial epoch the organization of social and economic life presupposes a unitary culture presided over by the state as its political guardian. But as Kedourie points out in his rejoinder to Gellner, "The areas ... where industrialism first appeared and made the greatest progress, i.e., Great Britain and the United States of America, are precisely those areas where nationalism is unknown." Kedourie, *Nationalism,* 143. The dispute here is partly a terminological one, since the forms of "national" culture subsumed by Gellner under the rubric of nationalism are clearly much broader than what Kedourie and other critics of nationalism have in mind.

23 Kymlicka, *Multicultural Citizenship,* 1 and 196 n. 1. In a quite balanced response to nationalism and its critics, Kymlicka states the essential normative point: "The boundaries of state and nation rarely if ever coincide perfectly, so viewing the state as the possession of a particular national group can only alienate minority groups. The state must be seen as equally belonging to all people who are governed by it, regardless of their nationality." "Misunderstanding Nationalism," in *Theorizing Nationalism,* ed. Ronald Beiner (Albany: State University of New York Press, 1999), 139.

11
1989: Nationalism, Internationalism, and the Nairn-Hobsbawm Debate

What happened in 1989? It's possible to give two radically opposed accounts of the meaning of 1989 with respect to the problem of nationalism and cosmopolitanism. Which of these two opposing accounts you opt for will determine where you stand on one of the most difficult and profound normative issues that it's possible for a political philosopher to address.

The first, which I'll refer to as the Hobsbawm account, goes roughly as follows. After 1989, various societies in Eastern Europe, owing to massive social disorientation and dislocations in the wake of the trauma of the collapse of highly centralized and statist regimes, embraced robust forms of nationalism, which in turn brought about the fragmentation of multinational states and the creation of a host of nationally defined mini- and micro-states. This is a pathological condition, and, one hopes, when these societies have time to adjust to their new post-Cold War circumstances, the nationalist fever will ease and these societies will be able to lessen their grip on the "banister" of national consciousness needed to give meaning and direction to life in this new (post-traumatic) social world.

The second, which I'll refer to as the Nairn account, goes roughly as follows. There is nothing pathological about the flourishing of new sovereignties based on national identity subsequent to 1989. The real pathology is the repression of national identities by multinational entities, not excluding the United Kingdom as hitherto constituted. The spawning of all these new national states opens up a space of political creativity for which we should be thankful. It is something that should be celebrated, certainly by those on the left who champion freedom and equality.

So where does the pathology lie? In the preoccupation with national togetherness (however defined) as a necessary bond of meaningful citizenship? Or in multinationality as a principle of deliberately transnational citizenship? As stated above, a deep investigation in a philosophical, and not merely historical or sociological, register is required in order to begin addressing an issue of this scope and import. There are several reasons why it might

be especially interesting to pose these questions in the context of the intellectual confrontation between Tom Nairn and Eric Hobsbawm. First of all,
both of them are powerful and penetrating social theorists, and since they
disagree radically, the debate between nationalism and anti-nationalism is
likely to be conducted by them at a level of depth and sophistication that
allows us to learn something important from each of the contenders. Second,
they know themselves to be implicated in a conscious dialogue that had its
start long before 1989 – back in the 1970s, when Hobsbawm responded to
Nairn's brilliant book, *The Break-up of Britain,* with a lengthy and intellectually ambitious review essay, and the dialogue has continued subsequent to
the events of 1989.[1] This means that there is a continuity to their dialogue,
not limited to the consequences of the end of the Cold War, but addressing
matters of principle that are theoretically paramount both pre-1989 and
post-1989. Third, both thinkers are very able Marxists or post-Marxists,
anxious to relate their positions on nationalism to the Marxist tradition
and to what they know to be the tortured history of leftist responses to nationalism. This drives home the point that two social theorists can situate
themselves in the *same* overarching political-intellectual tradition, and yet
come to radically antagonistic conclusions with respect to the legitimacy of
nationalism. The fact that both bear allegiance to a broadly Marxist-leftist
mode of social analysis should help us to focus more pointedly on how the
national question serves to define a given politics, and how it divides those
whose intellectual and political commitments otherwise incline in a similar
direction.[2] In short, what we have here is a genuine intellectual encounter:
on the one side a very intelligent and learned defender of nationalism, and
on the other side a very intelligent and learned critic of nationalism, and
between them, a deliberate and reciprocal dialogue.

   Let's start with Nairn's account of 1989. According to Nairn, 1989 finally
debunks the old mythology shared by Marxists and liberals that national
differences would succumb to the universalism of a modern world economy,
and that the reality of a modern-industrial-cosmopolitan civilization would
force inhabitants of particular cultures to realize that they would have to
forgo "medieval particularism" (Lenin's phrase) in order to win their human
emancipation. The liberal-Marxist faith was that progress was inherently
internationalist, and that it would leave discarded national allegiances in its
wake just as the modern world reduces rural social experience to an irrelevant
rump. This is not what happened subsequent to the Industrial Revolution,
nor is it what is happening now, as we struggle to cope with other technological and globalizing social-economic revolutions. What happened and
continues to happen is a *reinforcement* of national allegiances, which leads
one to think that the strength of contemporary nationalism is not just an unfathomable fluke, but is positively and inextricably related to the supposedly
globalizing tendencies of our world economy. There is an intelligible and

explicable dialectic at work here. This is in fact the social-theoretical thesis that Nairn borrows from Ernest Gellner.[3] Nairn calls the fact of a global economy and the mass idiot-culture that goes along with it "international-ity" (namely, present-day multinational capitalism). But internationality doesn't stamp out national cultures; on the contrary, it somehow, in a dialectical reversal, vivifies them and motivates them to politicize their cultural identity through struggles over national sovereignty. This, in turn, elicits "internationalism" as the cosmopolitan creed of intellectuals who can't stomach the excessive particularism of modern nationalist politics.[4] The dialectic can be summed up neatly in the following formula: inter-nationality provokes nationalism, as a defensive response, which in turn provokes internationalism, as a counter-nationalist politics. All three belong to one and the same sociological universe: the world of modern globe-encompassing industrialization and technologization. Just as "nationalism is not a reflection, a mirror of ethnic variety [but rather] a set of levers (which are sometimes weapons) through which ethnos is [in modern circumstances] driven into a new salience in human affairs," so internationalism "is not a mirror of internationality, but a complex range of reactions to national-ism." Internationalism "is a constituent of the same nationalist universe"; nationalism and internationalism are "the Siamese twin brothers of a single world-historical process."[5] The same can be said of nationalism's relation-ship to internationality:

> The overwhelmingly dominant political by-product of modern inter-nationality so far has been nationalism ... Even before 1989 it was clear that medieval particularism still had a future. Only after that year could it be more convincingly argued that it had *the* future too. I fail to see how one can avoid suspecting that there is some connection here. It cannot simply be a chain of accidents, as internationalists pretend ... All those Big Macs and IBM salesmen must have actually (materially) fostered or created this result, no doubt unintentionally. "Balkanization" must not be a doomed and mindless resistance to the advance of progress, but that progress itself. It must be what actually happens, as distinct from the ideological virtual reality offered up by the determinists, the multinational salesmen, and the internationalists. Ah yes, we always thought we knew that the poor Macedo-nians would have to resign themselves to progress – to the erosion of their antique and colourful ways, to becoming more like everybody else. Now, we also know that progress must resign itself to being Macedonian.[6]

This is a terrific statement of Nairn's basic analysis. But it doesn't yet spell out his normative stance toward nationalism, since one can view its stubborn persistence in the face of (and, according to Nairn's thesis, as a by-product of) internationalizing social-economic realities *either* as a kind of nuisance that happens to be inescapably inscribed in the sociological imperatives of modern life (which is more or less how Ernest Gellner views it) or as something to be celebrated. Although the celebration is not unqualified, Nairn tends to embrace the second of these two ways of responding to nationalism. In an essay entitled "The Owl of Minerva" in *Faces of Nationalism,* Nairn refers to "the great return to reality of 1989," as opposed to "internationalist delusions"; and he expresses the hope that nationalism will not vanish from the scene "at least until the last great empire has been Balkanised."[7] (But since every nationalist aspirant, unlimited in number, will see his or her people as the victim of imperial rule, there will always be another empire still waiting to be Balkanized!)

Eric Hobsbawm is a superb exemplar of the kind of intellectual that Nairn has in mind when he lampoons "internationalists." In the essay summarized above, he specifically cites Hobsbawm's fear that the United Nations "is soon likely to consist of the late 20th century equivalents of Saxe-Coburg-Gotha and Schwarzburg-Sondershausen."[8] According to Nairn, even though Hobsbawm knows that his own residual Leninist internationalism is impotent in the face of the accelerating trend whereby multinational states splinter along national and ethnic cleavages, Hobsbawm refuses to relinquish the faith that "as long as some functioning multinational states like the United Kingdom, the Soviet Union, and Yugoslavia survived, all [is] not lost."[9]

> From that point of view, all *was* lost in 1989. The last shards of the [internationalist] doctrine dropped through the grating, as the Eastern working class opted decisively for a mixture of "bourgeois democracy" and nationalism. The key overarching states fell apart. The United Kingdom is still there, true, though much worse afflicted than in the 1970s. So are China and India. Yet one need only cite this short list to see how hopeless the position may soon be. The internationalist ethic had survived only by being preserved in the Cold War aspic along with so much else.[10]

What is Hobsbawm's response to this charge of impotent moralism and unreasonable fear of legitimate particularisms? Hobsbawm's arguments against contemporary neo-nationalist secessionism include the following:

1 Other things being equal, smaller nations are more vulnerable than larger nations to the dictates of transnational or multinational capital.[11]
2 By definition, the moral imagination of those within a nationalist movement is limited to the boundaries of their own nation: the national question necessarily takes precedence over transnational moral-political objectives, for instance, a concern with global social justice.[12]
3 The nationalist illusion that the world is divisible into monocultural national units prevents nationalists from facing up to the real problem of

contemporary societies, which is "how to organize the actual coexistence of different ethnic, racial, linguistic and other groups"; instead, if the secessionist movement succeeds, this problem is simply replicated within smaller political units. In general, this is likely to worsen the problem rather than ameliorate it: "the case against *Kleinstaaterei* today, at least in its ethnic-linguistic form, is not only that it provides no solution for the actual problems of our day, but that, insofar as it has the power to carry out its policies, it makes these problems more difficult. Cultural freedom and pluralism at present are almost certainly better safeguarded in large states which know themselves to be plurinational and pluri-cultural than in small ones pursuing the ideal of ethnic-linguistic and cultural homogeneity."[13]

4   Nairn's principle seems to be: the more nation-states the better. But is this a coherent political principle? Hobsbawm obviously thinks not. There is no finite number of real nations because nations are not real to begin with: they are the contrivances either of states or of state-aspiring nationalist movements. There are no constraints upon the proliferation of new nationalisms other than the perhaps limited reserves of politi-cal creativity at the disposal of the nationalist intellectuals, ideologists, and politicians who mobilize popular support for their cause. Given the *chutzpah* of an Umberto Bossi, for instance, a new nation can be conjured up more or less out of thin air.[14] This line of thought goes a long way toward accounting for the Western "hysteria" that Nairn associates with critics of nationalism such as Hobsbawm. Sure, we can accord recognition to the new claimants in the queue, but where will it end? The answer, Nairn and Hobsbawm agree (though with wildly different valuations), is: anywhere or nowhere.

Hobsbawm of course doesn't limit himself to condemning nationalism. Like other theorists of nationalism, he offers some explanatory hypotheses. According to Hobsbawm, the one thing on which Lenin and Woodrow Wil-son agreed was the legitimacy of trying to draw political boundaries that match ethnic-linguistic communities. "The Wilsonian plan to divide Europe into ethnic-linguistic territorial states," he says, was "a project as dangerous as it was impracticable."[15] The crucial catalyst for nationalist mobilization is social disorientation; Hobsbawm quotes Miroslav Hroch's suggestion that "language acts as a substitute for factors of integration in a disintegrating society. When society fails, the nation appears as the ultimate guarantee."[16] Modern societies in general expose their populations to social transforma-tions of astonishing scale and rapidity. The social earthquake that hit in 1989 required a still more radical adjustment to a new social world. "When the landmarks which seem to provide an objective, a permanent, a positive delimitation of our belonging together disappear," people grope for readily available markers that will help them reassemble their lives.[17] In such situations, "the obvious fall-back positions are ethnicity and religion, singly or in combination."[18] The retreat to the "nation" as an obvious "fall-back position" is especially attractive "in those parts of the globe whose frontiers were drawn on Wilsonian-Leninist lines after 1918," since the fracture lines for ethnic separatism are ready-made; similar happenings elsewhere in the world can be partly accounted for by "the demonstration effect of central and eastern Europe."[19] These things "are comprehensible as symptoms of social disorientation, of the fraying, and sometimes the snapping, of the threads of what used to be the network that bound people together in society."[20] For those who don't share Nairn's enthusiasm for the spawning of new nation-states, the internationalist hope is that as the pace of historical change becomes more manageable and societies adjust to the radical upheavals thrust upon them, nationalist passions will correspondingly diminish.

From Nairn's point of view, Hobsbawm's aversion to the new nationalisms represents simply an irrational attachment to the international status quo, a failure to embrace the dislocations of ethnic politics as the opening for a new kind of political creativity. He quotes Benedict Anderson in support of the possibility "that on the whole the nationalist course of history after 1989 may be preferable to what went before, and may not be treatable by any recourse to the old multi-national or internationalist recipes": the language of "'fragmentation' and 'disintegration' – with all the menacing, pathological connotations these words bring with them [–] makes us forget the decades or centuries of violence out of which Frankensteinian 'integrated states' such as the United Kingdom of 1900, which included all of Ireland, were constructed ... Behind the language of 'fragmentation' lies always a Panglossian conservatism that likes to imagine that every status quo is nicely normal."[21] But if a principled aversion to redrawing of political boundaries in general strikes Nairn and Anderson as excessively conservative, an undiscriminating embrace of as many new nations as possible strikes many of us as alarmingly reckless. And Nairn indeed seems to revel in recklessness, at least in his moments of more unbounded enthusiasm, such as when he invokes Jane Jacobs's idea of a (presumably unbounded) "multiplication of sovereignties," welcomes a "proliferation" of smaller entities ("mini- and micro-units"), and speaks of a new "anarchist" internationalism.[22]

As a citizen of a political community presently imperilled by the nationalist upsurge saluted by Nairn and cursed by Hobsbawm, it's hard for me not to lean in Hobsbawm's direction. From a Hobsbawmian perspective, nationalism stands for a gratuitous and politically damaging attempt to ideologize cultural identity.[23] However Nairn does an effective job of ruling out as illegitimate the presumption that one inhabits a neutral space of non-ideological politics. Rather, according to Nairn, there are two warring ideologies here, nationalism on the one side and imperialism or neo-imperialism on the other side, with no neutral space between the warring contenders. For example, one might imagine that the designation "British politics" is reasonably neutral, ideologically speaking. No such thing, from Nairn's point of view. He sees multinational political communities as a residuum from the age of empires, and as carrying their own ideological baggage. Nairn's use of the language of "metropolis" and "periphery" underlines this imperialist legacy. London is the centre, Scotland is the periphery, and this ideological reality is masked by the centre's conduct of the business of state in the name of neutral-sounding "Britain" (so the very designation of Scotland and Wales as "periphery" implies English neo-imperialism). Empire is the only real alternative to the nation-state, and we should be thankful that in the past two centuries there have been plenty of "nativist fools around consistently to thwart imperialism," for without them, "one form or another of the empire would have to get its boots permanently on humanity's windpipe."[24]

This argument poses a challenge that we shouldn't rush to dismiss. The underlying assumption is basically that internationalism naturally goes along with a nostalgia for multinational coexistence and co-citizenship during the era of European and colonial empires. Scratch a cosmopolitan and you'll find an imperialist just below the surface.[25] One encounters the same argument in Michael Walzer's challenge to leftist internationalism: "The 'internationalism' of the left owes a great deal to Hapsburg and Romanov imperialism."[26] *Pace* Hobsbawm and other internationalists, the Soviet Union was not a genuine multinational political community but rather an empire, and Yugoslavia, as well, was a kind of empire on a smaller scale (and perhaps the same thing applies to Britain).[27] In the modern age, there are two kinds of polities that we know to be real: nation-states and empires. Some of the political communities that were thought not to be nation-states turn out on closer inspection to be in fact empires (or quasi-empires). The great hope of the internationalist left was to cultivate a form of class-based citizenship that would be "neither imperial nor national": the citizenship of a transnational proletariat.[28] But the internationalist left was mistaken. This internationalist wager came up empty: no such third possibility, both non-imperial and transnational, exists. After "the last great empire has been Balkanised," only nation-states will exist; and *every* political community, even those that present themselves as non-nationalist, must mobilize allegiance on some kind of national basis.

Nairn of course doesn't deny that post-1989 nationalism produced some notable horrors.[29] But his view is that once the storm of 1989 dies down, life among the old and new nations, "normal"-sized as well as mini- and micro-nation-states, will fall back into the kind of pacific and routinized pattern that one associates with a sane international order. As nationalist passion simmers down and returns to life as usual, the anti-nationalist hysteria of the West will likewise put things back into perspective and reconcile itself to the new, somewhat reconstituted constellation of national communities: "In the short run nationality politics [in post-1989 Central and Eastern Europe] may be more salient; but over a longer period either democracy or its failure will fix its shape and meaning," Nairn writes. "One must distinguish between initial shock waves and the longer term pressures for change ... When an old order dismantles itself ... 'nationalism emerges with all its vigour, but with few of its rivals' [quoting Ernest Gellner]. The rival forces of civil association, representative politics and local government were more severely repressed and take far more time to build up."[30]

In the passage quoted by Nairn, Gellner actually leaves it as an open question whether "irredentist nationalism ... or a diminution of ethnic conflict ... will predominate."[31] But in another essay from the early 1990s, Gellner seems to presume, like Nairn, that the storm will pass. Let's assume that modern nationalism is preordained for the sociological reasons that Gellner lays out. But the carving up of the world into Gellnerian culture-state pairs doesn't easily yield a political-ethnic stability, for the obvious reason that many or most of these culture-state units contain minorities that upset the prescribed one-to-one correspondence of state and culture. After the stage at which non-ethnic empires give way to smaller states based on a nationalist-ethnic principle, these new smaller units are frustrated to find themselves "just as minority-haunted as the larger ones which had preceded them."[32] This tension between the assertion of the nationalist principle and frustration of its complete fulfillment can give rise to horrifying atrocities, ranging from forced expulsion of minorities to genocide. But one needn't expect these convulsions to be permanent.[33] Gellner presents this theory not as a commentary on post-1989 but as the typology of a general historical pattern. The last stage of the typology anticipates subsidence of the nationalist fever: "High level of satiation of the nationalist requirement, plus generalized affluence, plus cultural convergence, leads to a diminution, though not the disappearance, of the virulence of nationalist revendications."[34] All of this may be true. Still, I think there is a problem of how to respond normatively to any particular nationalist challenge to reconfigure the system of states so as to accommodate a set of ethnic or cultural aspirations not yet accommodated – and it is a problem that Gellner's sociology doesn't address or even try to address (whereas Nairn and Hobsbawm do, although in opposing directions). The fact that nationalism doesn't necessarily lead to endless bloodshed certainly doesn't suffice to vindicate it normatively. According to Gellner's acute formulation, we enter the age of nationalism when "the old world of endless cultural diversity and nuance, only very loosely connected, if indeed connected at all, with political boundaries [gets replaced] by a world in which each culture has its political roof, and in which political units and authorities are only legitimated by the fact that they protect and express and cherish a culture."[35] This invites the normative challenge posed by Hobsbawm and other critics of nationalism: what's wrong with two (or more) cultures under one political roof, and why can't a single political unit protect and cherish two (or more) cultures?

I think it's an accurate description to say that Nairn is not a strictly nationalist but rather nationalist-sympathizing left-Gellnerian.[36] It's not easy for a Gellnerian to be a nationalist, or even a nationalist sympathizer, although, on the other hand, it's also quite difficult for a Gellnerian to be an out-and-out militant anti-nationalist. This requires some explanation.

As Nairn observes in the Introduction to *Faces of Nationalism,* Gellner's own stance toward nationalism is consistently both reductionist and sardonic (not to say brutally cynical): "Although it redeemed nationalism theoretically, the distinctive bias of Gellnerism was in fact always towards perceiving it as an effect ... rather than a motor, a chain of resultant phenomena rather than an originating or causative impulse. From 1964 onwards he nearly always couched this argument in the form of a standard put-down of naïve-nationalist belief."[37] A hard-boiled sociologist accustomed to cracking sharp jokes at nationalists' expense is not likely to be himself very receptive to any particular nationalist commitment. Nairn, on the other hand, is of course moved by genuine national sentiment. But for all Gellner's social-scientific detachment from and wit at the expense of nationalism, he wouldn't be capable of the kind of scorn toward nationalism summoned up by Elie Kedourie. The reason is that for Gellner, unlike Kedourie, the modern world is unthinkable without nationalism; in particular, nationalism can't be judged in abstraction from its formidable capacity for mobilizing populations for modernization, for fully equipped membership in the modern world. (This is what Nairn means in saying that Gellner's theory "redeemed nationalism theoretically.")[38]

The most important respect in which Nairn is *not* a Gellnerian is that Nairn clearly considers nationalism a fit topic for normative judgment; and he clearly considers those who hang tightly onto their "internationalist delusions" to be fit objects of normative criticism. Gellner, by contrast, expresses his judgments strictly through sarcasm – but it is a sarcasm directed at something that is an inescapable feature of modern life, and to that extent beyond meaningful normative approbation or disapprobation. There is something rather odd about this view. There are evidently a host of ways in which a society can embody its participation in a modern way of life. Even if it were true that all societies are required to consolidate a national existence *in some sense* in order to pass through the portal of modernity, it isn't at all clear that the kind of politics required to do this is in each case equally or in a comparable sense "nationalist" (especially since Gellner is quite precise about what he counts as nationalism, namely a unique alignment of culture and state). In any case, once the consolidation of a nation-state has done its job of equipping a given population for the travails of modernity, the nationalist ideology that has served this function would seem to be henceforth dispensable. As Liah Greenfeld has put the point in a recent article: "if nationalism is a product of a certain stage of economic development – presumably early capitalism and industrialization – then the passing of this stage must imply the passing of nationalism. Now we today, it is claimed, live in the period of late capitalism and, possibly, in the post-industrial society," so why is nationalism still around?[39] To offer a ready illustration: Quebec (Scotland too, for that matter) is already a modern industrial society.[40] It will remain a modern industrial (or postindustrial) society whether or not its nationalist cadres succeed with their project of aligning culture and state through national sovereignty. If the point of a nationalist movement is to equip a cultural unit for parity with other modern societies, then this particular nationalism seems strictly redundant: Quebec will be a part of the modern world whether or not its intelligentsia and trade unions are fervently nationalist. But if, contrary to Gellner's theory, such a nationalism is functionally dispensable, then the question of whether or not to embrace Québécois nationalism is once again a topic of legitimate normative inquiry. (Strictly speaking, what Gellner's theory explains is not the upsurge of this or that particular nationalism, but rather, the coming-into-being of a whole world of national – that is, culturally segregated – political units, which serves to displace an older pre-industrial world in which nations in this sense make very little sociological sense.)

If we were to go all the way with Gellner, we would come to the following conclusion. While social-scientific understanding of the sociology of nationalism would make it difficult if not impossible for sophisticated intellectuals to be taken in by the ridiculous national myths propagated by committed nationalists, this same sociological awareness would resign these students of nationalism to the inescapability of nationalist political commitment as a necessary concomitant of the modern world. I want to resist going all the way with Gellner because it would have the consequence of rendering normative engagement with nationalism utterly redundant, or very nearly so. Gellner can indeed sneer at nationalist intelligentsia for their credulity and myth-mongering, but he can't really criticize them – because what is sociologically determined is not an appropriate object of normative judgment. Gellner is certainly right to criticize social theorists who, in the grip of idealist assumptions about "the *Allmacht des Begriffes*," treat nationalism as "the offspring of philosophy."[41] There of course *is* a sociology of nationalism that has its basis in the social reality of modernity rather than merely in the wild delusions of modern intellectuals. But Gellner himself goes so far in the opposite direction (that is, in the direction of sociological determinism) that he removes nationalism as a legitimate object of normative inquiry.

As a sociologist, especially one inclined to the design of grand explanatory models, Gellner can permit himself the luxury of standing outside nationalism and theorizing its possible relationship to aspects of modern social existence (mobility, the relation between elite culture and mass culture, the place of bureaucracy in a modern society, a modern economy's need for standardized educational and cultural norms, and so on). But as citizens needing to respond to the political challenges of nationalism in the post-1989 world, we have no such luxury. Our relationship to the politics of nationalism is internal rather than external: we need to know whether to embrace the kind of politics that nationalist movements promote, whether to resist them, or whether to accommodate them grudgingly. Having available to us the kind of knowledge that Gellner's sociology provides concerning functional advantages of nationalism for distinctively modern societies doesn't by itself answer this question. For if it did, the question itself would be pointless: if nationalism were as deeply inscribed in the sociological requirements of a modern society as Gellner tends to suggest, a politics indifferent to or agnostic about or actually hostile toward national concerns would be off the map of political possibilities. But we know that this is not the case. It remains open to citizens (including those belonging to ethnic communities that are the site of nationalist agitation) to turn their backs on the claims of the ethnos, to put their energies into other political preoccupations or to resist the efforts of their fellow citizens to make national self-expression the central preoccupation. For instance, in Canada today (and for more than a generation – since 1968 in fact!), the key political actors in the resistance to the project of Québécois sovereignty have been Québécois federalist politicians in Ottawa. No sociological theory compels them to locate their politics on the nationalist side: anti-nationalism as well as the accommodation of national identity within a multinational state remain political possibilities. Nairn may be right that their cause is hopeless, and that in our modern world, constituted as it is sociologically, nationalist politics almost always wins, at least eventually. But the sociologist's (external) point of view and the citizen's (internal) point of view are mutually exclusive.[42] As a citizen one has to presume that agency counts, and that political choices are multiple, and therefore that one acts on the basis of choices that are either normatively well founded or normatively misguided. It follows that nationalism is a topic of normative-philosophical, and not just sociological-explanatory, reflection. It follows, in turn, that the outcome of the Nairn-Hobsbawm debate is a matter not just of which of these two theorists has got it right sociologically (whether the historical conditions of the modern world strongly favour nationalist outcomes or whether the sociology of modernity leaves room for possibilities outside the horizon of nationalist politics), but more important, which of the two opposing normative visions is more defensible.

Source
This chapter was originally published in *Archives européennes de Sociologie* 40, 1 (1999): 171-84.

Notes
1 Tom Nairn, *The Break-up of Britain: Crisis and Neo-Nationalism,* 2nd, expanded ed. (London: New Left Books, 1981); Eric Hobsbawm, "Some Reflections on 'The Break-up of Britain,'" *New Left Review* 105 (1977): 3-23. For a very instructive and insightful account of Nairn's intellectual career, see Joan Cocks, *Passion and Paradox: Intellectuals Confront the National Question* (Princeton, NJ: Princeton University Press, 2002), 111-32. For critical discussion of Hobsbawm, see Tom Nairn, *Faces of Nationalism: Janus Revisited* (London: Verso, 1997), 40-2, 47-56, 148. Cf. Benedict Anderson, "Introduction," in *Mapping the Nation*, ed. Gopal Balakrishnan (London: Verso, 1996), 13.
2 Ernest Gellner suggests that the very fact of Nairn's sensitivity to nationalism proves that there is little real content to his residual Marxism: see "Nationalism, or the new confessions of a justified Edinburgh sinner," in Gellner, *Spectacles and Predicaments: Essays in Social Theory* (Cambridge: Cambridge University Press, 1979), 265-6.
3 The thesis is nicely summarized as follows: "The general process of industrialisation has consistently rendered all the factors of nationality (ethnic, linguistic, physiognomic, sometimes religious) more, rather than less, important. In one sense, all 1989 showed was that this is continuing: command-economy failures in the East have generated an overdue reaction which like others before it has to assume a primarily nationalist form. In other words, nationalism ... is no counter-current or side eddy, interfering with the majestic mainstream of Progress: nationalism is the mainstream" (Nairn, *Faces of Nationalism*, 48).
4 Tom Nairn, "Internationalism and the Second Coming," in *Mapping the Nation*, ed. Balakrishnan, 267-80; for a lengthier statement of the same argument, see "Internationalism: A Critique," in Nairn, *Faces of Nationalism*, 25-46.
5 Nairn, "Internationalism and the Second Coming," 270. Cf. *Faces of Nationalism*: "Internationalism and nationalism are, in a curious way, perfectly twin ideologies. They are parts of a single, overall, modern thought-world ... Even the most berserk chauvinist is a sort of 'internationalist' – a fact recorded in the 'ism' of his nationalism" (41-2).
6 Nairn, "Internationalism and the Second Coming," 269-70.
7 Nairn, *Faces of Nationalism*, 49, 48.
8 Nairn, "Internationalism and the Second Coming," 272. The quotation is from Hobsbawm's 1977 review essay on Nairn (see n. 1 above). Hence Nairn's judgment: "Internationalists knew defeat was coming well before 1989."
9 Nairn, "Internationalism and the Second Coming," 273.
10 Ibid.
11 Hobsbawm, "Some Reflections on 'The Break-up of Britain,'" 7-8.
12 "Nationalists ... are by definition unconcerned with anything except their private collective" (ibid., 7); "nationalism by definition subordinates all other interests to those of its specific 'nation'" (ibid., 9); nationalism's place in the socialism versus capitalism nexus "is of no significance to nationalists, who do not care what this relationship is, so long as Ruritanians (or whoever) acquire sovereign statehood as a nation" (ibid., 11).
13 E.J. Hobsbawm, *Nations and Nationalism since 1780: Programme, Myth, Reality,* 2nd ed. (Cambridge: Cambridge University Press, 1992), 185. One of the illustrations offered by Hobsbawm is the relationship of the Slovakian nation to its ethnic-Hungarian minority (ibid., 185-6); another is the relationship of the Québécois nation to minorities in Quebec ("Some Reflections on 'The Break-up of Britain,'" 8 n. 9).
14 Eric J. Hobsbawm, "Ethnicity and Nationalism in Europe Today," in *Mapping the Nation*, ed. Balakrishnan, 260.
15 Ibid., 259.
16 Ibid., 261.
17 Ibid., 265.
18 Ibid., 261.

19 Ibid., 262.
20 Ibid., 264.
21 Nairn, *Faces of Nationalism*, 62; the quotation is from Benedict Anderson, "The New World Disorder," *New Left Review* 193 (1992): 5.
22 Nairn, "Internationalism and the Second Coming," 277-9. It would be interesting to know how Nairn would answer Hobsbawm's question of why one should desire "the division of the Indo-Burmese-Chinese frontier region into twenty separate sovereign 'nation-states'" ("Some Reflections on 'The Break-up of Britain,'" 13).
23 For a more general argument by Hobsbawm on the perils of identity politics, see "Identity Politics and the Left," *New Left Review* 217 (1996): 38-47.
24 Nairn, "Internationalism and the Second Coming," 272. Cf. *Faces of Nationalism:* "The alternative to antagonistic, ethnically biased development was never in fact cosmopolitan growth or 'internationalism.' It could only have been one form or another of empire" (51).
25 Nairn, "Internationalism and the Second Coming," 271-2. According to Nairn, internationalist intellectuals are typically "metropolitan" creatures, with their own metropolitan interests at stake. See Nairn, *Faces of Nationalism:* internationalism is the ideology of Enlightenment elites, "the ideology most consonant with their location and class interests ... In practice, this ideology has of course served the big battalions" (48-9).
26 Michael Walzer, "The New Tribalism: Notes on a Difficult Problem," in *Theorizing Nationalism*, ed. Ronald Beiner (Albany: State University of New York Press, 1999), 205. Interestingly, nationalists too can harbour a nostalgia for imperialism. At the end of his essay "The First Person Plural" (*Theorizing Nationalism*, ed. Beiner, 279-93), Roger Scruton switches from a defence of English nationalism to an appeal for a return to the age of empires.
27 On Britain as a (domestic) empire, see Nairn, *The Break-up of Britain*, 74-5.
28 Nairn, "Internationalism and the Second Coming," 272.
29 Still, his response to Yugoslavia seems a bit flip: "The post-Yugoslav war has given a momentary boost to old-style Atlantic Leftism, but I doubt it will last long" (ibid., 275).
30 Nairn, *Faces of Nationalism*, 160.
31 Ernest Gellner, *Encounters with Nationalism* (Oxford: Blackwell, 1994), 31. Cf. n. 34 below.
32 Ernest Gellner, "The Coming of Nationalism and Its Interpretation: The Myths of Nation and Class," in *Mapping the Nation*, ed. Balakrishnan, 111-12.
33 The same conclusion is implicit in the last line of Hobsbawm's "Ethnicity and Nationalism in Europe Today."
34 Gellner, "The Coming of Nationalism and Its Interpretation," 112. Cf., "Nationalism can now be tamed ... Finally, with the coming of generalized affluence and the diminution of cultural distance through late industrialization and a universal market and standardized lifestyle, there comes a certain diminution of intensity of national sentiment. That ... is the trajectory one would naturally expect" (126-7). Also, 131-2, where Gellner explicitly applies his model to post-1989 Europe: the Russian Empire managed to avoid the fate of the Ottoman and Habsburg empires (or at least to defer this fate) by submitting its population to an even more overwhelming ideology than nationalism; however, as soon as Marxism lost its credibility as a secular religion, nationalism emerged from its post-1917 (and in the case of satellite states, post-1945: cf. 138) cryogenic state. Gellner explains that one can't be sure whether the outcome will be ethnic conflict at its worst or "that stage of diminished ethnic hatred which, one hopes, goes with very advanced industrialization" because when these societies resume their suspended nationalisms, frozen until 1989, it's hard to determine at which of the various stages of his typology this resumption will occur (cf. the passage cited in n. 31 above).
35 Gellner, "The Coming of Nationalism and Its Interpretation," 115.
36 The fact that Nairn is not orthodoxly nationalist is easy to document. For one thing, he is too schooled in Gellner's sociology to take nationalist dogmas at face value. He is obviously committed to Scottish nationalist aspirations over against "metropolitan" England; at the same time, he is, like most Scottish and other European nationalists, enthusiastic about the European Community. But more fundamentally, he is skeptical of the classical nationalist vision of a world parcelled neatly into culturally homogeneous states, each monopolizing

sovereignty within a medium-sized territory. Nairn is as interested in autonomous city-states as he is in more conventional nation-states. (See *Faces of Nationalism*, 133-49; "Internationalism and the Second Coming," 277-9.) His hope is for a "new nationalist system," a new order of political communities consisting of "bastards, mongrels, odd interstices, and breathing spaces, as well as 100 per cent isomorphs like Slovenia and Poland ... any such system will need its buffers, zones of confluence, no-man's-lands, and enclaves in order to function tolerably at all. Andorra, the Isle of Man, Sarajevo, Singapore, and Gibraltar may be as important in it as the more neatly theorizable ethnic building blocks" ("Internationalism and the Second Coming," 277). Such a new nationalism would also engender a "new style of internationalism": "The old internationalism was often uncomfortably close to 'all-the-same-ism.' I feel confident that this will never be said of post-1989 nationalism. Internationalism will find a far more natural foothold there as a moderating tendency of the system, rather than as a futile holding operation against its realization" (ibid.). One should also note that Scottish nationalists themselves aren't necessarily impressed by Nairn's nationalist credentials: see Craig Beveridge and Ronald Turnbull, *The Eclipse of Scottish Culture* (Edinburgh: Polygon, 1989), chapter 4.

37 Nairn, *Faces of Nationalism*, 7.

38 Nairn is by no means uncritical of Gellner. See, for instance, the critical remarks in *Faces of Nationalism* (which must be taken not just as criticism of Gellner but also in large measure as self-criticism): "Modernisation theory [is subject to the suspicion that it is] simply over-rational and 'bloodless' as an explanation for processes in which so much unreason is typically manifested, and so much literal blood has been spilt. It leaves too much out; it accounts for the material or vested interests in nationalism rather than its 'spell.' It is articulated around high-cultural politics rather than low-cultural glamour and popular identity ... [Gellnerite modernization theory] reacts against earlier nonsense about nationalism being a tale of Dark Gods and resurgent tribalism by stressing how much of it is novel, unprecedented and forced from the press of modernity. Correct as this is, one may doubt whether it is sufficient for analysing the resultant brew" (9). Here Nairn aptly cites a similar judgment by Perry Anderson in a luminous essay on Weber and Gellner: "Gellner's theory of nationalism might be described as immoderately materialist. For what it plainly neglects is the overpowering dimension of collective *meaning* that modern nationalism has always involved: that is, not its functionality for industry, but its fulfilment of identity ... Whereas Weber was so bewitched by the spell of nationalism that he was never able to theorize it, Gellner has theorized nationalism without detecting the spell. What was tragic fate for the one becomes prosaic function for the other." "Max Weber and Ernest Gellner: Science, Politics, Enchantment," in Anderson, *A Zone of Engagement* (London: Verso, 1992), 205-6.

39 Liah Greenfeld, "The Worth of Nations: Some Economic Implications of Nationalism," *Critical Review* 9, 4 (1995): 556.

40 In his review of Nairn (see n. 2 above), 275, Gellner acknowledges that Scottish nationalism "did not seem to fit the theory," namely, the modernization theory that he and Nairn share. The account he goes on to offer (275-6) is much more crudely reductionist than any likely to be furnished by Nairn.

41 Gellner, *Spectacles and Predicaments*, 266, 267. Gellner of course refers in this context to his eternal nemesis among students of nationalism, Elie Kedourie.

42 This raises interesting questions about a possible tension between Nairn's "first-order" political commitment (as a Scottish nationalist) and his "second-order" Gellner-inspired functionalist explanation of nationalism. (Consider, for instance, *Faces of Nationalism:* "It couldn't have been otherwise" [51]). Is *being* a nationalist existentially consistent with believing that nationalism is causally determined by industrialization, etcetera?

12

Civicism between Nationalism and Globalism: Some Reflections on the Problem of Political Community

> If living together is impossible, then life itself is impossible as well.
>
> Miladin Zivotic

The nature of political community is puzzling. Political philosophers generally don't do enough to retain a sense of the philosophical puzzles that drew them into theoretical reflection in the first place. Instead, we get confident-sounding or confident-looking arguments that lay out proposed solutions for these puzzles. But the initial puzzles are surely at least as important as the solutions. For if this weren't the case, we wouldn't go on reflecting theoretically on these problems: we would write our articles, solve the puzzles, and retire from further reflection on those sets of issues. Yet in actual fact, this isn't how theorists conduct themselves – they keep circling back to the puzzles that drew them into initial reflection on the problem – and, in writing about problems of political philosophy, we need to do more to convey that the initial puzzles *remain* puzzles. So it is with the problem of political community. Why is it that when we think of ourselves as citizens, we comport ourselves as members of this rather than that community of fellow citizens: Québécois or Canadian, Scottish or British, and so on? The *easy* answer (if one thinks there is an easy answer) would be that there is a political identity here that is inscrutably contingent, as when an individual happens to become romantically attached to one partner rather than another. It might seem intellectually bizarre to come up with a philosophical theory to account for this inscrutable contingency. And we might think of political identity in similar fashion: it would be intellectually bizarre to theorize the fact that someone "loves" her Scottish identity but not her British identity.

I don't think this easy solution works for the problem of political community. After all, when we reflect for a moment on the kinds of examples I've just mentioned, we realize that the conflicting identities that are at stake are not on the same level, normatively speaking, and so are not reciprocally exchangeable (or "swappable"). Each side of a given pair like this represents a distinct normative vision of suitable political community, that is, a distinct political commitment requiring normative grounding. All of this, of course, is implicit in political identity, but theoretical reflection draws it out and makes it explicit. To privilege Scottish or Québécois identity, I would argue, is to aspire to a vision of uni-national political community, whereas to embrace Canadian or British identity (even if not all Canadians or Britons see their political community in this way) involves a commitment to the idea of a multination political community.[1] When I say they're not "swappable," this doesn't mean people can't drop their commitment to Scottish nationalism and accept the legitimacy of shared British citizenship. What it means is that in doing so they haven't exchanged one uni-national identity for another; rather, they've dropped a uni-national vision of political community for a *different kind* of conception of political community, and it seems appropriate to say that each of these two views of political community invites a separate political philosophy to give it normative justification. Theorizing here *is* appropriate.

Of course, it's possible to do political philosophy without addressing the problem of political community. Just to refer to one very famous and hugely influential example, John Rawls's *A Theory of Justice* devoted six hundred pages to analyzing important issues of political philosophy without speaking of the problem of political community, except to say that he wouldn't address it: "I assume that the boundaries of [the schemes of justice being considered] are given by the notion of a self-contained national community."[2] Well, where exactly does the notion of a self-contained national community come from? Rawls doesn't attempt to answer this question, nor does he offer anywhere else in his book any acknowledgment that the problem of the boundaries of political community is (at least out there in the real political world) a problem – and in many parts of the world, a fairly intractable one. Again, one certainly can write works of political philosophy in abstraction from the question of what gives discrete political communities their boundaries. It is perhaps easier to do so when one lives in a society (such as Rawls's society) where those boundaries are presently uncontested. But consider how much of the substance of contemporary political life is put to one side if one starts off one's political philosophy by deliberately removing this as a question to be addressed. And this is especially so in a time such as ours, when the politics of nationalism in so many conspicuous areas of political interest is in such a dramatic upswing.

It goes without saying that particular instances of nationalist politics will be articulated in terms of a particular, historically generated set of cultural grievances. We can only assess the validity of these grievances in the context of the particular historical and political situation that defines those grievances. The general form of such a claim is: majority cultural group X within the larger political community, as it currently exists, denies us (minority cultural group Y) the opportunity to maintain our culture; political institutions as they exist give us insufficient means to control our collective destiny; and our freedom and self-determination as a people require a political community of our own. Judging the legitimacy of these nationalist claims therefore presupposes knowing quite a lot about the history of relations between groups X and Y, and about distributions of political authority embodied in current political arrangements in that society. All of this strongly suggests that nationalism as a political project can only be judged on a case-by-case basis, in the light of the historical contingencies that ground a particular set of claims. As I suggested earlier, however, there's more of a place for a general normative theory of political community (a weighing of nationalist versus non-nationalist visions of political community) than these considerations seem to imply. In certain cases, to be sure, the grievances advanced seem overwhelming: to take an extreme case, it's difficult not to feel sympathy for the people of East Timor, suffering clear oppression and genocide by the government of Indonesia, and it's reasonable to think that anyone living in these circumstances would be an East Timorese nationalist. Here this is simply a function of the unhappy history these people have suffered. Or Yugoslavia: while civic coexistence of different peoples may once have been possible or even flourished in some respects, there comes a point where one must make the judgment that that civic possibility is no longer available, not because it isn't normatively to be preferred but simply because the history that has unfolded between these peoples is so bitter that even peaceful separation looks like a substantial achievement.[3] One may say something similar about the history of Jews and Palestinians in the Middle East: while there might have been a point in that difficult and complicated history when binational arrangements within a shared state were an option, and therefore an argument might have been mounted for a normative political vision other than a nationalist segregation of these peoples, we seem to have moved definitively beyond that point. A nationalist separation of peoples now seems the only option (though the details are still subject to negotiation)[4]; therefore a normative contest between nationalist and non-nationalist politics is not a meaningful possibility.

But consider again those cases where the cultural grievances of nationalists are not decisively borne out by the facts of the political situation: perhaps those grievances are warranted, perhaps not. Here there *is* room for what we can call a pure normative theory of political community. In these cases, for instance Quebec and Scotland (unlike East Timor), an individual isn't driven inescapably into nationalist politics by a set of undisputed grievances against a majority cultural group (or against a minority cultural group, in cases where the minority has more power). Rather, it's the normative appeal of one vision of politics or another that determines whether citizens will assemble a narrative of grievances or supposed grievances. Those Scots or Québécois who are drawn to a vision of the normative attractiveness of uni-national political community will then start assembling a catalogue of grievances that justify their political commitment (or at least it's possible that the positive vision of political community comes first; in some cases, perhaps, it's the sense of mounting grievances that "push" an individual, reluctantly, into a nationalist commitment). In any case, if this argument is correct, a space is opened for independent normative reflection on the merits of nationalist versus non-nationalist conceptions of political community (as opposed to merely responding to a set of historical specificities, including inscrutable feelings of identity for one community rather than another).

The Civic Idea

So far, I've limited myself to referring, negatively, to "non-nationalist politics" as an alternative to nationalism. I now want to give a more positive-sounding name to this politics, which I'll call the civic idea. Although it's easy to give a name to this political vision, it's much more difficult to specify its content. To simplify the task, let me situate it between two competing approaches to the problem of political community: 1) According to the first – the globalist approach – the nation-state is obsolete, or rapidly en route to becoming so. We should let it go, and focus our political energies on reconstituting transnational networks of communication, exchange, and political activity. 2) According to the second – nationalism – the *national* principle is more relevant than ever. The more that certain aspects of modern life get globalized, the more we require a strictly national (ethnocultural) basis of political community to sustain a coherent political existence. It may be conceded that both of these diverging conceptions of political community (which sometimes work in concert against existing states) have considerable force to them in current circumstances; in particular, there's no point denying that the idea of multinational political communities has suffered stunning defeats in the years following 1989 (Czechoslovakia, Yugoslavia, the Soviet Union). Nonetheless, we'll try in what follows to argue the case for a notion of political community that is neither strictly national nor strictly transnational.

The idea of being a political animal as a required part of our human nature, in a normative sense, has been a leading idea in the history of Western political philosophy going back to Aristotle, and I think that this notion, as old as it is, continues to retain a great deal of intellectual force (though admittedly not precisely in the version held to by Aristotle). The civic idea, we might say, is a liberalized and diluted late-modern version of Aristotle's idea of citizenship. To get a handle on this civic conception, we should start by reflecting that we don't live our lives just as individuals. All of us live also in a social context heavily conditioned by political decisions and structures of political authority. Therefore autonomy (the core idea of most versions of liberalism) can't be fully meaningful unless individuals have some possibility of being politically involved in these larger political structures that shape social existence. To be sure, modern political communities offer most citizens modes of civic involvement that are mainly symbolic, or severely mediated, or vicarious, or nonexistent. But channels of more meaningful civic participation are in principle available for those for whom citizenship is indeed a central purpose (ideally, everyone; in reality, only a minority).

Being a citizen in the full sense would require something closer to the Aristotelian archetype – taking an active part, through public deliberation, in shaping and defining the political conditions of one's life. The vision of modern citizens regularly deliberating the very foundations of their political existence doesn't seem plausible, yet something of this kind is at work even within the much more modest dimensions of contemporary citizenship. (Just having opinions is already a civic attitude.) One could say that however much pluralism (either individual pluralism or group pluralism or both) there may be within a political society, its very character as a political society confers upon it a shared way of life (in some important respects). And this shared way of life then becomes the ultimate object of public deliberation in that society (insofar as there is any) – for instance, a change of government in the society becomes in some respect an initiative to change aspects of the shared way of life. The "way of life" becomes the ultimate unit of analysis in thinking about political community in a way analogous to how "an individual life as a whole" is the ultimate unit of analysis in ethical deliberation. If I decide to make some significant change in my life, the ultimate question is how it will affect my life as a whole, and something like this (our fundamental way of life as a political society) is at stake in modes of deliberation conducted within the political community.[5] (This analogy helps explain why the liberal idea of state neutrality toward conceptions of the good is incoherent, for a society can no more be neutral about its core collective purposes than an individual can be neutral about the fundamental purposes of his or her life.) To be a citizen is to have access to this "existential deliberation" on the part of one's society, at least in principle.

To be sure, this is an idealization. In a world of ideal citizenship, members of the political community would experience political life embedded in a firm civic identity; the notion of a civic common good would be intelligible; civic agency on the part of ordinary citizens would be meaningful and visible in its results; and politics would figure importantly among the ends of life of most people. But we don't live in that kind of civic world. The problem of scale is certainly a major challenge in all modern political communities: these are very large societies, where the civic activity of one citizen is rarely perceptible. The information needed to participate meaningfully in important social decisions is in the hands only of a few. Political elites dominate the political agenda. Many people are too preoccupied with the struggle to win a livelihood for their families to be able to devote much energy to the luxury of politics. Or they are more interested in projects of private consumption than in projects of shared civic agency. There is widespread apathy and de-politicization. Even voting in elections once every four years or so is regarded more as a grudging exercise than as an act of civic affirmation. Even in the more well-governed of modern societies, the civic idea is in bad shape.[6] Yet the civic article of faith is that citizenship in modern societies, as attenuated as it is, offers a sufficient trace of genuine attachment to a community of citizens and sufficient possibility of viable civic agency that there are at least intimations here of citizenship as a meaningful normative standard (even if the societies that yield these intimations are themselves very remote from meeting the standard of full-blown citizenship). As we suggested earlier, all of this serves as a weaker late-modern version of Aristotle's conception of the human being as a political animal.

A core idea of liberalism is that individuals ought to have space in which to decide on their own ends, their own purposes of life. Therefore, for many contemporary liberals, there appears to be something unavoidably illiberal about the notion that all human beings should be *obliged* to rank political experience very highly among their other ends. And perhaps there is indeed something illiberal in this notion. But one might just as well say that there is a tension between liberalism (defined as I have defined it above) and the whole enterprise of political philosophy as an effort to reflect on desirable ends of life; if so, I'd rather see this as an argument against liberalism than as an argument against the enterprise of political philosophy. (In fact, liberalism itself can't avoid taking a stand on the question of more desirable and less desirable ways to live a human life, and therefore can't object to the civic idea because it privileges a certain vision of the good life; and more civic versions of liberalism don't object to it on these grounds.)

One set of questions that this civic ideal raises is the sort of social and economic policies that would ideally accompany (and bolster and sustain) a regime of robust citizenship or civic co-involvement.[7] Another perhaps more basic set of questions concerns what defines the boundaries according to which citizens feel and know themselves to be in fact co-citizens. I've already conceded that not everyone will accept the idea of being a politi-cal animal as an obligatory norm. But if you *do* accept this idea, you will be forced to confront what I've called the problem of political community, or the problem of the boundaries of citizenship. For surely one can't be a political animal on one's own. There must be a community of citizens with whom one *shares* civic ends: a *locus* of citizenship that specifies those par-ticular other human beings *with whom* being a political animal is possible. Now for most people, the locus of citizenship isn't deliberately chosen, but is given – we're born into a political community, and accept it as setting the horizons of our citizenship unless something in our political thinking (such as a nationalist commitment) renders it problematical for a particular subgroup, or unless as individuals there's some compelling reason to leave it and settle in some other society. On the other hand, it would be a bit strange for anyone who takes citizenship seriously to say: "any political community will do. I want to be a political animal, and *any* community of fellow citizens that's at hand will serve well enough." To the contrary, this would trivialize political membership, and that in turn would trivialize citizenship. Citizens, if they think politics is important, *care* about the fact that they belong to one political community rather than another. That, in fact, is why certain citizens become nationalists: for them, one of the central questions of their political existence (or often *the* central question) is whether they enact their political life within *this* locus of citizenship or *that* locus of citizenship.

All political communities inhabit boundaries that are partly or wholly arbitrary. A sense of political community is a given for any state that is able to sustain itself in a stable way. But it's far from clear why members of these communities *should* share political identities with or feel political attachments to co-citizens who happen to reside on this side rather than that side of these arbitrary boundaries, which is a crucial part of the reason why I began by referring to political community as a puzzle. If the nationalist idea that there are natural or quasi-natural boundaries between national communities is false, however, what alternative is there? (Clearly, an important part of what makes the nationalist vision of political community attractive is that it confers a greater sense of fatedness on civic boundaries than is really warranted.) One obvious alternative is to say that we should be able to enact citizenship *without* boundaries. Some, though not many, would say that a world state is possible, and that globalizing trends at the beginning of the twenty-first century are moving in that direction.

A more moderate view would be that international legal norms, world markets, new technologies of communication, and cross-national modes of political agency are all making national sovereignty increasingly irrelevant. Without doubt, boundaries between national states are vastly more permeable than they were a generation or two ago, and this has incalculable implications for the political authority of states and the meaning of citizenship. It's not an overstatement to say that citizenship means something quite different in an age when state governments must defer to international courts, when they're answerable in formulating their economic policies to international agencies and financiers around the world, and when the Internet opens up possibilities of political initiatives conducted on a planetary scale. And one should not underestimate the impact of the EU – a grand experiment in shared sovereignty and new permutations of multinational political community. For its most ambitious proponents, the EU already gives political embodiment to "Europe" as a new kind of political community (although the reality seems to fall decidedly short of this target).[8] In any case, the question is what to make of all this, normatively speaking. Many today very much welcome these new vistas and are eager to push further in that direction. But if civic existence is as important as we have suggested it is, and if a form of political community that meets the civic standard must be a bounded community (so relations between fellow citizens can deepen and civic identity can be rendered coherent), then these globalizing trends may be cause for concern as much as or more than cause for celebration. We can see this quite strikingly in the frustration some citizens feel when global banking and trading arrangements make a mockery of a given political community's belief that it can control its own social and economic destiny. On the one hand, there seems good reason to say that if being a political animal is important, one should grab possibilities of civic agency wherever one can find them – locally, or in the European arena, or through planetary initiatives. On the other hand, if it is already supremely difficult to exercise citizenship effectively in bounded national states, what are the chances of meaningful identity as a citizen in Europe or in the world as a whole? Hence those who are persuaded of the importance of citizenship are probably well advised not to look too far beyond national states as they currently exist, while remaining attentive to the increasing limits of the efficacy with which those states exercise their political authority. Of course, those who are politically aware will be interested in what is going on politically in other societies and devote some portion of their civic imagination to public affairs in those societies and the fate of their citizenry. But there must still be a privileged *locus of citizenship* (or locus of civic agency) if citizenship itself is to make any sense. If one can't find political community in a world state, one must find it *somewhere*.

The main purpose of articulating the idea of civicism is to highlight the fact that people can only be together as citizens if they feel bound together as a civic community. David Miller (from a left-wing liberal-nationalist point of view) cites criticisms of liberalism by conservatives such as Roger Scruton according to which liberalism is deficient insofar as "it fails to address the problem of social unity: what ties together all the various associations and subgroups into a cohesive whole? The liberal looks to the state itself to perform this unifying function: we are held together by our mutual subscription to the authority of the state and its laws, but on the conservative view this is a shallow answer. Political legitimacy depends upon a pre-political sense of common membership. We have to feel that we belong together in a common society before we can address the question of the political institutions that will govern us."[9] To which we might add that the more cultural and religious diversity there is in one's society, the more urgent this task. But this "being bound together as a civic community" *doesn't* have to take the form of a national identity (in a cultural or ethnonational sense).[10] Again, we should face up honestly to the fact that multination states have not been faring well in the past decade or so: it suffices to think of ex-Czechoslovakia, ex-Yugoslavia, and the former Soviet Union. Yet there are still many multi-nation states that have not succumbed to nationalism (e.g., Canada, Britain, Spain, Belgium, Switzerland); and as long as this is the case, we should not rush to give up on the civic idea as an alternative to nationalism.

Earlier in this chapter I mentioned that binational political community is no longer an option for Jews and Palestinians in the Middle East, and therefore the civic idea is in that respect ruled out, which I think is true. But we shouldn't assume that this was a preordained fate: if enough people on both sides saw the normative attractions of a civic rather than national community (and historically, some did), maybe a different kind of political community could have been forged than the separate Jewish and Palestinian states that will be the final outcome of this long political drama. No doubt there is a detailed historical narrative to be told about why these two peoples opted for national rather than civic community. In fact, though, the civic idea remains necessarily relevant in Israel at least, for even after the final release of the West Bank and Gaza from Israeli tutelage, and the formation of a fully Palestinian Palestine, Israel will continue to include a substantial Arab minority. Can these Arabs be given full civic status? For Israel, binationality will remain inescapable, and the test of its civic principles will be whether it can embrace its Arab population in a full civic community.

The National Idea

From what I've said above concerning the civic idea, it should be clear that there are important characteristics that it shares with the idea of nationalism. Being a nationalist is one way of being a political animal. For nationalists, politics looms very large among the ends of life, because the nation can only fulfill its full destiny by becoming politically free and self-determining. Citizenship understood from within a nationalist horizon is necessarily bounded, and the location of the boundaries matters immensely. The definition of political community is close to the core of what counts as humanly impor-tant. Thus far, the national idea appears as a variation of the civic idea, and perhaps in some measure it is. But the differences are also decisive.

In our analysis in the previous section, we saw that the first crucial attribute of the civic idea is that it is a *bounded* citizenship – with citizens on this side of the boundary and non-citizens on the other side of the boundary. Where exactly the boundary falls will of course be a product of the history of one's own civic community and of its neighbours (or in some cases, of its colonial masters). That is, it will depend on a narrative full of historical contingen-cies. As soon as there emerges a form of civic life, norms and practices of citizenship, a shared political history, and a politically defined way of life, there is a basis for individuals relating to each other *as* citizens (as opposed to as co-religionists, members of the same ethnic group, of the same gender or sexual orientation, and so on): the distinctively civic relation. This whole conception is sometimes called civic nationalism (or what Jürgen Habermas calls constitutional patriotism). To use the term *civic nationalism* is to suggest that this is one variety of nationalism, which seems to me confusing. It has also often been taken as suggesting that civic bonds have force in abstraction from cultural attachments. Critics of Habermas have focused especially on this apparent implication of his constitutional patriotism idea (although the criticism also applies to theories of civic nationalism more generally).[11] Habermas's constitutional patriotism tries to make the constitution itself (and the political institutions that envelop it) the sole basis of civic solidarity, which is admittedly a questionable proposition.[12] Civicism no less than nationalism requires markers of identity, symbols of collective existence, even shared myths. But the crucial difference is that according to the civic vision, these markers of identity are relevant for *every member of the civic community*, whereas the national vision applies only to members of *the nation*, which may be a subcommunity of the existing civic entity (e.g., Jews within Israel or Estonians within Estonia). So the difference is not the existence of a politically relevant shared culture, but the class of citizens among whom this culture is shared.

Is nationalism (or ethnonationalism) inherently illiberal? The national idea would not be an illiberal political project if the various societies on earth were culturally segregated, or if there were a way of drawing boundaries between them in such a way that these boundaries delimited culturally discrete units. The original theorists of nationalism such as J.G. Herder had such a picture in mind. But our world is simply not like that – there is far too much cultural and ethnic intermixture, entailing the cohabitation of cultural minorities and majorities, and our world is rapidly moving further away from the nationalist picture rather than moving toward it. There is a strong association between the idea of citizenship and the idea of (political) equality, and in any political community that is multiethnic or multinational (which is what almost all modern states now are), any robust appeal to "the nation," where this has any kind of ethnic connotation, will make it very difficult to sustain the idea of the equality of all citizens.

Anyone who wants to discredit nationalism as an attractive vision of political community will find no shortage of horror stories to tell from many parts of the world. I want to relate only one story since I think it nicely illustrates the kind of pathologies that nationalism generates. The story comes from a sad and thoughtful book written by an anglophone Quebecker with a distinguished record of public service in Quebec in order to explain, not without a considerable amount of pathos, why he has reluctantly and unhappily come to the conclusion that the continued project of shared

Canadian-Québécois political community is a hopeless one. The story concerns a meeting that took place in January 1977, soon after the election of the Parti Québécois as the new government of Quebec; Reed Scowen, the narrator of this story, was a member of the Quebec civil service at the time:

> It seemed obvious that interesting and important things were about to happen in my province and I wanted to be involved. So I flew back to Quebec City and called on Louis Bernard, the *chef du cabinet* of the new premier of Quebec, René Lévesque. Bernard was about to become secretary of the Executive Council, the most important civil servant of the Quebec government, and I asked him to reintegrate me into the public service. His answer was surprisingly clear. He told me he thought I should resign, because there was no more place for anglophones in the Quebec civil service. Please keep in mind that my conversation with Louis Bernard was in French. I spoke French, but to the new government he represented, I was an "anglophone." And consequently, a career in the public service of my own province was no longer possible. With several generations of family history in Quebec behind me, this came as a big surprise.[13]

This is an example of pure ethnic politics (one can call it "ethnocracy": rule by an ethnos). It illustrates what Hannah Arendt once referred to as "the conquest of the state by the nation."[14] The message is simple: not all those who reside within the civic boundaries are full citizens. Naturally, few nationalists in the world today will admit that their politics has an ethnocratic basis (Quebec nationalists certainly don't admit this), but the real test comes in whether the actual practices of the political community honour or fail to honour the civic identity of those belonging to what is regarded as another ethnos. If a political community composed of different national groups begins to assert itself in the guise of a robustly national regime that reflects only one of these groups (even if it claims to be representing a civic nation), then minority nations are cast into a kind of civic "limbo."[15] It shouldn't be assumed that all aspects of Quebec nationalism are as unflattering as the aspect exposed in this story. But it discloses certainly a *part* of what motivates sovereigntists in Quebec to frame their vision of political community in nationalist terms: we want to be *"maîtres chez nous,"* and not all residents within the territorial boundaries of Quebec are legitimate participants in this *nous*.[16] Perhaps one could say that citizenship involves accepting – and embracing – the untidiness of the human condition that lands one rather fortuitously in a particular political community, whereas nationalism yearns for a neater world, with a more exact alignment of culture and politics.

I don't want to suggest that the politics of ethnicity is the only kind of politics that offends against the civic idea. Sectarian religion also violates the civic idea, and so do conceptions of citizenship defined according to class, race, or gender (which is what has existed under regimes where only males, only Europeans, or only the propertied have been enfranchised). In fact, it's reasonable to say that I'm focusing on the challenge of nationalism just as a way of simplifying the theoretical problems raised by a much broader set of challenges to the civic idea. When we reflect on how Serb-centric or Estonian-centric politics undermines ideas of shared citizenship between citizens of different ethnicities, we could easily substitute similar dilemmas raised by Hindu-centric or evangelical Protestant-centric politics.

Civicism and Nationalism: The Mill-Acton Debate
The canonical history of political philosophy offers few theoretical resources for tackling the problem of the respective normative attractions of uni-national versus multinational political communities. To be sure, there are some texts relevant to nationalism in the history of political thought, but these either assumed that nations could happily coexist and flourish side by side without encroaching on each other's boundaries (Herder) or assumed that the cause of the nation (their own, naturally) was a righteous one (J.G. Fichte). There's very little that's attractive about Fichtean nationalism; and Herderian nationalism isn't very helpful for the set of questions that concern us because, as we'll discuss, humanity doesn't divide off into nations along neat cleavage lines (which seems obvious today but wasn't obvious to nationalists such as Herder). The problem we need to address arises precisely where nations or different cultural communities share territory and boundaries are contested. Some theoretical resources for further reflection are made available in an important nineteenth-century debate between two liberal political theorists – John Stuart Mill and Lord Acton – with the former highlighting the virtues of uni-national political communities and the latter seeking to argue the case for multination political communities.

The debate centred on a claim made by Mill in chapter 16 ("Of Nationality") of *Considerations on Representative Government,* published in 1861. (Acton's response, contained in his essay "Nationality," was originally published in 1862.) Mill's claim was that "it is in general a necessary condition of free institutions, that the boundaries of governments should coincide in the main with those of nationalities."[17] Mill said that "where the sentiment of nationality exists in any force, there is a prima facie case for uniting all the members of the nationality under the same government, and a government to themselves apart."[18] What does he mean here by a "nationality"? "A portion of mankind may be said to constitute a Nationality, if they are united among themselves by common sympathies, which do not exist between them and any others – which make them co-operate with each other more willingly than with other people, desire to be under the same government, and desire that it should be government by themselves or a portion of themselves, exclusively."[19] Mill goes on to list identity of race and descent, community of language, and community of religion as commonly relevant factors. Geography, too, is typically significant. But Mill doesn't exclude more specifically political considerations: a cause of the feeling of nationality ("the strongest of all," he writes) "is identity of political antecedents; the possession of a national history, and consequent community of recollections; collective pride and humiliation, pleasure and regret, connected with the same incidents in the past."[20] This definition of nationality clearly straddles ethnonational and civic aspects. For instance, Mill recognizes Switzerland as possessing "a strong sentiment of nationality, though the cantons are of different races, different languages, and different religions."[21] One can see that Mill's argument is not a strictly nationalist one from the fact that the very next chapter of *Representative Government* is devoted to an account of the advantages of federal governments.[22] Mill also takes it for granted that Bretons and Basques are better served by access to general French citizenship than by "sulking on their own rocks," and that the Scots and Welsh are better off as members of the British nation – which pretty obviously tramples on nationalist sensibilities.[23] Indeed, Mill goes so far as to state that "whatever really tends to the admixture of nationalities, and the blending of their attributes and peculiarities in a common union, is a benefit to the human race. Not by extinguishing types, of which, in these cases, sufficient examples are sure to remain, but by softening their extreme forms, and filling up the intervals between them."[24] But the clearest evidence that Mill's argument can't be considered a strictly nationalist one is that the core reasons he offers for basing government on nationality are explicitly civic ones: a political community can only cooperate effectively and exercise freedom in concert if it feels itself to be an integral community of citizens – sharing relevant experiences, partaking of the same or similar political concerns, and having enough of a shared background for a common civic sensibility – rather than an aggregation of subcommunities that view the world politically in ways that are (for reasons connected with differences of culture, language, religion, and so on) fundamentally alien to each other.[25] The point is not to put politics in the service of national self-affirmation as a good in itself, but rather to identify conditions of effective citizenship.

After stating his "general principle," Mill immediately hedges it with important qualifications.[26] He recognizes that there are many societies where strict enforcement of this principle is neither realistic nor desirable: societies "in which different nationalities are so locally intermingled, that it is not practicable for them to be under separate governments," or in which the minority nation is not large enough to form a viable state.[27] Presumably, if Mill were reconsidering this argument today, he would concede that what he presents as the norm is now the exception, and what he saw as the exception is now the norm. There are national minorities in virtually every political society on earth, and Mill certainly wasn't the kind of theorist of national citizenship to want to undo this condition. No doubt, Mill has a complicated view of how nationality relates to citizenship (surely he recognizes the Irish as possessing a distinct sentiment of nationality, yet that doesn't seem to him a decisive reason for independent Irish statehood).[28] But what *is* unmistakably clear is that civic considerations (what binds people into possibilities of free and effective citizenship) are all-important for him. As he puts it, appeal to the principle of nationality "is merely saying that the question of government ought to be decided by the governed": "One hardly knows what any division of the human race should be free to do, if not to determine, with which of the various collective bodies of human beings they choose to associate themselves."[29] In other words, what we have called the problem of political community (making a judgment about the relevant body politic, the group of human beings capable of regarding each other as fellow citizens) takes priority over any other substantive issue of political life.

There are fewer tensions in Acton's argument, and his political vision is more straightforwardly plurinational. Acton begins by tracing the awakening of the theory of nationality to the partition of Poland, which he says had the effect of "converting a dormant right into an aspiration, and a sentiment into a political claim."[30] This violation of Polish national existence (which alone among European states remained cut off from the dynastic principle) put into question the legitimacy of the territorial boundaries of all states in Europe, since these had precisely only a dynastic (that is, non-national) basis. Depriving a nation of "its right to constitute an independent community" highlighted the notion that "the arrangement of States [in general] was unjust."[31] Acton writes that the Mazzinian challenge to existing divisions of territory, judged according to the standard of an idea of national sovereignty, was just as revolutionary as the Rousseauian challenge to social and political inequality and communism's challenge to property. Of these three revolutionary doctrines, Mazzini's challenge is, according to Acton, "the most recent in its appearance, the most attractive at the present time, and the richest in promise of future power."[32] Although the spirit of national independence was decisive in overturning Napoleonic domination, the defeat of Napoleon ended in an uncompromising reassertion of the dynastic principle, with the result that the principle of nationality, denied political recognition, "was matured ... into a consistent doctrine." Dynastic absolutism, in resisting the liberal movement in post-Napoleonic Europe, gave rise as an unintended side-effect to a quite different system of thought, namely "the idea that national claims are above all other rights."[33] National rights were no longer "auxiliaries in the struggles for freedom, but now nationality became a paramount claim, which was to assert itself alone."[34] Nationalism "grew into a condemnation of every State that included different races, and finally became the complete and consistent theory, that the State and the nation must be co-extensive" – a doctrine that Acton takes to be asserted in Mill's thesis in chapter 16 of *Representative Government.*[35]

What are Acton's reasons for rejecting Mill's thesis? A core objection to what Acton calls the French view of nationality is that it posits "a fictitious unity," and tempts the state to overrun liberty, as is the case "whenever a single definite object is made the supreme end of the State."[36] Opposed to this view is a contrasting theory (the English view of nationality) according to which nationality is represented "as an essential, but not a supreme element in determining the forms of the State."[37] This second view "tends to diversity and not to uniformity, to harmony and not to unity ... While the theory of unity makes the nation a source of despotism and revolution, the theory of liberty regards it as a bulwark of self-government, and the foremost limit to the excessive power of the State"; "the presence of different nations under the same sovereignty is similar in its effect to the independence of the Church in the State."[38] Certainly, one important consideration for Acton is his anxiety about excessive state regulation, and he therefore finds attractive the notion that "national diversities" within the state will constrain the power of the state: "This diversity in the same State is a firm barrier against the intrusion of the government beyond the political sphere ... into the social department."[39] But that doesn't tell the whole story. The idea that national diversities will inhibit state action is a negative reason for preferring multinationality; Acton, however, has a positive vision of the attractions of multiple nations living and coexisting within the boundaries of the same state. He conjures up a picture of a "fertilising and regenerating" interaction between nations, and this "can only be obtained by living under one government": "The combination of different nations in one State is as necessary a condition of civilised life as the combination of men in society ... Where political and national boundaries coincide, society ceases to advance, and nations relapse into a condition corresponding to that of men who renounce intercourse with their fellow-men."[40]

Acton concludes with the problem that is the central one for any liberal-minded critic of nationalism: the problem of the quality of citizenship for minority nations. As Acton puts it, the theory of nationality is itself the "greatest adversary of the rights of nationality": "By making the State and the nation commensurate with each other in theory, it reduces practically to a subject condition all other nationalities that may be within the boundary. It cannot admit them to an equality with the ruling nation which constitutes the State, because the State would then cease to be national, which would be a contradiction of the principle of its existence."[41] Acton is convinced that the project of "making the nation the mould and measure of the State" is a wildly revolutionary doctrine, and also a wholly unrealizable one: "it is a chimera. The settlement at which it aims is impossible ... it can never be satisfied and exhausted, and always continues to assert itself."[42] Since polities are fated always to contain multiple nationalities, what national agitation brings about is not a uni-national state, but rather a final result completely different from the one it intended: "the liberty of different nationalities as members of one sovereign community."[43] Acton isn't of course committed to the proposition that there is *no* political relevance to the concept of nationality. But he is insistent that national identity flows from politics rather than being a basis *for* politics. Nationhood "is derived from the State, not supreme over it. A State may in course of time produce a nationality; but that a nationality should constitute a State is contrary to the nature of modern civilisation. The nation derives its rights and its power from the memory of a former independence."[44] Acton therefore carries further the implicit view in Mill that nationality isn't just a function of pre-existing ethnicity or culture, but is shaped by a history of shared political experience.

Although Acton presents his political theory as diametrically opposed to Mill's, the contrast between them is less stark than Acton assumes.[45] (As we saw earlier, Mill's view of nationality is more nuanced and qualified than his "general principle" suggests.) More to the point, both theories are relevant to our current circumstances. Acton is right that appeals to the notion of a robust unity of the nation are not an attractive way to conceptualize modern political community. Internal diversity enhances freedom within a political community, and a militant ideology of shared nationhood can intimidate diversity, and therefore limit freedom. Equally, Mill can teach us that if different sections of the political community feel too far removed from each other in their political concerns, in their sense of what matters politically, and in their ultimate notion of what they belong to, then it will be hard for them to experience their relationship as a community of shared citizenship, and civic agency (the pursuit of shared purposes) will be impaired. A quick glance at contemporary theories of multiculturalism might help to highlight this dual relevance of the Mill-Acton debate.

Civicism, Nationalism, and Multiculturalism

Civicism and liberalism are both political philosophies that are suspicious of ethnocultural politics and politics based on a strong appeal to the special claims of subnational groups, but for different reasons. The liberal principle is that a political community is to be admired insofar as it gives individuals space in which to decide their own ends, make up their own minds, and form opinions that reflect their authentic view of life. Therefore the liberal fear is that types of politics based on too robust a sense of communal identity and shared culture will inhibit or constrain the exercise of individual autonomy. The civic principle is that the political community is to be judged according to a standard of the vibrancy and quality of the experience of citizenship enjoyed by its members. Therefore the anxiety from the civic point of view is that cultural attachments within the political community will overwhelm civic attachment to the political community, and that members of various races, religions, ethnicities, and those of a given gender or sexual orientation will allow these identities to trump their civic identity. However, it has to be said that there are some versions of liberalism that come extremely close to the civic view in their articulation of ideas of civic equality.[46] How these two systems of thought, partly overlapping and partly in tension, relate first to nationalism and then to multiculturalism is anything but simple. Just for a sense of these complexities, what follows are brief summaries of the thinking of a few important figures in these debates.

On the face of it, one might expect that nationalism (affirming uni-national political community) and multiculturalism (affirming a robust cultural pluralism) would offer diametrically opposed principles. However, the theoretical landscape is more complicated. Nationalism and multiculturalism have at least this is common: both involve political claims on behalf of "thick" cultural communities. Both involve a politics of culture: a politics of cultural self-maintenance or cultural self-defence. Therefore, liberal theorists who have theoretical sympathy for one will often also display theoretical sympathy for the other. (Conversely, uncompromisingly individualist versions of liberalism will resist both.) A good example of a liberal political philosopher whose arguments run in the direction of simultaneous support for multiculturalism and (moderate) nationalism is Will Kymlicka. Prior to Kymlicka, one might have assumed that rigorously individualistic philosophical premises (focused on individual autonomy as an ultimate principle) would run counter to a politics of robust group rights. However, Kymlicka makes individual autonomy conditional on a secure cultural context, and this has the effect of rendering liberal individualism compatible with (according to Kymlicka's argument, indeed *requiring)* special political protections for minority cultures and for national cultures. There are two ways of characterizing Kymlicka's contribution. One can either say that he has expanded the boundaries of liberalism in order to accommodate the concerns of communitarians, multiculturalists, and nationalists. Or one can say that he has put liberalism in the service of multiculturalism (to the displeasure, no doubt, of some liberals).

Another important defender of multiculturalism worth mentioning briefly is Charles Taylor. Taylor is hard to classify with respect to the problem of political community since his thought is simultaneously liberal, civicist, nationalist, and multiculturalist. In Taylor's case as well, the impulse to be more sensitive to the legitimacy of collectivist aspirations generates arguments that support both multiculturalism and nationalism. In fact, Taylor's famous and highly influential essay "The Politics of Recognition" presents a bit of a theoretical oddity: it appeals primarily to the legitimacy of moderate nationalist policies in Quebec in order to construct an argument for multicultural policies. But can't one object that the tension-laden relationship

between nationalism and multiculturalism (representing the cultural-
political aspirations of different groups) forces one into having to choose
between them? *Either* legal and political norms in Quebec are geared toward
Québécois cultural survival, to which multicultural aspirations must take a
back seat, *or* the flourishing of multicultural diversity is seen as a supreme
good, which will have adverse consequences for the project of promoting
Québécois nationhood. I put this challenge to Taylor in a public discussion
of his work in 1999.[47] His response, basically, was that absorption of immigrants into a French-language milieu in Quebec (what he calls "a language
of convergence") is no more subversive of multiculturalism than absorption
of immigrants into an English-language milieu in the rest of Canada is
subversive of multiculturalism. Minority cultural identities can flourish in
either language, but the English language is secure in North America whereas
the French language requires special protections and political support. Fair
enough: but I think this response discounts the fact that what is at stake for
nationalist Québécois is not just preservation of a language, but the longing
for nationhood in a fairly strong sense – the political affirmation of their
(whose?) existence as a distinct people. (A strong way of describing this
would be to say that Taylor offers a rendering of nationalism according to
which nationalism is neutered of "the nation," or in which appeals to the
nation somehow drop out of sight; perhaps more aptly one could say that
Taylor's "liberal nationalism" isn't a form of nationalism at all, but really a
form of liberalism concerned with promoting the preservation of the French
language.) These hegemonic, "ethnocratic" implications of the national idea
seem to me to account not only for the resistance to the nationalist project
on the part of ethnic communities in Quebec (including francophone immigrants, in some cases), but especially for the universal hostility to the
nationalist project on the part of Aboriginal groups in Quebec.

What about the relationship between multiculturalism and civicism?
Consider the following analogy between liberalism and multiculturalism.
Just as liberals are fearful of an overly robust conception of civic identity
and civic purposes, lest this conception impinge upon the space needed by
individuals to define their own purposes, so multiculturalists are fearful of an
overly robust definition of citizenship lest it impinge upon the space needed
by cultural groups to define *their* distinctive purposes.[48] According to the
multiculturalist vision, the need for cultural groups to flourish on their own
terms trumps the need of the political community as a whole for a shared
civic identity. Thus multiculturalism as a distinct political doctrine privileges
the claims of cultural groups, even if this requires trumping the needs of
general citizenship, just as liberalism as a political doctrine privileges the
self-elected ends of individuals, even if these are in tension with the needs
of general citizenship. Neither doctrine *necessarily* cancels out the claims of
citizenship (with respect to group claims, for instance, all kinds of tradeoffs

and accommodations are possible), but there is always the possibility of a tension between the civic idea and these other political philosophies, since they ground their political vision on a basis other than the principle of general citizenship.

In the case of civicism and multiculturalism, how serious the tension is will depend very much on the kinds of examples on which one focuses. For instance, if we think of Will Kymlicka-type examples such as allowing Sikhs in the Royal Canadian Mounted Police to wear turbans in order to integrate them more effectively in central civic institutions of the larger political community (by demonstrating respect for their cultural identity), then there can certainly be no objection from a civic point of view: Kymlicka seems right to argue that this serves the cause of citizenship rather than subverts it. If, on the other hand, we think of Susan Okin-type examples of respecting the attitudes of certain minority cultures with respect to the status of women, here there is indeed a real danger that basic principles of shared and equal citizenship will be undermined.[49] We can't assume that civic and multicultural principles will necessarily be in conflict, but nor can we assume that they will necessarily be in harmony (of course it depends on what group claims are at issue). The question is – in cases where the two principles are *not* in harmony, should we allow multicultural considerations to trump the needs of citizenship, or should the principle of citizenship trump multiculturalism?

Does civicism entail a general stance toward multicultural policies (either favourable or unfavourable)? I don't think so. Civicists will certainly favour culturally diverse political communities, for reasons that are spelled out in this chapter; but this is not the same thing as favouring policies that promote multiculturalism. Culture is undeniably important, for minorities no less than for majorities, and one should try to locate ways of accommodating cultural attachments consistent with loyalty to one's *civic* identity. In many cases, the principle of civic equality will encourage us to treat the cultural identity of constituent groups within our society with special respect, since lack of respect toward their culture will entail lack of respect for these groups (hence violating the civic principle). For instance, it is impossible to treat Aboriginal citizens in Canada as equal members of the political community without giving special recognition to their cultural distinctiveness. But there are limits: where cultural identity and civic identity pull in opposing directions (which they sometimes will), there is indeed a problem. An obvious example is how to deal with cultures that fail to affirm the equal citizenship of women. Whether multiculturalism is pro-civic or anti-civic will depend (in particular instances) on whether the cultural practices that are being bolstered are consistent with the principle of active and equal citizenship (sometimes they will be and sometimes they won't be). Again, the decisive question is whether multicultural policies are viewed as being in the service of citizenship, or whether citizenship is being knocked down to size in order to suit the cause of multiculturalism.

I end these reflections not very far from where I began them: with a strong conviction of the importance of trying to shed light on different conceptions of political community by means of normative reflection, and a weak conviction about how to do so convincingly. If there is such a thing as a knock-down argument in favour of one's preferred understanding of political community, I haven't found one. (Or put otherwise: a large part of the purpose of theorizing is merely to clarify one's own thinking.) But this doesn't mean that opting for a certain mode of political community is a matter of sheer contingency, beyond theoretical judgment. How one conceives political community expresses an implicit theory of what it is to be a citizen, and political philosophy ought to be able to illuminate that.

Source
This essay was written while I was a visiting fellow at the Centre for Philosophy and Public Affairs, Department of Moral Philosophy, University of St. Andrews, and I'd like to express my gratitude for the hospitality of the Centre and especially of its director, David Archard.

Notes
1 I don't want to pretend that this is a neutral description: for instance, Québécois nationalists sometimes say that part of their grievance is that a uni-national Canadian identity is being imposed on them (they may say that precisely this was Pierre Trudeau's political project, which was anti-Québécois nationalist but pro-Canadian nationalist), and that Canadian political community offers insufficient acknowledgment of their distinct nationhood. I hope that the arguments presented later in this chapter offer some further justification for this (admittedly contestable) characterization.
2 John Rawls, *A Theory of Justice* (Oxford: Clarendon Press, 1972), 457. Cf., "Let us assume, to fix ideas, that a society is a more or less self-sufficient association of persons" (4); and "I shall be satisfied if it is possible to formulate a reasonable conception of justice for the basic structure of society conceived for the time being as a closed system isolated from other societies" (8).
3 Affirming the normative superiority of one political condition over another (e.g., the superiority in principle of a multiethnic Yugoslavia to an ethnically segregated Yugoslavia) is compatible with recognizing that the normatively superior condition is no longer realizable, or simply not attractive in the given circumstances. For instance, while a federal Yugoslavia is in principle preferable to a uni-national Yugoslavia, who could blame the Montenegrins for wanting to go their own way, after what the Serbs have done to their various former partners in the Yugoslav federation?
4 Cf. Jeff Spinner, *The Boundaries of Citizenship: Race, Ethnicity, and Nationality in the Liberal State* (Baltimore, MD: Johns Hopkins University Press, 1994), 144-5.
5 Think of what's at stake for the Israeli electorate in electing Ariel Sharon rather than Ehud Barak.
6 Alasdair MacIntyre cites Philip Pettit's articulation of the republican ideal of individuals who "deliberate together *qua* republican citizens," but then firmly rejects the notion that "such a form of shared deliberation [is] open to those whose politics is the politics of the nation-state." MacIntyre, "A Partial Response to My Critics," in *After MacIntyre: Critical Perspectives on the Work of Alasdair MacIntyre*, ed. John Horton and Susan Mendus (Notre Dame, IN: University of Notre Dame Press, 1994), 303. MacIntyre offers an important challenge to the idea of state-based citizenship, but my fear is that he applies such a stringent standard of shared deliberation that the idea of civic deliberation is abolished altogether. For a fuller discussion, see chapter 5 above.

7 Thus there are important things to be said about the social conditions/entailments of civicism – which I won't attempt to address here. What I have in mind is the notion that the political community must guarantee access for all citizens as citizens to education, housing, medical care, reasonable prospects of employment, pensions for the elderly, and so on, since these things are essential for effective exercise of one's citizenship. These can be viewed either as civicism's preconditions (in order to have a fully civic regime, the political community must be committed to ensuring that all citizens are provided with X, Y, Z) or as its necessary entailments (if you are committed to civicism as a normative ideal, you should be equally committed to X, Y, Z for all citizens). For some relevant discussion, see my essay, "Is Social Democracy Dead?" in *Governing Modern Societies,* ed. Richard V. Ericson and Nico Stehr (Toronto: University of Toronto Press, 2000), 225-41; see also Brian Barry, "The Continuing Relevance of Socialism," in *Liberty and Justice: Essays in Political Theory 2* (Oxford: Clarendon Press, 1991), 274-90.

8 It is reasonable to think that the EU still has quite some way to go in becoming a meaningful locus of citizenship. In the British general election of 1997, 71 percent of the British electorate voted (considered very low by British standards); in the European Parliament election of 1999, a mere 23 percent of the British electorate voted.

9 David Miller, "Communitarianism: Left, Right and Centre," in *Liberalism and Its Practice,* ed. Dan Avnon and Avner de-Shalit (London: Routledge, 1999), 176.

10 Scruton clearly regards the United States as meeting this standard of "a pre-political sense of common membership": see Roger Scruton, "The First Person Plural," in *Theorizing Nationalism,* ed. Ronald Beiner (Albany: State University of New York Press, 1999), 289-90. Yet the United States is unquestionably (in my categories) a civic rather than national political community. A republican ideology such as that in post-Revolutionary France can also serve this bonding function on a non-ethnic basis, though it is certainly not culturally neutral.

11 For two powerful examples of such criticisms, see Bernard Yack, "The Myth of the Civic Nation," in *Theorizing Nationalism,* ed. Beiner, 103-18; and William James Booth, "Communities of Memory," in *Canadian Political Philosophy: Contemporary Reflections,* ed. Ronald Beiner and Wayne Norman (Don Mills, ON: Oxford University Press, 2001), 263-81.

12 Cf. the quotation from David Miller in the previous section.

13 Reed Scowen, *Time to Say Goodbye: The Case for Getting Quebec out of Canada* (Toronto: McClelland and Stewart, 1999), 14-15. Scowen goes on to inform us (32) that although a representation of anglophones in the public service proportionate to their numerical importance in Quebec would have required about a 10-percent presence, and despite the fact that the political party elected to government in 1985 had committed itself to achieving proportionate representation, by 1997 anglophones held only 0.8 percent (411 out of 51,000) of positions in the Quebec civil service.

14 For discussion, see chapter 8 above.

15 One could object that these "ethnocratic" aspects of nationalism are likely to be more conspicuous during the stage of a nationalist movement at which it is trying to win independent political existence. Once the nationalist struggle for independent statehood has been won, the regime can more confidently liberalize and "civicize" itself. This seems to me a fair point.

16 For a very clear and perceptive account of how Quebec's "civic nationalism" naturally and unavoidably slips into a more ethnic key, see Jeremy Webber, "Just How Civic Is Civic Nationalism in Quebec?" in *Citizenship, Diversity, and Pluralism: Canadian and Comparative Perspectives,* ed. Alan C. Cairns et al. (Montreal and Kingston: McGill-Queen's University Press, 1999), 87-107. Webber argues persuasively that this slippage from civic to ethnic nationalism is brought about by tensions that are endemic in the very concept of civic nationalism, since civic nationalism aspires to be a kind of nationalism that abstracts from culture, whereas in reality any form of nationalism cannot help but be moved by cultural concerns.

17 John Stuart Mill, *Three Essays* (London: Oxford University Press, 1975), 384.

18 Ibid., 381.

19 Ibid., 380.

20 Ibid.
21 Ibid.
22 "When the conditions exist for the formation of efficient and durable Federal Unions, the multiplication of them is always a benefit to the world" (Mill, *Three Essays*, 398).
23 Ibid., 385. Mill makes the same argument with respect to Ireland, namely that it is to the advantage of the Irish to remain part of Britain (ibid., 387) – again, sure proof that Mill's argument doesn't necessarily favour nationalist politics. One would certainly think that his general principle leans toward an endorsement of Irish independence, but his own explicitly stated political position leans the other way.
24 Ibid., 385.
25 "Free institutions are next to impossible in a country made up of different nationalities. Among a people without fellow-feeling, especially if they read and speak different languages, the united public opinion, necessary to the working of representative government, cannot exist. The influences which form opinions and decide political acts, are different in the different sections of the country. An altogether different set of leaders have the confidence of one part of the country and of another. The same books, newspapers, pamphlets, speeches, do not reach them. One section does not know what opinions, or what instigations, are circulating in another" (ibid., 382).
26 "Several considerations are liable to conflict in practice with this general principle" (ibid., 384).
27 Ibid., 384, 386-7.
28 See n. 23 above. He also thinks it is very much to the credit of British political culture and British political traditions that England and Scotland can be governed by very different laws and very different administrative arrangements without breaching "legislative unity" (Mill, *Three Essays*, 399-400). One can assume that he wouldn't object strenuously to a separate Scottish Parliament (as now exists), but he would probably be more resistant to Scottish-nationalist aspirations for an independent state, for the same reasons that he prefers that Ireland remain content with equal citizenship within Britain. It seems clear that Scottish nationalists, for instance, would view the argument of *Representative Government* as smugly "metropolitan" rather than as pro-nationalist.
29 Mill, *Three Essays*, 381. Acton's gloss on this statement is that "the theory of nationality is involved in the democratic theory of the sovereignty of the general will," therefore "the national theory" is a natural beneficiary of "the triumph of the democratic principle." John Emerich Edward Dalberg-Acton, *The History of Freedom and Other Essays* (London: Macmillan, 1907), 287. In effect, nationalism "piggybacks" on the rise of democracy.
30 Acton, *The History of Freedom and Other Essays*, 275. Acton cites Burke's protest against the second partition of Poland in 1793 (after the original partition in 1772), but the full partition of Poland took place in 1795.
31 Ibid., 276.
32 Ibid., 273.
33 Ibid., 283. Cf., "The absolutism which has created [the national theory] denies equally that absolute right of national unity which is a product of democracy, and that claim of national liberty which belongs to the theory of freedom" (288). Acton refers to the former as the French view of nationality and to the latter as the English view of nationality, and claims that they "are in reality the opposite extremes of political thought."
34 Ibid., 285.
35 Ibid., 285.
36 Ibid., 288.
37 Ibid., 289.
38 Ibid.
39 Acton, *The History of Freedom and Other Essays*, 290. When Acton writes that "the co-existence of several nations under the same State is a test, as well as the best security of its freedom" (ibid.), security means security against an overactive state. David Miller highlights this aspect of Acton's argument: see "Nation and Nationalism," in *Routledge Encyclopedia of Philosophy*, vol. 6 (London: Routledge, 1998), 660.
40 Acton, *The History of Freedom and Other Essays*, 290.

41 Ibid., 297. Admittedly, one may well be uneasy about the conclusion that Acton draws from this theoretical principle, which is that multinational empires constitute "the most perfect" type of state (298). Cf., "When different races inhabit the different territories of one Empire composed of several smaller States, it is of all possible combinations the most favourable to the establishment of a highly developed system of freedom" (296). When Acton speaks of different nations participating in a "fertilising and regenerating process" (290), this is also heavily shaped by imperialist notions. Acton has a picture of superior nations elevating inferior nations, which is precisely the kind of imperialist presumption that (rightly) infuriates nationalists.

42 Ibid., 299, 298. Cf. Margaret Canovan, *Nationhood and Political Theory* (Cheltenham: Edward Elgar, 1996): "It is of the essence of nationalism ... to be a revolutionary doctrine" (11).

43 Acton, *The History of Freedom and Other Essays,* 298.

44 Ibid., 292. Cf., "The nationality formed by the State ... is the only one to which we owe political duties, and it is, therefore, the only one which has political rights. The Swiss are ethnologically either French, Italian, or German; but no nationality has the slightest claim upon them, except the purely political nationality of Switzerland" (294-5).

45 Consider the following: "The great importance of nationality in the State consists in the fact that it is the basis of political capacity" (that is, shared national character forms a base for self-government) (ibid., 297). This comes very close to restating Mill's central idea.

46 See, especially, Brian Barry, *Culture and Equality: An Egalitarian Critique of Multiculturalism* (Cambridge: Polity Press, 2001), chapters 3 and 8. Another powerful statement of Barry's view, particularly with respect to his concept of civic nationality, is offered in "A Commentary on Jacob T. Levy, *The Multiculturalism of Fear* and Bhikhu Parekh, *Rethinking Multiculturalism,*" paper presented at the American Political Science Association annual meeting, Washington, DC, 2000.

47 Panel on "The Work of Charles Taylor," meetings of the Association for Canadian Studies in the United States, Pittsburgh, 20 November 1999. My contribution to the panel ("Some Questions Concerning Charles Taylor's Liberal Nationalism") has been published in *Cahiers du PÉQ* 19 (June 2000): 10-13, with a response by Ruth Abbey (13-22).

48 For instance, this is how I interpret the theory of minimal citizenship offered in Melissa Williams, "Citizenship As Identity, Citizenship As Shared Fate, and the Functions of Multicultural Education," in *Collective Identities and Cosmopolitan Values,* ed. Walter Feinberg and Kevin McDonough (Oxford: Oxford University Press, forthcoming). By way of contrast, see what David Miller says about "the left critique of multiculturalism" and the need for "a doctrine of strong citizenship" ("Communitarianism: Left, Right and Centre," 178). Miller writes: "If people define their identities through a plurality of specific communities without at the same time giving priority to an inclusive politically organized community, there is a danger that the social fabric will begin to unravel, with the different communal groups becoming increasingly alienated from and hostile to one another ... an exclusive emphasis on the celebration of specific cultural identities may be incompatible with preserving just that form of political community which allows such separate identities to co-exist in relative peace" (178).

49 See Will Kymlicka, *Multicultural Citizenship* (Oxford: Clarendon Press, 1995); and Susan Moller Okin, *Is Multiculturalism Bad for Women?* ed. Joshua Cohen, Matthew Howard, and Martha C. Nussbaum (Princeton, NJ: Princeton University Press, 1999). Jeff Spinner argues persuasively in *The Boundaries of Citizenship* that being open to the legitimate claims of ethnic, racial, and national groups doesn't mean that one should defer to all imaginable claims of such groups. There are larger civic considerations (relating to freedom and equality) that shouldn't be trumped by the demands of subnational groups. See Spinner, *The Boundaries of Citizenship,* x, 3, 62, 68-73, 76-7, 177-8.

Index

Printed and bound in Canada by Friesens

Set in Stone by Artegraphica Design Co. Ltd.

Copy editor: Cheryl Cohen

Proofreader: Gail Copeland

Indexer: Noeline Bridge